1986

BEHOLD THE MIGHTY WURLITZER

Recent Titles in
Contributions to the Study of Popular Culture

Tarzan and Tradition: Classical Myth in Popular Literature
Erling B. Holtsmark

Common Culture and the Great Tradition: The Case for Renewal
Marshall W. Fishwick

Concise Histories of American Popular Culture
M. Thomas Inge, editor

Ban Johnson: Czar of Baseball
Eugene C. Murdock

Putting Dell on the Map: A History of the Dell Paperbacks
William H. Lyles

BEHOLD THE MIGHTY WURLITZER

The History of the Theatre Pipe Organ

JOHN W. LANDON

Contributions to the Study of Popular Culture, Number 6

Greenwood Press
Westport, Connecticut · London, England

Copyright Acknowledgments

Grateful acknowledgment is made for permission to reprint the following: Excerpts from *The Best Remaining Seats* by Ben M. Hall. Copyright © MCMLXI by Ben M. Hall. Used by permission of Clarkson N. Potter, Inc.; "Bigger Than Stereo," *Time*, copyright 1962 Time Inc. All rights reserved. Reprinted by permission from TIME.

Library of Congress Cataloging in Publication Data

Landon, John W., 1937–
Behold the mighty Wurlitzer.

(Contributions to the study of popular culture, ISSN 0198-9871 ; n. 6)
1. Organ—History. I. Title.
ML557.L16 1983 786.6 83-5557
ISBN 0-313-23827-8 (lib. bdg.)

Library of Congress Catalog Card Number: 83-5557
ISBN: 0-313-23827-8
ISSN: 0198-9871

First published in 1983

Greenwood Press
A division of Congressional Information Service, Inc.
88 Post Road West
Westport, Connecticut 06881

Printed in the United States of America

10 9 8 7 6 5 4 3 2

CONTENTS

ILLUSTRATIONS

PREFACE

The theatre organ is really an extraordinarily remarkable piece of mechanism. It was basically evolved by Hope-Jones from the church organ for one single purpose—to provide an accompaniment for silent motion pictures with a sound removed as far as possible from that of a church organ and designed to take the place of the inadequate "relief pianist." It was virtually a "one-man" band and, with its vast range of beautiful solo stops and tonal combinations, it became, almost overnight, a marvelous instrument of entertainment. In a few years, it had evolved so rapidly that by 1924 Jesse Crawford, dean of American theatre organists, was playing a big four manual Wurlitzer in the Chicago Theatre, and a couple of years later, had become world-famous at the New York Paramount, mainly through his duets with his wife Helen on two consoles.

The difficulty in those early years was to find suitable performers to play these strange instruments. It was useless to employ a church organist, as he would not have the essential ability and experience in playing the variety of light music required; equally it was no good using the pianist out of the orchestra, as he couldn't play with his feet and had little idea what to do with the stops. In the hands of a capable performer, the theatre organ could produce a magical accompaniment to every variety of silent movie, especially the comedies where the organist could improvise and fit the movements on the screen far better than any orchestra. One of the most famous organists in America was C. Sharpe Minor, who although he could not read a note of music, toured around opening new theatres. He could virtually make an organ talk and had his audiences in stitches with his clever reproduction of all the missing sounds.

When the talkies came in in 1929, the movies proceeded to provide their own musical and speaking background as well as all the other various sounds which had hitherto been missing, so organists and orchestras were no longer necessary and were discharged virtually overnight. As a result, all the beautiful organs were closed down and left to deteriorate.

England was several years behind America in these matters, though several English organ builders did their best to provide a similar instrument—notably Compton who, in the course of time, eventually produced a few superb organs, especially the BBC Theatre Organ installed in 1936.

Wurlitzer began to come into Britain in 1924, and two years later, I was lucky enough to become organist of the New Gallery Kinema in Regent Street on the third one imported. It was quite a small instrument, a style "F" with two manuals and eight ranks, but it sounded so completely different from anything anyone had ever heard that it created an immediate sensation. I began broadcasting on it in June 1926, and within a few weeks, it was famous throughout the British Isles and northwestern Europe; my first "His Master's Voice" recording made on it sold three and one-fourth million copies.

England has traditionally been a more organ-minded country than America, so when the talkies came in, although all the orchestras were let go, most of the organists were retained, given a ten- or fifteen-minute interlude in every show with names featured on the front of the theatre. It was found that audiences enjoyed the live organ solo played by a man in a spotlight as a pleasant contrast to the canned music from the screen. In fact, English organists improved on their American friends by presenting a pleasant selection of tuneful music rather than lazily putting on a "sing-along" with words on the screen.

Radio theatre organ programs on the BBC became so popular that, in order to be independent of the movie theatres with their tight program schedules, the BBC purchased its own four manual, twenty-three rank organ from Compton who built the finest theatre organ the Compton Company ever made. I was fortunate enough to be chosen from 350 applicants to be the BBC staff theatre organist, and within a matter of weeks, my name became a household word.

At the end of 1951, I came to America to live; the following year, I was approached by Emory Cook to make some recordings at the Mosque, Richmond, Virginia, on a fine Wurlitzer Style 260, which after ten years of disuse had been completely restored to mint condition by two enthusiasts, Harold Warner and Bill Jones. Until that time, the theatre organ in America had apparently been dead and forgotten, and I have been told many times that it was those Mosque recordings which brought the theatre organ back to life once more and resulted in many of them being rescued from oblivion and rejuvenated into the immense popularity that they are enjoying today. Practically all the theatre organs have been removed from theatre pits and storage rooms and rebuilt almost entirely by enthusiastic members of the American Theatre Organ Society and reinstalled in homes and concert halls where they are once again giving an immense amount of pleasure to untold numbers of lovers of theatre organ music.

Reginald Foort

Clearwater, Florida
September 1977

ACKNOWLEDGMENTS

The author is grateful to all those without whose help this book could not have been written. Any list will naturally be incomplete but special thanks belong to the following:

Leah Agnoni, Mildred Alexander, Don Andersen, William H. Andrews, Roger G. Angell, Ruth Hines Ashcroft, Vincent C. Astor, Lowell C. Ayars, Jerry Bacon, Doug Badham, Don Baker, Karl Baker, C. M. "Sandy" Balcom, Thelma Barclay, William G. Barnes, Richard Barons, Bill Bartlow, Helen M. Barton, William H. Bauer, R. Frederick Becker, Fred Beeks, Ralph Bell, Gordon Belt, William Benedict, Tom B'Hend, Bill Biebel, Ray Bingham, Lawrence Birdsong, Jr., Clealan Blakely, Roger and Dorothy Bloom, Esther Bodycombe, Ray Bohr, Al Bollington, Trevor Bolshaw, Q. David Bowers, Mary A. Bowles, Roy Brooks, Raymond A. Brubacher, William Bunch, Paul C. Burgess, Franklin Butte, Mike Candy, Opal Cansler, Helen Dell Carson, Robert Spencer Carson, Gaylord Carter, J. Paul Chavanne, N. Francis Cimmino, Cinema Organ Society *Journal*, Robert H. Clark, Jr., Len Clarke, Bob Coe, Columbia Broadcasting System, Clara Conner, *Console* magazine, Donald Cooper, Brother Andrew Corsini, Mike Coup, Lucy Crawford, David L. Cross, Andrew Crow, Frank Cunkle, Ian Dalgleish, Jackson Davis, Norman J. Dawe, John DeMello, Clyde Derby, Michael Detroy, *Diapason* magazine, David Dickey, Melvin Doner, J. Wilson Doty, David Dunlap, Wallace Dunlap, Bob

Dunn, Orrill Dunn, Robert Elmore, EMI Records, Harry Farmer, Fred Feibel, Dennis Ferrara, Tom Ferree, Nathaniel W. Finston, Eldon Firmstone, James N. Flanagan, Bill Floyd, Reginald Foort, John Foskett, Virgil Fox, Barnard Franklin, Paul D. Gable, Connell Gallagher, Doris Garrett, Fred Garrett, John Gart, Nancy L. George, Bob Gesslein, Gene Gladson, Irma Glen, Robert Gliddon, W. Stuart Green, G. Edgar Gress, J. Llelyn Haggart, Chauncey Haines, Ben Hall, Jane Hamlin, Eddy Hanson, Richard Hargar, Jack and Jan Harris, Mark Harris, Charles E.J. Hayles, Porter Heaps, Richard Heisler, Terry Helgesen, Tom Helms, George L. Hergesheimer, Dean Herrick, Doug Hickling, Mary Jane Higby, Robert S. High, Warren Vander Hill, Stuart Hinchliffe, Lewis E. Hodson, Clay Holbrook, Dwight Hoover, Marie Hoscheid, E. A. Houlden, Georg Huber, Jr., Len Hudson, Arlo Hults, Henry W. Hunt, Louis B. Hurvitz, Vic Hyde, Stanton Hyer, Opal C. Snodgrass Ingersoll, Frances Wood Irving, Dennis and Heidi James, Forest Johnson, Lance E. Johnson, Debra Jones, Virginia Kahapea, Stan Kann, Harriett Hall Kaufmann, Preston J. Kaufmann, David Kemp, Sylvan Ketterman, Gordon Kibbee, Roger D. Kinkle, Lloyd E. Klos, Don Knights, Harry and Catherine Koenig, Rex Koury, Miles Kreuger, Bill Lamb, Eileen Lambertson, Thomas O. Landrum III; Bill Langford, Lyn Larsen, Jean Lautzenheiser, Arthur Lawrence, Eddie Layton, James Leaffe, Leroy N. Lewis, Rudy Lewis, Jerry Limbert, Jim Lindsay, Edwin A. Link, Jan Locher, Tom Lockhart, Thomas Lockwood, Richard E. Loderhose, Bob Longfield, Joan Lord, Warren Lubich, Mel Luchette, H. W. Luebke, George L. Lufkin, Jesse Macartney, Tina McCarthy, R. R. McCombs, Ian R. McIver, William McMains, Johnny Mack, Ray McNamara, Dean McNichols, Erskine MacPherson, John Mann, Clifford Manning, Lou Marder, Mike Marsden, Frank and Frances May, Byron Melcher, George T. Merriken, Ken Michelson, Allen R. Miller, Ashley Miller, Edwin F. Miller, Jr., M. P. Moller Company, Peter Möller Daniels, Tim Moody, Alberta Morgan, Tony Moss, Ed Mullins, Mark Muntzel, Jr., John Muri, Music Library of the Library of Congress, Billy Nalle, National Association of Music Merchants, Inc., National Broadcasting Company, Tim Needler, T. L. "Red" Newberry, New York Public Library staff,

Donna Nickel, Buddy Nolan, Ruth Noller, Jonas Nordwall, Everett Nourse, Eugene M. Nye, Orpha Ochse, Hector Olivera, Oral Roberts University, *Organist* magazine, E. F. "Eddie" Osborn, Robert J. Palian, Theresa Papp, C.A.J. Parmentier, Geoffrey Paterson, Elizabeth Pattengill, Joe Patton, James Paulin, Jr., Harold and Mary Pearrell, Vladimir Pech, Dion Peluso, Dick Penberthy, J. T. Peterson, John Potter, Charles Powers, Frank W. Pratt, Jane Price and her fellow staff members at the University of Kentucky Photographic Services Office, *Punch* magazine, E. J. Quinby, Len Rawle, Les and Edith Rawle, RCA Consumer Services, Virginia Byrd Rechtoris, Eric M. Reeve, Wynola Richards, William H. Rieger, Joseph G. Roberts, Jr., Harvey Roehl, R. C. Rolfing, Al Rollo, Dorothy Roser, James C. Roseveare, Allen W. Rossiter, Mrs. Edward Saling, Bernard J. Schaefer, W. Charles Schrader, Hubert Selby, Ben Selvin, Earl C. Sharits, John D. Sharp, Patrick J. Sheehan, Marjorie Shelden, David Shepherd, Helen Sherman, Barry Simmons, Richard C. Simonton, J. J. Slingerland, J. B. Smiley, Carlton Smith, George Smith, Scott Smith, Tony Bernard Smith, Ray F. Snitil, Nick Snow, Jessie Crawford Speer, Spencer Turbine Company, Marilyn J. Stabelton, John Steele, Reginald Stone, Joanne Ganne Strader, John J. Strader, Robert J. Stratton, Walter Strony, Ian Sutherland, Bill Taber, John B. Terwilliger, Don Thompson, George Thompson, Taco A. Tiemersma, Stan Todd, Jim Tolle, C. Orian Truss, Robert Turman, Harold Turner, John Varney, Robert F. Vaughn, Richard S. Villemin, Wesley Vos, Roy Wagner, Judd Walton, Claire Watson, Eddie Weaver, Jim Weisenborne, Christopher Wesson, WGN Radio-TV, Dorothy MacClain Whitcomb, Lorin Whitney, Stanley Whittington, Martin Wick, Luella K. Wickham, Wicks Pipe Organ Company, Harry Wilkinson, Janus Wilson, Charles Wright, Ken Wright, M. Searle Wright, Farny Wurlitzer, Cheryl Young, John T. Zander, all presidents, vice-presidents, secretaries, historians and other officials and members of the local chapters of the American Theatre Organ Society across the country and in other countries, officials and members of the Cinema Organ Society of Great Britain and the Theatre Organ Club of Great Britain, and officials and members of the Theatre Organ Society of Australia.

BEHOLD THE MIGHTY WURLITZER

ONE
AN INTRODUCTION

In the earliest days of silent movies, no one thought a thing about musical accompaniment. It was exciting enough to watch the flickering images on the screen. True, the penny arcades often boasted mechanical pianos which played away merrily while patrons shut one eye and squinted into the kinetoscope, but there was no effort to coordinate the music to the "peep show."

As new inventions enabled films to be projected on a screen before an audience, they took on a greater respectability. Entrepreneurs became anxious to exploit this new field of entertainment and sought ways to attract plenty of paying customers. No one knows who first got the idea of putting a piano into his storefront theatre, but it proved profitable. Somehow, live music helped to set the mood and convey emotion more effectively than the silent film alone. Some theatre operators bought electric pianos, which sometimes included drums, traps, and other noisemakers, and played long piano rolls of several musical selections.

Silent films gradually increased in quality, and more sophisticated audiences were attracted to movie theatres. As an evidence of "culture," live piano music, perhaps augmented by an occasional violinist, came into widespread use. As the storefront theatres were gradually replaced by more luxurious film houses, the piano and violin were augmented by additional instruments until orchestras of various sizes came to be featured. Orchestra conductors followed the example of theatre pianists, piecing together musical scores from snippets of classical music, the semiclassics, and the ballads of the day. Quite early in the evolution of film presentation came the development of a whole new medium of musical accompaniment—the introduction of the pipe organ into film theatres. No one knows for sure when or where this first occurred, but surely one of the first exponents of the organ for film theatres was Thomas L. Talley of Los Angeles. In 1905 Talley built a theatre in Los Angeles specifically for film presentation. He had in mind a theatre which would charge only modest admission (ten cents) but which would be a quality house, deluxe in every way. Perhaps it was his love of music which prompted his choice of an organ. Orchestras were expensive. You had to pay a number of musicians to perform, and a piano did not provide the right aura of quality and luxury that he wanted. Thus, he decided upon a pipe organ. Other exhibitors scoffed. The organ had always been identified with sacred and "high-brow" classical music. Film patrons wanted entertainment. Talley was not dissuaded, however. A large expensive Murray M. Harris pipe organ was installed and a classically trained organist (name unknown) was hired to play it. It turned out to be a huge success.[1]

Other theatre operators eventually followed Talley's example. Not many could afford to hire a vast orchestra of musicians to accompany silent pictures. In the deluxe houses these orchestras boasted upwards of fifty or sixty musicians. The alternative was to install a pipe organ outfitted with all sorts of sound effects and percussions. The organist could play while the picture was showing, as the early silent movie pianists had done, but he could skillfully evoke many more moods through the use of various stops or voices of the organ.

In many ways the organ was more flexible than an orchestra for silent picture accompaniment. An orchestra would have to rehearse as a group, and circumstances sometimes prevented the picture being previewed all the way through before the public performance, but in the early days the orchestra leader had to piece together his program from the theatre's own library of music. In later years complete printed scores were available.

A single organist, with a specially designed instrument, could do many things the orchestra could not. He could play music from memory, making smooth transitions from one piece to another. He could time his playing and the use of special effects to fit the actual movement taking place on the screen. Above all, he could improvise musical accompaniments using fragments of ballads, classical and semiclassical themes, incorporating the organ's special sound effects.

In a very real sense, the organ changed the movies and the movies changed the organ. Use of the organ provided a much more realistic accompaniment to the action on the silent screen. This was particularly true because of the sound effects played from the organ such as door bells, steamboat whistles, railroad bells, sirens, bird calls, auto horns, wood blocks, drums, and cymbals. Marimbas, xylophones, all kinds of chimes and bells, and grand pianos were attached and could be played from the console at the flick of a stop tablet (an electrical switch). Further, the organ helped create a certain atmosphere of luxury and culture, thus helping to attract an audience of higher calibre (and greater affluence). At the same time, the movies themselves improved remarkably in a technical and artistic sense. Theatres changed from storefronts to movie palaces and cathedrals of the film. This in turn changed the organ itself. The first organs in theatres were usually built by church-organ builders. They were called straight organs because they were best equipped to play classical and sacred music.

The theatre organ was the result of the achievements and inventions of many persons. Chief among them was Robert Hope-Jones. Hope-Jones did not set out to invent, design, or build an organ specifically to accompany silent pictures. His inventions were designed, rather, to produce an orchestral organ capable of reproducing many of the sounds of an orchestra. This would permit playing serious orchestral works on the organ. This becomes clear when one realizes that many of his major inventions predate 1907, several years before it became a widespread practice to install organs in motion picture theatres.

Hope-Jones built the first reliable electric action pipe organ. An electromagnet was placed at the bottom of each pipe, which opened the valve to admit air to sound the note when a key was depressed at the console. This meant the organ console—the portion of the organ that houses the keyboards (organ keyboards are known as manuals)—could be placed anywhere, connected to the pipes only by a cable of electric wires. Formerly, the console had to be directly attached to the pipes themselves. Hope-Jones perfected this idea in building an organ for a church in England in 1886. He staged a startling demonstration by putting the console out in the churchyard. There he sat amidst tombstones, playing to an audience who heard the sound issuing from the pipes within the church itself.

Hope-Jones was born in England. He migrated to the United States early in the 1900s to avoid prosecution on a morals charge. Although already an organ builder in England, upon arriving in the United States, he set to work at once inventing and designing. Eventually his patents became the property of the Rudolph Wurlitzer Company of North Tonawanda, New York. The Wurlitzer Company marketed a theatre organ known as the "unit orchestra," because it was designed to imitate all sounds produced by an orchestra, using ranks (sets of pipes) each producing its own distinctive tone quality. Wurlitzer made heavy and expert use of advertising and was eminently successful. Just as almost every refrigerator in the 1920s was known as a Frigidaire and every phonograph as a Victrola, so every theatre organ became known as a "Mighty Wurlitzer." There were many well-known makes such as Robert Morton, Kimball, Marr and Colton, Kilgen, Barton, Möller, Page, and others, but the Mighty Wurlitzer became the "Rolls-Royce" of the theatre organ world.

Developments by Hope-Jones and others made possible very rapid changes of organ volume from a whisper to a thundering crescendo. Newly designed instruments permitted very rapid playing and not just the sustained, mellow smoothness of previous organs. It was not the demands of silent picture presentation which led to the invention of the theatre organ. Rather, it was new developments in organ design, most of which preceded the silent film era, which made it possible to use the organ, with minor adaptations, for silent film accompaniment. The demands of silent picture accompaniment resulted in the addition of nontonal percussions such as sirens, horses' hoofs, steamboat whistles, and the like, but the basic design of the unit organ came well before its use in theatres.

Organ pipes were installed in one or two chambers or rooms usually located at either side of the theatre proscenium. Often the console (keyboard desk) was located on an elevator to permit it to be raised into view when needed. It could also sink from sight, eliminating audience distraction during silent film accompaniment.

Anyone who aspired to become a theatre organist could take instruction in one of the special schools in the larger cities such as schools run by Emil Velazco or Lew White in New York, Del Castillo in Boston, or Bill Knauss' school in Chicago. If this was not feasible, he could buy a variety of do-it-yourself books and learn at home. Among those available were: *How to Play the Cinema Organ—A Practical Book by a Practical Player*, authored by a noted British organist, George Tootell; *Musical Accompaniment of Moving Pictures* by Edith Lang and George West, and *Musical Presentation of Motion Pictures*, by George W. Beynon.[2] Each of these books contained a wealth of practical advice. If the organist were accompanying a picture with romantic love scenes, he was advised to play the old favorite "Hearts and Flowers." Neutral music was needed for those "in-between" scenes, and for this Mendelssohn's "Song Without Words" or Liszt's "Consolations" was recommended. Nothing was better for a chase scene where speed was necessary than Chopin's "Minute Waltz" or Wagner's "Ride of the Valkyries." Edvard Grieg's "In the Hall of the Mountain King" was considered best for depicting a "villainous character," and specific suggestions were made to accompany "impending tragedy," the "aftermath of tragedy," and "death" itself.

As if this kind of instruction were not enough, other books featuring the use of special effects appeared. One such delightful volume was C. Roy Carter's *Theatre Organist's Secrets*.[3] In his introduction, Carter set the theme of his book:

An audience will often be more favorably impressed by the organist who takes advantage of appropriate situations for putting in some clever trick or effect than by one who might possibly be a better musician but lets these scenes pass unnoticed. Remarks like "Wasn't that a clever Banjo effect the organist played for that Negro scene?" or "Wasn't that Rooster-crow imitation he put in a scream?" are much more frequent than "Didn't the organist play that Chopin Nocturne beautifully?"[4]

No wonder "legitimate" organists turned up their noses at their counterpart in the cinema.

Carter's book contains instructions and short musical passages which an organist could use to produce effects such as a snore, laughter, a yell or scream, a kiss, a railroad train, an "aeroplane," thunder, a rooster crow, a pig grunt, a cat meow, a lion roar, and many others. Some organists were known for their development and use of a particular effect. Nobody could imitate a barking dog quite as well as Lew White, chief organist of the Roxy Theatre, New York. In England, organist Terance Casey was justly renowned for his interpretation of a man on a sea voyage who becomes quite seasick and very obviously throws up!

Using special effects could be a tricky business if the organist missed his cue. Often there was not an opportunity for the organist to see the film through completely, to plan what he was going to play, before he had to begin his public performance. Former BBC organist Reginald Foort tells of one such time when the silent picture hero, carrying a bouquet of flowers, walked upon the porch of the heroine's home. As he reached for the doorbell, Foort rang it loudly from the organ. Unfortunately, the hero changed his mind, didn't touch the bell, but turned and walked away.

The organ came to have a wider use in theatres than simply for accompaniment of silent pictures. Organ music was played to "empty the house"—while those who had just seen the feature film left, and a new group of patrons entered. Gradually, the organ came to be featured for brief ten- to fifteen-minute solo periods in the larger, more luxurious theatres. Some of the organists themselves became show business "personalities" sharing billing on the theatre marquee with the stars of films and stage shows. Entire full-length organ concerts were given in the theatres, a favorite time being Sunday noon when most theatres opened. Some organists were able to add to their popularity through the medium of phonograph records and live radio broadcasts. Through these media, they became known to thousands who never heard them perform in person. Many persons came to the theatre just to hear the organist play, regardless of the other features of the entertainment bill. Names such as Jesse Crawford—"The Poet of the Organ," Lew White, Fred Feibel, Milton Charles, Ann Leaf—"The Mighty Mite of the Mighty Wurlitzer," Don Miller, Milton Slosser and many others became known widely to many radio and theatre audiences.

The silent movie era eventually came to an end. The birth of "talkies," plus the catastrophic stock market crash, spelled the beginning of the demise of the theatre organ in the United States. With a few notable exceptions, organs fell silent around the country by the mid-thirties.

In the 1950s, the theatre organ experienced a surprising and unexpected comeback. The coming of high fidelity made it the perfect instrument for demonstrating what wide-range sound equipment could do. Thus, rediscovered, the theatre organ became the object of attention by groups of enthusiasts who began printing and circulating newsletters, salvaging organs from theatres and installing them in their own homes, or rebuilding them in their old locations. Silent film series with pipe organ accompaniment became popular, and theatre organ concerts here and there across the country drew enthusiastic crowds. Pizza parlors equipped with theatre pipe organs became all the rage. People of every age bracket seemed interested, not just those who recalled the silent picture era. Young, well-trained, serious musicians began to take a second look at the theatre organ as a unique musical instrument.

The story of the theatre organ is a fascinating one, long deserving the attention of serious research. In the following chapters its history is carefully traced from its origins to the most recent developments.

NOTES

1. Benjamin B. Hampton, *History of the American Film Industry*, 2d ed. (New York: Dover Publications, Inc., 1970), pp. 99–100. This book

is a slightly corrected unabridged reprint of Hampton's, *A History of the Movies* (New York: Covici, Friede, 1931).

2. Each of these three books was probably published in the early 1920s. Only Lang and West carries a copyright date—1920.

3. Carter's book carries no copyright date but undoubtedly comes from the early 1920s. It carries an interesting subtitle, "A Collection of Successful Imitations, Tricks, and Effects for Motion Picture Accompaniment on the Pipe Organ." Compiled and published by C. Roy Carter, Los Angeles, Calif.

4. Ibid., Introduction, no page number.

TWO
THE BEGINNINGS OF THE THEATRE PIPE ORGAN

From the beginning the theatre organ evolved as a very important part of the theatre entertainment package. Many persons came to motion picture theatres because they preferred music to the films or vaudeville acts. It had not always been so. There were many theatres which had graduated from a piano or nickelodeon to a pit organ before moving on to install a full-fledged unit orchestra or organ of its genre.

A theatre of only a few hundred seats usually installed an organ of some kind—frequently a "pit-organ." A pit organ was a small pipe organ or perhaps combination organ/piano with many kinds of special effects such as door bells, fire gongs, tom-toms, tambourines, and castanets. Usually these instruments could be played with rolls (just like piano rolls) or from the keyboard.

> By pulling handles, pushing buttons and stepping on foot pedals the photoplayer operator could orchestrate the fast changing movie scenes by providing march music, romantic interludes, funeral dirges . . . or whatever the flickering scene demanded.[1]

The Robert Morton "Fotoplayer," the Seeburg "Pipe-Organ Orchestra," or the Wurlitzer "one man orchestra" were the more common brands. All helped to enliven the silent picture.

By 1912 and thereafter the Wurlitzer Company, perhaps the

best known of all, began shipping pipe organs to theatres on a regular basis. The pipe organ had begun to take its place as an integral part of the motion picture theatre:

> The Mighty Wurlitzer (and its counterparts) was as much a part of the movie palace as the electric lights that danced around the marquee, or the goldfish that swam in the lobby fountain. Inside the theatre the music seemed to bubble up and soar into the darkness of the balcony. Far below, bathed in a rose spotlight, was the organist perched in the maw of the great golden console. A flick of the finger, and chimes would call Ramona back beside the waterfall. A dramatic sweep of the hand and all would be silent save for the sobbing of the broken-hearted Tibia—languishing in the left loft as it was comforted by its mate, the crooning Vox Humana over on the right—to the tune of "Prisoner of Love." A quick kick at the crescendo pedal, a lightening jab at the combination pistons, and the mood would change to joy again—all glockenspiels, trumpets, tubas and snare drums—as an invisible MacNamara's Band marched across the balcony.[2]

In addition to its use as accompaniment to silent pictures, the organ, with as many dramatic possibilities as these, soon was being featured in brief ten- to fifteen-minute concerts as a part of the regular theatre production.

By the mid-twenties, when movies were still silent, a new device was added. Dick Huemer and Max Fleischer introduced the first "bouncing ball" sing-along cartoon film at the Circle Theatre, Columbus Circle, New York City, in 1924.[3] The idea was to use a cartoon figure or a bouncing ball to hop, skip, or jump from one word to the next of the song lyrics to help the audience get the right tempo for the song. Before long this device became very popular. People liked to sing as a part of a group, so organists added "community sings" to their other bag of tricks and substituted or alternated with ordinary song slides with the lyrics printed on them. It was a good way to forget one's problems and worries for a short while at least.

Certainly motion picture entertainment provided a medium of "escape." The later movie palace complete with theatre pipe organs assisted in producing the aura of make-believe, and doubtless there were many in Hollywood who honestly sought to produce films with this goal in mind. Hortense Powdermaker, an anthropologist of some note, used anthropological techniques to study the film makers. Her conclusion was that Hollywood was a "Dream Factory."[4]

To many it seemed as if the world had lost its bearings after the Great War (World War I). Hollywood provided a medium of escape from the uncertainties of the postwar world. Certain themes were frequently repeated in the average film fare of that time:

> The Good Guys always win in a world where romance is of the essence. Crises are almost always personal, and crises are always successfully resolved. Winning is all-important and winning, although deferred until the last scene, invariably happens. There is little inner conflict, there is no complexity of characterization. The hazards are external, and they are divorced from reality, from the very nature of life.[5]

As part of motion picture theatre entertainment, the theatre pipe organ made its contribution.

Those in the business of motion picture production probably didn't consciously examine their motives in providing a medium of escape. Profit was sufficient reason for creating the kind of mass entertainment which "sold."

By 1914 movies had taken their place as America's fifth largest industry, employing over 100,000 people and representing an estimated total investment of a half-billion dollars.[6] Attendance was estimated at 15 million per day with daily admissions totaling a million dollars.[7] The availability of movies in an increasing number of communities, from small to large, is probably one factor in the tremendous growth of the industry. Another factor was the large return on a small initial investment. Almost any entrepreneur with a very limited amount of capital could go into business as a motion picture exhibitor or even as producer. These factors, among others, led to the phenomenal growth of the motion picture business.

Huge fortunes were built. William Fox, Adolph Zukor, and Louis B. Mayer became known in financial circles as the captains of the industry. When more capital was needed for expansion, Wall Street came to the rescue and the motion picture industry became, more than ever, a huge empire. Gertrude Jobes called it a "Wall Street invasion."[8] The complicated mergers and financial arrangements defied explanation.

Meanwhile Hollywood itself developed into a dream world of its own.

> Well paved boulevards extended for miles where for generations muddy paths had been the only roads. Building after building covered what had been pasture land before. Palatial studios replaced tottering shacks. Millionaires' Lane supplanted Poverty Row. The world's most glamorous city emerged on the site of an unknown sleepy village. In Hollywood were reflected the expansion, the magnitude of the motion picture industry. Its suburbs were studded with estates. A forty-room bungalow was built by the sea for Marion Davies. At Pickfair, Mary Pickford and Douglas Fairbanks, now married, received in imperial style. . . . The men and women of Hollywood were publicized as the best dressed persons in the world. The parties of Hollywood were reported as important social events. The guests of Hollywood were feted as royalty, Hollywood style. The doings of Hollywood personalities became looked-for gossip, the private life of Hollywood, newspaper items.[9]

This make-believe existence was a logical outgrowth of an industry dedicated to escape from reality's world. The theatre pipe organ in no small measure helped extend the dream-world illusion as motion picture theatres grew to motion picture palaces.

By the twenties, movie theatres had become an accepted institution in this country. From coast to coast they were being feverishly constructed to provide for increasingly larger audiences. They also were becoming more lavish. Ben M. Hall in his book, *The Best Remaining Seats*, discusses the evolution of the movie theatre from the tiny storefront hall where flickering images were projected on an ordinary white sheet to the elaborate, gaudy movie palaces such as New York's Roxy or Paramount theatres and a host of lesser "Paramounts" from one end of the country to the other.

From a handful of movie houses in the first years of the twentieth century, the motion picture industry grew to 22,624 theatres by 1900.[10] In the vast majority of those of any size, a theatre pipe organ could be found in daily use. No country of the world ever accepted the theatre organ as fully; America's closest competitor for this honor was England. But why was the theatre pipe organ so popular?

Many reasons might be advanced to explain the rapid development and use of the organ in theatres. First, the organ, as has been suggested, was much more versatile than an orchestra in accompanying silent pictures and live stage acts. In the hands of the gifted performer, near-perfect synchronization could be achieved.

Second, the theatre operator was in business to make a profit. Many of the motion pictures of the twenties fell far below their artistic potential, but they seemed to please the public. The theatre owner had his choice of paying union wages to an orchestra with a minimum of six or seven musicians. Some deluxe houses had orchestras of over one hundred musicians. The theatre organist might earn slightly more than the average trombone player, but he alone could provide a satisfactory substitute for an orchestra pit full of instrumentalists. The theatre operator pocketed the profit.

But versatility and economy were not sufficient reasons for the spectacular rise of the theatre organ. The organ had particular power to express emotion and to convey moods that went far beyond the inherent limitations of the lonely pianist of the early days. From the thundering power of cathedral effects to the soft whispers of the Vox Humana and Celeste, the gamut of human feelings could be expressed.

Roderick Nash writes of the "nervous generation," nervous because of tensions arising from increasing urbanization, shifting absolutes, and the uncertainties of the postwar world.[11] How easy it was for Mr. Smith of Junction City to escape the tensions of the age by visiting one of the local movie palaces. If he desired the less complicated life of an earlier age, he could return to it vicariously through the flickering images on the screen and the mellow tones of the pipe organ. The golden West of which Zane Grey was writing was immortalized then as now in "westerns" which, although often bloody and violent, presented a picture of life in which absolutes were certain and secure, right and wrong were easily distinguished, and the hero always rode the white horse.

For Mother, the serials, such as *The Perils of Pauline* starring Pearl White, provided a week-by-week episode of danger and romance and escape from the boredom of daily life. Would the splendor of love have seemed as vivid or would hearts have fluttered without the ubiquitous organ playing "Hearts and Flowers," as the hero took the heroine in his arms?

Nor were children forgotten by Hollywood. Rin-Tin-Tin, the dog superstar, "was voted the most popular film performer in 1926."[12] The Saturday matinee was geared to the kiddie crowd.

Theatres usually attempted to schedule pictures of more general family interest on the weekends. Dad, Mama, and Junior might go separately during the week but often went as a family on the weekend. Frequently they went on Sunday to the growing distress of the clergy. Estimates of weekly theatre attendance put the figure at 85 million people at the end of the decade of the twenties.[13] Allowing for the tremendous growth in our population since then, contrast those attendance figures with an average of 14 million per week in 1973.[14] This increased somewhat to 21 million per week in 1980.[15]

The films of the twenties and thirties have been described as "devoutly escapist."[16] Poet and critic John Gould Fletcher made the following observation about them: "The American film has served as propaganda for the emotional monotony, the naive morality, the sham luxury, the haphazard etiquette and grotesque exaggeration of the comic, the sentimental and the acrobatic that are so common in the United States."[17] Yet the American public bought it, and in ever-increasing numbers.

Ben Hall, in *The Best Remaining Seats*, has suggested that the movie palace, lavish and opulent, provided not only an escape, but the opportunity to enjoy surroundings more luxurious than royalty could afford. He suggests that this fact may, in itself, have prevented more serious conflicts between the upper and lower socioeconomic classes.[18] The poor could enjoy the same luxury as the rich at twenty-five cents per ticket. The pleasure of being treated like a "somebody" was a part of the appeal of the movie palace. The doorman would throw open the door, and a uniformed usher would show one to a seat. The deep pile carpets and red plush upholstery, to say nothing of the crystal chandeliers and marble balustrades, created an impression of bona fide elegance, and this was standard fare from coast to coast. At the movie theatres, all were equals and everyone was treated alike.

The theatre pipe organ contributed to the whole effect of the movie palace. Samuel Rothafel, the dean of motion picture theatre operators, had dubbed the New York Roxy, his flagship theatre, the Cathedral of the Motion Picture. The organ made the cathedral complete. In fact, Roxy, as Rothafel was called, had formally dedicated his "cathedral" by having a figure dressed as a monk emerge from total darkness on opening night, unfold a scroll and read in a voice of deep conviction:

> Ye portals bright, high and majestic, open to our gaze the path to Wonderland and show us the realm where fantasy reigns, where romance, where adventure flourish. Let Ev'ry day's toil be forgotten under thy sheltering roof—O glorious mighty hall—thy magic and thy charm unite us all to worship at beauty's throne. . . .
>
> Let there be light.[19]

and suddenly the theatre was flooded with light and the orchestra and grand organ pealed forth an anthem appropriate to the occasion. In the lesser Roxys and Paramounts from the Atlantic to the Pacific, theatre managers emulated, to some degree, Samuel Rothafel. The movie palace became the cathedral of the new cinema art and the haven of escape for the nervous generation.

Ben Hall in *The Best Remaining Seats* has perfectly described the experience of theatre attendance in the 1920s in a series of paragraphs which must be read in full in order to aid the reader's imagination in recapturing the flavor of the times:

> For Mama, another world lay beyond the solid bronze box office where the marcelled blonde sat (beside the rose in the bud vase) and zipped out the tickets, sent the change rattling down the chute, read Photoplay, and buffed her nails—all without interrupting her telephone conversation. Heaven only knew what exotic promise waited

behind the velvet ropes in the lobby, what ecstasy was to be tasted in the perfumed half-darkness of the loges. . . .

As she entered the Grand Foyer and surrendered her ticket to the generalissimo at the door, Mama could *feel*, more than hear, the rumbling majesty of the Mighty Wurlitzer in the still-distant auditorium. Not to be fooled by the dashing grenadier who chanted "For the best remaining seats, take the Grand Staircase to the left," she would tighten her grip on her shopping bag and forge ahead to the orchestra floor. Here she would be greeted by a cadet from the court of Franz Josef who would usher her into the auditorium with a deference usually reserved for within-the-ribbons guests at society weddings. Down the aisle he would escort her until just the right seat was found. Then, with a smile and a quick salute, the usher would vanish and leave Mama to settle back in the crimson plush, slip off her Enna-Jetticks and lose herself—body and soul—in Never Never Land.

Many nights Mama came with the whole family. Usually a certain evening each week was set aside for going out to the movies, and usually they went to the same theatre every week. As the dishes were usually hurriedly dried and the milk bottles set out, nobody bothered to look at the paper to see what was playing. It really didn't matter; the picture on the screen at the Xanadu was secondary to the total adventure. It might be bad more often than not, but it was always over in little more than an hour, and then the fun began.

This time Papa bought the tickets and Junior scrunched down in his lumber jacket so he could get in for a dime. Mama and Sister, who had stopped by Liggett's to buy Necco Wafers and Tootsie Rolls (this was before the days of candy counters, and popcorn was something you got only at the circus), joined them in the outer lobby. For Junior (and secretly for the others) this stroll along the polished terrazzo, across the colored rubber mats, past the bronze showcases with the stills for next week's show mounted behind cutouts in the silver-flittered compo boards, past the fountain where giant goldfish who had never seen the light of day swam slowly beneath the changing colored spotlight, past the polished brass doors, past the ticket-taker beside his ornate gold ticket chopper, and finally into the Grand Foyer. . . this was a journey of almost insupportable suspense. Then, if the orchestra could be heard playing mutedly beyond the glass partitions at the back of the auditorium (the stage show had already begun!), Junior could stand it no longer. He broke ranks and ran for the Grand Staircase and the balcony that lay beyond.

In the evenings they always sat in the balcony. It was nice to be able to look up and see the stars twinkle, even if it was raining outside. And those lovely clouds . . . how *did* they do it? Mama never knew.

So there they were. Who cared if the ferns in the porch box at home were dying or if the Essex needed new tires? They were sitting in the midst of a crowd of happy people in the most beautiful place they had ever seen, while way down below a stageful of talented performers was going to see to it that they had a wonderful time.[20]

All this was to be had for fifteen cents to a quarter—a chance to enter a world of beautiful make-believe and to escape from the drudgery and boring routine of daily life. This was a part of the kind of world in which most of our citizens lived.

Escape was likewise offered in the music of the decade. Mark Sullivan who chronicled the twenties does not hold to the theory that the history of a nation is written in its popular songs, but he wrote:

. . . the decade of the 1920's had as its overture the serene and confident *Smiles*, it rose to a fortissimo which might be expressed in a paean of exuberant affluence, *My God, How the Money Rolls In*, and—it ended, after the panic of 1929, with a crashing finale—"crashing" is in this connection an especially apt adjective—the universally familiar and uniquely appropriate song of indigence, *Brother, Can You Spare a Dime*?[21]

Yet one might develop an inaccurate picture of the music and mood of the twenties from this description. The popular songs of the twenties were not all the fast, frenetic pieces often associated with the decade. "Five Foot Two" (1925), "Running Wild" (1922), and "Charley My Boy" (1924), were certainly popular, but likewise the slow, sentimental ballad and the love song had significant places. The top ten best-selling records of the decade included at least six selections of the "Moon-June-croon" variety, such as "My Blue Heaven," "In a Little Spanish Town," and "Sleepy Time Gal."[22] None of these were rousing or raucous. Such popular songs as "Ramona," "Girl of My Dreams," and "The Sweetheart of Sigma Chi" were all written in the twenties and served as vehicles for a new vocal style—the crooner—personified in Gene Austin and Rudy Vallee.

There was certainly an element of escape in this music. Many songs expressed unabashed sentimentality. The organist often used colored slides for his organ solos with the words of the songs projected on the screen, and he urged the theatre audience to sing. More often than not the slides would show a rural scene, of privacy and isolation—a little cottage with morning glories growing around the door—such as that depicted in songs like "Just a Cottage Small By a Waterfall" or "My Blue Heaven." The visual and auditory stimuli helped transport the theatre patron back to an idyllic rural existence. It was escape, pure and simple.

The extent to which the theatre organ contributed to the escapism of the twenties will probably never be fully known. Very little research has been done in this area both in terms of the music itself that predominated and the role of the organ as an instrument uniquely fitted to set the mood. Yet one may well conclude that the movie palace provided institutionalized escape for the nervous generation.

NOTES

1. Q. David Bowers, *Put Another Nickel In* (Vestal, N.Y.: Vestal Press, 1966), p. 29.
2. Ben M. Hall, *The Best Remaining Seats* (New York: Clarkson N. Potter, Inc., 1961), pp. 183–84. (Used by permission.)
3. Harry "J" Jenkins, "The Saga of Koka and His Bouncing Ball," *Theatre Organ Bombarde*, 11, No. 5 (October 1960): pp. 6–10.
4. Hortense Powdermaker, *Hollywood, The Dream Factory* (Boston: Little, Brown and Company, 1950).
5. Arnold W. Green, *Sociology: An Analysis of Life in Modern Society* (New York: McGraw-Hill Book Company, Inc., 1960), p. 579.
6. Gertrude Jobes, *Motion Picture Empire* (Hamden, Conn.: Archon Books, 1966), p. 123.
7. Ibid.
8. Ibid., pp. 193–279.
9. Ibid.
10. "World Theatres," *The Motion Picture Almanac* (1930), p.165.
11. Roderick Nash, *The Nervous Generation* (Chicago: Rand McNally, 1970), p. 3.
12. Maitland Edey et al., eds., *This Fabulous Century*, Vol. 3: *1920–1930* (New York: Time-Life Books, 1969), p. 228.

13. Ibid., vol. 4, *1930–1940*, p. 180.

14. "To Open in Oshkosh," *Time*, October 1, 1973, p. 66.

15. Britannica, *Book of the Year*, 1981, p. 543.

16. "To Open in Oshkosh," *Time*.

17. Ibid.

18. Interview with Ben M. Hall, author of *The Best Remaining Seats*, Noblesville, Ind., September 1964, and Hall, *The Best Remaining Seats*, p. 93.

19. Ibid., p. 8.

20. Ibid., p. 24.

21. Mark Sullivan, *The Twenties*, vol. 6 of *Our Times* (New York: Charles Scribner's Sons, 1935), p. 444.

22. Ibid., p. 470.

THREE
THE MANUFACTURERS OF THE THEATRE PIPE ORGANS

The theatre pipe organ would never have come into existence except for the contributions of Robert Hope-Jones. Although he was not the first to invent electric action for pipe organs, his may be called the first successful and practical electric action.

The first known organ with an electric action (to open a valve, admitting air to sound the pipes) was a two manual instrument constructed by an organ builder named Barker for the Salon, Bouches du Rhône, France, in 1866. Two years later the first electric action instrument to be built in Britain was opened at the Theatre Royal, Drury Lane, London. When this instrument drew its first breath, May 26, 1868, it caused quite a sensation. The pipework was located on stage behind the scenery with the console more than fifty feet away in the orchestra pit. This instrument, although very small, was apparently successful. It was built by the then rather well known British organ building firm of Bryceson.[1]

There had been many early attempts to perfect an electric action for the pipe organ dating almost as far back as the invention of the electromagnet in 1826. Hope-Jones is often credited with being the inventor of electric action, but it would be more correct to say that he refined it and made it fully workable. He was able to eliminate many of the problems that plagued other experimenters. Particularly, he should be credited for reducing the voltage carried by the wiring system of the pipe organ, making it safer and decreasing the likelihood of electromechanical failure. That he succeeded in this enterprise is testified to by the fact that of the approximately thirty organs he built in England, many are still functioning well with their original electric actions and, eighty years or more old, require only routine maintenance.

Hope-Jones was born in Hooten-Grange, Cheshire, England, in 1851.[2] He developed from a precocious child into a somewhat erratic genius. He played the organ himself but found more pleasure in tinkering with the mechanical aspects of the instrument. In 1886, when he built the now famous organ for St. John's Anglican Church, Birkenhead, hardly anyone had ever seen an organ where the pipes and console (keyboards) were detached. Formerly the organist pressed a key at the console, which was connected directly by means of rods to a valve at the bottom of a single pipe, opening it to admit air to sound the note. Hope Jones' use of electricity with an electromagnet to open the air valves made it possible to place the organ console anywhere, connected to the pipes only by a cable of electric wires. It was at Birkenhead that Hope-Jones staged his dramatic demonstration of playing the organ within the church from a console located outside the church, placed amidst the tombstones in the churchyard. Perhaps it was this flair for the dramatic that led to his receiving many contracts to build similar instruments.

It was the Austin Pipe Organ Company that first hired Hope-Jones when he arrived in this country, rather suddenly, in 1903. He had been allowed to leave Britain rather than to be prosecuted for corrupting the morals of a minor.[3] He did not remain with Austin long, but worked for a succession of organ builders including Ernest M. Skinner, before he finally established his own company at Elmira, New York, in 1907.[4] Although he was something of a mechanical genius, his business acumen did not match his inventive skill. Yet he was able to interest such persons as Mark Twain and Diamond Jim Brady in investing as stockholders in his company.[5] He built a number of notable instruments while in business for himself such as the organ in the enormous 10,000-seat auditorium in Ocean Grove, New Jersey. The organ remains playable today.

Hope-Jones did not purposely direct his efforts toward the invention of the theatre pipe organ. In the days of his earliest inventions, theatres were not using organs. Yet the sum total of his contribution to organ building made the theatre organ possible. This list of his inventions and adaptations is startling indeed. It was he who first designed the "horseshoe" console (with stop board shaped like a horseshoe) to put all stops within easy reach of the organist. He also pioneered the use of a stop tablet rather than a drawknob. He slightly tilted the keyboards toward the organist to make the instrument easier to play. He invented the "Double Touch," which allowed the organist to bring a second set of organ voices into play by applying a little extra pressure to the keys. From this came his invention of the "Pizzicato Touch" which produced a staccato or plucking effect, like a violinist plucking strings.

William H. Barnes believes Hope-Jones' most significant discovery to be the so-called unit system. The unit system (or unification)

> is the ability to use the same set of pipes at all pitches (16; 8; 4; $2^2/_3$; 2; $1^3/_5$) on all manuals and pedals. Consequently, a Concert Flute, for example, could be played at any pitch or on any keyboard. . . . Unification is the reason the largest theatre organs have so few ranks of pipes compared to the largest church organs.[6]

It was this invention which, more than any other except electric action, revolutionized organ building.

The list of Hope-Jones achievements and refinements in organ building is almost too numerous to catalog. Hope-Jones himself described a number of his own innovations in a lecture he gave in 1910 for the National Association of Organists explaining his design of the famed Ocean Grove Auditorium organ. His address not only described the organ but gave some idea of his philosophy of organ building. Some excerpts from his lecture follow:

> *Expression*: Is it not obvious that every stop and every pipe of every organ should, as a matter of course be enclosed?

> *High pressure*: Twenty years ago a pressure sufficient to lift a column of water three or three and a half inches, was practically universal. In

this organ before you the pressures employed are ten inches, twenty-five and fifty inches.

Diaphone (Patent): The basis of this organ we have been examining is the Diaphone. It is the most powerful foundation stop in the instrument. This particular Diaphone resembles a Diapason in tone quality, but many distinct colors of tone can be produced from a Diaphone. This one that I hold in my hand is a diaphonic flute. It consists, as you see, of a small aluminum piston which rapidly and freely vibrates in an enclosing cylinder. Though the whole thing is scarcely larger than my two fists it wouıd (if supplied with sufficient pressure) produce a sweet musical note that could be heard twenty miles away.

Unit Organ (Patent): This Ocean Grove instrument is a "Unit Organ," though from the limitation in funds, necessarily a skeleton one. Months before its completion the "Unit Organ" had developed on the following published lines.

The old departments of Pedal, Great, Swell, Choir, and Solo are abandoned in favor of Foundation, String, Woodwind, Brass, and Percussion departments. Each of these latter is enclosed in its own independent cement swell box. The whole organ is treated as a unit. Practically any of the stops may be drawn upon any of the manuals (or on the pedal) at any pitch.

The Foundation department contains the Diaphone, the Tibias, and two or three Diapasons. The Strings department contains a couple of mild and robust Gambas, two or three very keen Viol d'orchestres, a Quintation Flute for furnishing the deep body tone often heard in strings, a Vox Humana Celeste, and perhaps my new Vox Viola—in fact any stops that go to make up a thrilling mass of "live" string tone.

The Wood Wind department contains the Oboe, Orchestral Oboe, Clarinet, Cor Anglais, Kinura, Concert Flutes, etc.

The Bass department contains the Trombones, Trumpets and Tubas.

The percussion department embraces the Tympani, Drums, Triangle, Glockenspeil [sic], Chimes, etc.

A set of stop keys representing all or most of these stops, at various pitches, is provided in connection with the great manual. Another set is provided in connection with the swell; another in connection with the choir, another with the solo, and another with the pedal. By their means any selection of the stops from the various departments may be freely drawn and mixed on any keyboard quite [in]dependently of what may at the same time be in use on the other keyboards. Because of limited funds this organ has but 14 stops. It is easily the most powerful instrument in the world, and I fancy it would be difficult to find any fifty stop organ giving equal variety of effect.

Suitable Bass (Patent): On each keyboard there is provided a double touch or piston labeled "Suitable bass." Upon touching this tablet the pedal stops and couplers instantly so group themselves as to provide a bass that is suitable to the stops at the moment in use upon that particular manual. If the tablet be pressed much more firmly it will become locked down and then the pedal stops and couplers will continue to move automatically so as to keep the bass suited to that particular manual, whatever changes may be made in registration. This locked suitable bass tablet will release itself the moment the performer touches any of the pedal stops or couplers by hand or touches the suitable bass tablet belonging to any other manual.

All the combination pistons in the Unit Organ are provided with double touch. The first touch moves the manual stops only, but a firmer touch will provide a suitable bass for the particular combination in use.

Double Touch: In the Unit Organ all keys and pedals are provided with double touch. The first touch is an ordinary or normal one and the key is brought to rest against an apparently solid bottom in the usual way. When, however, great extra pressure is used the key will suddenly give way again about a sixteenth of an inch and a strengthening of tone, either of the same or of another quality, will be brought into play.

We have heard much said against "degrading the organ" and "prostituting our art"—I cannot see the matter in this light. Such remarks are indeed forceful when applied to the Church organ; but I fail to see that you thereby hinder yourselves from performing the highest classical compositions on the Church organ when the proper times and seasons arrive. . . .

"Degrading our art" indeed! Let me tell you that there is scope for the exercise of the highest art any of you can bring to bear, in rendering effectively good popular composition on the new orchestral organ or "Unit Orchestra" as I prefer to call it. If any of you will successfully study this new art I can promise you will not lack remunerative employment.[7]

Hope-Jones continued to amaze laymen and musicians alike with his new ideas. On one occasion he set up a unit orchestra in the Baptist Temple in Philadelphia and for sixteen days gave daily recitals. He charged an admission of twenty five cents per person for the poorer seats and up to fifty cents for the best. About 300 persons attended the first concert. By the close of the series "the police had to be called out to disperse the crowds unable to obtain even standing room" in the 3,000-seat structure.[8]

The "unit orchestra" fitted naturally into the environment of the silent picture theatre. One person, making skillful use of the voices and sound effects, could make the action on the screen come alive. A full orchestra of live musicians was not necessary. In fact, one person could provide superior, well-coordinated picture accompaniment. Reginald Foort, famous British theatre organist, remembers:

> The organist . . . could either play suitable music from memory, sliding smoothly from each piece into the next without a break, or he could improvise. Above all, playing entirely by himself, he could time his playing when necessary to fit the actual movement taking place on the screen.[9]

The first pipe organs installed in the theatres were usually built by church organ builders and thus were merely translated church instruments appearing before the silver screen rather than before the altar. Many builders sold and installed such instruments. Eventually a great many companies began to manufacture pipe organs designed specifically for theatres. No one knows exactly how many companies were engaged in such business, but they ranged from Wurlitzer, Kimball, Robert Morton, Möller, Barton, Marr and Colton, and others which produced hundreds or thousands of instruments to some tiny business enterprises which may have produced only one or two instruments in a garage on a back lot somewhere.

The *Exhibitor's Herald-World* of October 25, 1930, carried a list of manufacturers making organs expressly for theatres. That list ran as follows:

Maxcy-Barton Company	—Chicago, Ill.
Beman Organ Company	—Binghamton, N.Y.
Bennett Organ Company	—Rock Island, Ill.
Estey Organ Company	—Brattleboro, Vt.
Geneva Organ Company	—Geneva, Ill.
Hall Organ Company	—West Haven, Conn.
Hillgreen-Lane Organ Company	—Alliance, Ohio
Geo. Kilgen and Sons Organ Company	—St. Louis, Mo.
W. W. Kimball Organ Company	—Chicago, Ill.
Link Organ Company	—Binghamton, N.Y.
Marr and Colton Organ Company	—Warsaw, N.Y.
M. P. Möller Organ Company	—Hagerstown, Md.
Robert Morton Organ Company	—Van Nuys, Calif.
National Theatre Supply Company	—New York, N.Y.
Nelson-Wiggin Piano Company	—Chicago, Ill.
Page Organ Company	—Lima, Ohio
Henry Pilcher's Sons Organ Company	—Louisville, Ky.
J. P. Seeburg Organ Company	—Chicago, Ill.
Wurlitzer Organ Company	—Cincinnati, Ohio

The names as they appear here are not necessarily the form in which they were used in the trade and in advertising. Although this is an impressive list, it is incomplete.

The same section of *Exhibitor's Herald-World* included a partial list of companies engaged in the manufacture of pipe organ rolls. It included such companies as the Automatic Music Roll Company of Chicago, Filmusic Company of Hollywood, the Geneva Organ Company of Geneva, Illinois, and the QRS-DeVry Corporation of Chicago. Not listed are many companies that manufactured rolls at this time including Wurlitzer, Austin, Aeolian, and others.[10]

The balance of this chapter has been divided into two parts. Part I includes the better-known manufacturers of theatre pipe organs—Wurlitzer, Barton, Estey, Kilgen, Kimball, Marr and Colton, Möller, Robert Morton, and Wicks. With the exception of Wurlitzer, these appear in the text in alphabetical order. These were not in every case the largest builders in terms of numbers of organs manufactured, but they were, perhaps, the most publicized and the most commonly known. All other builders are categorized as "Lesser-Known Builders." In many cases, these were firms that were well publicized and well known, but perhaps more for their church, concert, and residence instruments than for their theatre instruments. Others in this category were simply small concerns that did not manufacture many organs. The assignment of builders to one or the other of these categories is somewhat arbitrary and open to argument, and does not reflect the author's assessment of the quality of the instruments produced.

PART I: BETTER-KNOWN MANUFACTURERS

WURLITZER

By all odds, the best-known manufacturer of theatre pipe organs was Wurlitzer. Ben Hall in *The Best Remaining Seats* recalled:

> of course there were a score or more manufacturers of theatre organs, but the Wurlitzer basked in the same sweet sunlight of generic familiarity as the Frigidaire, the Victrola, and the Kodak. It might be a Kimball, a Robert Morton, a Möller, a Page, a Barton, or a Marr and Colton (a few of the better-known makes), but to the average moviegoer, if it rose up out of the pit at intermission with a roar that made the marrow dance in one's bones, if rows of colored stop-tabs, lit by hidden lights, arched like a rainbow above the flawless dental work of the keyboards, if it could imitate anything from a brass band to a Ford horn to a choir of angels gee, Dad, it was a Wurlitzer.[11]

The "Mighty Wurlitzer" was standard equipment in the average movie palace of the 1920s. It was as much a part of the theatre as curtains, orchestra pit, and screen.

The Wurlitzer pipe organ was the product of a family engaged in the manufacture of musical instruments for hundreds of years. The Wurlitzer family can trace its name at least as far back as the 1590s. The original Wurlitzer, Heinrich, was born in Schillbach, Saxony. His ancestors may originally have been from an area known as Wurlitz in Bavaria. It was not, however, until Nicholas Wurlitzer came on the scene in 1659 that we find the first recorded instance of this family making musical instruments. Nicholas did not become a swordmaker like his father, but rather spent his life making lutes. Other descendants were known to be violin makers.[12]

Rudolph Wurlitzer, the father of the American branch of the Wurlitzer family, was born in Saxony in 1831. Seeking greater opportunity than his father's general store provided, Rudolph set sail for America, landing on the East Coast in 1853 with no money and very little command of English. Ironically, his first job was in a New Jersey grocery store. But Rudolph had not crossed the ocean to do the kind of work he had left in Germany. This was the land of opportunity to him, and he was to make the most of it. Assiduously saving a portion of his meager earnings, he eventually accumulated $700. He sent the entire amount to his relatives in Saxony and asked them to ship musical instruments to him, which he, in turn, sold to retailers. He had found a job as a bank clerk in the predominantly German city of Cincinnati, but in his spare time he worked at his importing business, finally setting it up on a formal basis as the Rudolph Wurlitzer Company. He located in three small rooms over the Masonic Building at Fourth and Sycamore streets in Cincinnati, and a mere three years after his penniless arrival, was managing a thriving business.[13]

Rudolph Wurlitzer became a naturalized citizen in 1859, and his brothers, Anton and Franz, soon came over from Germany to join the business. Strangely enough, the Civil War provided much opportunity for expansion. The Union Army needed drums and trumpets, which Wurlitzer cheerfully supplied. In 1868, with the war over, Rudolph felt the time was right to marry Leonie Farny.[14] Six children were born of this union: Sylvia, Howard Eugene, Rudolph Henry, Leonie, Percy, and Farny Reginald, the youngest.[15]

The first keyboard instrument manufactured in this country under the Wurlitzer name was a piano in 1880. Soon, automatic and coin-operated musical instruments were added as a sideline. This came about through a merger with Eugene DeKliest of Düsseldorf, who had come to this country and set up the North Tonawanda Barrel Organ Works, locating there because of the availability of the kinds of wood he needed. He joined forces with Wurlitzer around the turn of the century, specializing in making and marketing military band organs, orchestrions, player pianos, and other like instruments.[16]

Farny Wurlitzer joined the firm in 1904 and soon became manager of the North Tonawanda plant. It was he who recognized a potential market in making instruments for the accompaniment of silent films. The next step was the manufacture of organs in piano-type cases.[17]

Before Wurlitzer acquired Hope-Jones' patents, Hope-Jones himself had manufactured and installed a considerable number of organs. His very first *unit* organ (1ater to be universally known as *theatre* organ) left the Elmira factory on February 3, 1907. For a period of about three years Hope-Jones marketed the type of instrument later to be known as "Wurlitzer" before the Wurlitzer Company had anything to do with it. One such early Hope-Jones instrument was a two manual, six rank organ (that had only "Hope-Jones" on the nameplate) installed in a small theatre on the main street of Canaan, Connecticut.[18]

In 1909, Hope-Jones became insolvent and his assets and patents were acquired by the Wurlitzer Company. Hope-Jones stayed on for a time in the capacity of supervisor. Farny Wurlitzer remembered him as "a genius, but not practical. We would have an organ already set up on the erecting room floor and Hope-Jones would get a sudden inspiration to make some basic change in it or add some new device." It was impossible to conduct a profit-making enterprise in that way. His inclination to make continual changes in an effort to improve instruments did not lend itself to mass production. Finally Hope-Jones' increasingly erratic behavior led to his being barred from the Wurlitzer factory. Disillusioned, he committed suicide on September 14, 1914. Sometime afterward the company changed the name of its instruments to Wurlitzer Unit Orchestras.

With the use of skillful marketing and advertising techniques, Wurlitzer became the best known and most prestigious builder of theatre pipe organs in the world.[19] The term "Mighty Wurlitzer" became, in the minds of many, synonymous with "theatre pipe organs." At the peak in 1926, the company was shipping one complete pipe organ from the factory every day. In 1931, *Fortune Magazine* estimated Wurlitzer business as grossing $6 million annually.[20]

The first genuine Wurlitzer theatre pipe organ was the Style L, which went on the market around 1912. It featured a regular, nonhorseshoe console with a concave pedalboard, roll-player mechanism, and detached pipe case. It cost around $9,000. One of the early successful horseshoe-console Wurlitzer pipe organs was the three manual, seventeen rank instrument installed in 1914 in the Liberty Theatre in Seattle, Washington. The theatre was designed just for photoplay productions and had only a shallow stage and no dressing rooms. The organ pipes were located in chambers on either side of the theatre and above the proscenium. The console was placed in the exact center of the orchestra pit. This was probably the first organ designed just for a theatre to carry the Wurlitzer nameplate. This organ cost $45,000 originally, and the Jensen and Von Herberg Company, theatre owners, made arrangements to pay for it on a contract basis, so much per week. It was paid off in one-quarter of the specified time because the theatre was so successful.[21] Interestingly enough, the original direct-current blower operated off the street car lines, so the organ could not be played after the power was shut off at midnight. The instrument survives today in the First Nazarene Church, Spokane, Washington.

This organ is of historic importance in another way as well. It was the first Wurlitzer pipe organ in Jesse Crawford's life. Crawford was destined to become the most famous theatre organist in the world, and he was fascinated as he heard this instrument played by Henry B. Murtagh.[22]

The Wurlitzer theatre pipe organ played a most prominent part in Crawford's career. From the time he went to Los Angeles to work for Sid Grauman, to his rise to fame in Chicago and to the pinnacle of his career at the New York Paramount where he was billed as the "Poet of the Organ," Crawford rarely played any other brand of instrument. In addition, from his first recordings to his last, the organ he played was almost always a Wurlitzer. In most of his sound films, both alone and with his wife Helen, and in nearly all of his radio broadcasts, it was the "Poet of the Organ at the Mighty Wurlitzer."

Crawford preferred the Wurlitzer for the vividness of its tone colors, the speed of its action, and its incomparable dynamic range. He felt that no other instrument had its capabilities, and he was, as a result, the best "salesman" Wurlitzer ever had. Probably because of this, the Wurlitzer Company gave him a four manual, twenty-one rank organ, which was installed in the Paramount Theatre studio on the ninth floor of the Paramount Building. Here, at the height of his career, he broadcast over all the major networks, made his most memorable 78 rpm recordings, and rehearsed for his solo productions to be presented on the four manual, thirty-six rank Wurlitzer in the theatre below.

The Wurlitzer Company is well remembered for the outstanding quality of its instruments. The New York Paramount Theatre Wurlitzer became the standard by which all others were judged. Wurlitzer also had the signal honor of manufacturing and installing the world's largest theatre pipe organ installed in a theatre. This organ featured two four manual consoles on either side of the proscenium, fifty-eight ranks of pipes, and was installed in the Radio City Music Hall, New York, for its opening in 1932. Remarkably, the organ is still in regular use.[23] Wurlitzer produced a considerable number of four manual instruments and a total of three organs with five manuals (a five manual, twenty-eight rank organ, Michigan Theatre, Detroit; and five manual, twenty-one rank organs in the Marbro and Paradise theatres, Chicago).

BARTON

Another of the better-known builders was the Barton Company of Oshkosh, Wisconsin. Organized in 1911, the company first manufactured a photoplayer device called the Bartola which employed an upright piano to which were added a few ranks of pipes, a set of chimes, and other percussive effects. A limited number of these were built in 1911 and thereafter by Daniel Barton, founder of the firm.[24] At the start, the manufacturing was done in the factory of the Oshkosh Metal Products Company in Oshkosh, Wisconsin. The first Bartola included the upright piano with a separate cabinet for the drums and traps and a separate cabinet for orchestra bells, xylophone, and marimba on the left. At the right of the piano was a cabinet containing two ranks of pipes—a flute and a violin.[25] Well-known theatre organist and music personality Eddy Hanson was invited by Dan Barton to try this first Bartola. It was the start of a long and fruitful friendship between these two men.[26]

From these beginnings, the Barton Company went on to manufacture some very fine theatre pipe organs, which compare favorably with the best output of any other manufacturer. The first sales office was opened in Chicago in the Schiller Building at 64 West Randolph Street. Later, the offices were moved to the Mallers Building at 5 South Wabash Avenue.

The Barton Company produced from 700 to 800 theatre organs, which varied from small to very large, including two dual console instruments. One notable installation was the three manual, fourteen rank instrument in the lavish Indiana Theatre in downtown Indianapolis. This organ boasted a gold console mounted on the usual lift but also on a turntable allowing the console to turn while it was being played. This instrument will always be associated in the public mind with theatre organist Dessa Byrd, who was well known in the Midwest through personal appearances and radio broadcasts.

Another widely publicized Barton was installed in the Rialto Theatre, Joliet, Illinois, on May 23, 1926. This four manual, twenty-one rank instrument is still maintained and used regularly. Organist Kay McAbee has recorded and concertized on it for a period of years.

The most famous Barton installation is in the Chicago Stadium. It has been described as the world's largest unit pipe organ—a statement that does spur controversy within the theatre organ world. The statistics alone are overwhelming. The organ console is considerably higher than the organist's head (when the organist is seated) and includes 6 manuals and 833 stop keys. The pipes are located in dust-proof chambers suspended from the ceiling of this vast auditorium. The organ is powered by a 100 horsepower Spencer blower. The seven and one-half ton console is finished in red and gold. It is mounted on a turntable.[27] It has been described by one writer as "the loudest organ ever built."[28] It required fourteen boxcars to move the organ from the factory to the stadium; a crew of thirty-six men worked for over three months to install it, and the final tuning required six weeks.[29]

Al Melgard was associated with this instrument for many years until his retirement in 1973. Activities in the Chicago Stadium include everything from hockey games to political conventions, and Melgard played for them all. Born in Denmark, Melgard came to Chicago at the age of six where he enjoyed a long career as a radio and theatre organist and pianist before going to the stadium in 1929.[30]

In 1929 the company took ads in various trade journals to announce its change of name from the Bartola Musical Instrument Company to the Maxcy-Barton Organ Company. The advertisement read: "to the many friends of the Barton Organ we assure that this makes no other change in personnel or manufacture and wish for their continued goodwill and patronage. 'The Same Golden-Voiced Organ.' " This phrase had been their advertising slogan for many years. Warren G. Maxcy bankrolled the new partnership, but the company went out of business when theatre organs went out of fashion. Dan Barton died April 26, 1974, just a few days short of his ninetieth birthday.[31]

ESTEY

The Estey Pipe Organ Company was founded in 1846 by Jacob Estey in Brattleboro, Vermont. It closed its doors forever in the early 1960s, but it was in the hands of the Estey family throughout its more than a century of life.[32]

Estey left its mark on America through the widespread sale of its reed parlor organs, which were very popular before the turn of the century, and the company continued to manufacture them until it finally went bankrupt. Electrified-reed organs were still being manufactured and sold even after the company had ceased building pipe organs. In 1974 small chord organs were being manufactured bearing the Estey name, but it is probable that there was no connection with the original Estey Company.

During its years of pipe organ manufacture, Estey is estimated to have built about 3,300 pipe instruments.[33] William Barnes and Edward Gammons in their book, *Two Centuries of American Organ Building*, indicate that the company was quite innovative. It was for Estey that William E. Haskell developed the Haskell pipe—"half length open basses for the longer open pipes."[34] Estey also owned patents based on Haskell's work for reedless oboes and saxophones.

Beginning in 1907 the company built pipe organs with stop controls in the form of an additional manual above the other manuals with the names of the stops imprinted on the fronts of the white keys. To turn on the stops, one pressed the nearest black key—a system which must have been rather confusing.

Beginning in 1923 the company began using a luminous stop control, often referred to as the "cash register" type of stop control. To turn on the stop, one pressed the glass stop knob which lighted up. To disengage the stop, one pressed it again and the light went out.[35] This system was delightful to use, but many problems resulted. It was possible for an organist to experience an electrical shock in playing an Estey organ thus equipped. The company replaced many of these stop control systems at its own expense and moved to the use of more conventional controls on later instruments.

The Estey Company built quite a few residence and concert instruments including a great many with fine quality automatic player mechanisms. Most of its instruments were built for churches. The number of theatre instruments that it produced represented a small fraction of its total output. Yet, several of these Estey theatre organs were quite distinctive in character. One was a three manual, fourteen rank instrument installed in the United Artists Studio in Hollywood which was later resold to Walt Disney for his studio. Other notable installations included the Clemmer Theatre, Seattle (three manual, twenty-eight rank) and the Capitol Theatre, Broadway and 51st Street, New York City.[36] (National Theatre Supply was, for a time, the exclusive dealer for Estey in the metropolitan New York City area.)

New York's Capitol Theatre was a remarkable movie palace. At the time it opened in 1919, it was the largest in the world. It seated over 5,000 persons. Major Edward Bowes was its first director, and he left his imprint upon it as did Samuel L. Rothafel, better known as "Roxy."[37] The Capitol featured a four manual, thirty-five rank Estey, the largest theatre instrument ever built by the company. The instrument was not highly unified but was a concert organ in design. Such organists as Dr. Melchiorre Mauro-Cottone and Dr. C.A.J. Parmentier were associated with this instrument.[38] Parmentier had followed Deszo Von D'Antalffy as chief organist, and when Parmentier left for the Fox Theatre, Philadelphia, he was succeeded by Carl McKinley.

The original console, of the tilting stop tablet variety, was replaced in July 1923 by an Estey luminous stop console. Four years later the Estey Company added twelve more ranks of pipes (to the original thirty-five ranks), a full set of traps, additional tonal percussions, and effects, a grand piano, and a horseshoe console. Estey took an ad in trade papers to advertise the finished product as "Broadway's Finest Organ." A later organist of the Capitol, Henry B. Murtagh, was not satisfied with the instrument however, and longed for a Wurlitzer.

At least one more notable Estey installation should be mentioned. This was the three manual, twenty-one rank organ in the Trinity Baptist Church in Camden, New Jersey. The Victor Talking Machine Company of Camden purchased the church in the early 1920s and used it as a recording studio. Many well-known organists recorded for Victor on this instrument.[39]

KILGEN

The Kilgen Organ Company was also one of the best-known manufacturers of pipe organs. Company brochures spoke of the ancient origins of this company in Germany as far back as 1640 in Duvlach.[40] George Kilgen, of that ancient family, came to the New World in 1851, and the Kilgen Organ Company established its home in St. Louis, Missouri, in 1873.[41] The Kilgen Company remained in the family until it ceased operation in 1960.[42] The Kilgen shield included the Latin inscription "Mirabile Auditu" which means "wonderful to hear."[43] From this came the advertising slogan, the Kilgen "Wonder Organ," which was widely used during the 1920s when Kilgen was deeply involved in the manufacture of theatre organs. The bulk of the company's total output was church instruments and included such important installations as those at St. Patrick's Cathedral and Carnegie Hall, New York.

Alfred G. Kilgen, grandson of the American founder, was perhaps most responsible for the theatre organ business of the company. He spent ten years as an apprentice in the Kilgen factory before attending St. Louis University and earning a degree in law. Although he passed his bar examination, he practiced law only briefly before taking a position as sales manager for Wurlitzer. Two and a half years later he returned to Kilgen where he remained until his retirement. He died in 1974. Other notable persons who were associated with Kilgen included Dr. Charles M. Courboin, tonal advisor for a time, and a grandson of Henry Willis who served as head voicer for a period of years.[44]

One of the most notable theatre installations by the Kilgen Company was the four manual organ in the Picadilly Theatre, Chicago. This organ was highly duplexed with 225 stop keys controlling its nineteen ranks, plus a piano and other percussions and effects. Featured at this organ for a time was the well-known Leo Terry of St. Louis.

Other noted Kilgen organs were installed in the Majestic Theatre in Houston; the Palace in Gary, Indiana; the Palace in Canton, Ohio; the Jayhawk Theatre in Topeka, Kansas; the Alamo in Chicago, and the "L" Lido in Chicago. Kilgen had a number of installations in well-known radio stations such as KMOX with studios in the Mayfair Hotel in St. Louis; WKY, Oklahoma City; and WHAS, Louisville.

KIMBALL

The Kimball Organ Company was one of the best known of all the builders of theatre pipe organs. In fact, it was one of the three largest builders in terms of total theatre output. Only Wurlitzer and Robert Morton built more theatre pipe organs.[45]

The Kimball Company was founded in Chicago in 1857 by William Wallace Kimball.[46] Like the Estey Company, Kimball became a large business concern by manufacturing reed parlor organs. Kimball had sold pianos upon arriving in Chicago, later adding reed organs to his stock. From the start, they sold well, and by 1878 Kimball was making and selling his own Parlor organs.[47] This is what made him the "king of the piano and organ industry in Chicago."[48] By the time the company ceased to manufacture reed organs (September 1922), it had made and sold over 400,000 of the instruments.

Kimball began manufacturing pipe organs in 1894 and ceased operations in 1942. All told it had built 7,326 instruments.[49] Around 1920, Robert Pier Elliott became manager of the organ department and from that time onward, some excellent instruments were built reflecting his ideas. Kimball organs were noted for their use of good materials and hence for their reliability. Their organ business might have turned more of a profit over the years had they cheapened the product. This they steadfastly refused to do. Dr. William H. Barnes estimates that 80 percent of the company's output in the 1920s was theatre organs.

The most famous Kimball theatre pipe organ was the three console, thirty-four rank organ in New York's Roxy Theatre—perhaps the most lavish and ornate movie palace ever built—and, at the time of its opening, March 11, 1927, the largest theatre, with 6,214 seats.[50] This remarkable organ had one main five manual console flanked by a three manual "brass" console and a three manual "woodwind" console. The Roxy theatre also boasted a studio organ and a lobby or rotunda organ built by Kimball. The famous Lew White was chief organist of the Roxy Theatre for many years. Other notable organists on the staff there included Dr. C.A.J. Parmentier, Dezso Von D'Antalffy, and George Epstein. The organ in the theatre was somewhat muffled as it was installed under the stage—a very uncommon practice in the United States. It was Roxy's idea to locate the organ there, so that the sound could merge with that of the orchestra. It was unsuccessful in this application because the orchestra lift, when elevated with eighty musicians aboard, completely covered the pipe chamber openings. This buried sound was partly compensated for by the three rank Fanfare organ installed high over the proscenium arch and to the right. These ranks included a Military Bugle, the Fanfare Trumpet, and a Fife.[51] Near the Fanfare chamber was installed a gigantic set of tower chimes. The Fanfare organ ranks and chimes gave out with a deafening sound but much of it was lost when heard in the theatre itself. Thus they were seldom used. Altogether the Roxy organs were a part of the $135,000 Kimball contract.[52]

Other outstanding theatre installations by Kimball included the Wiltern Theatre in Los Angeles (four manuals, thirty-seven ranks), which was originally installed in the Forum Theatre in Los Angeles. No one who has ever heard its beautiful string stops or the unique "Serpent" rank will ever forget it.

The Convention Hall Ballroom at Atlantic City, New Jersey, boasts the largest unit organ that Kimball built. It was designed by Senator Emerson L. Richards and has four manuals and fifty-five ranks.[53]

The Minneapolis Civic Auditorium organ has two consoles—one of the conventional style (five manuals) and another four manual horseshoe console, on separate elevators.[54]

Other important installations included the four manual organ in the Palace Theatre, Philadelphia; the three manual organ in the Stanley Theatre in Philadelphia; the three manual organ in the Stratford Theatre, Chicago; the three manual organ in the Roosevelt Theatre, Chicago (where Helen Anderson was playing at the time she met her future husband, Jesse Crawford, who was playing across the street at the Chicago Theatre); and the huge 6,616 pipe Kimball in the Public Auditorium, Pretoria, the Transvaal, Union of South Africa.[55]

Kimball installed its share of pipe organs in radio stations including WABC in New York City and WGN, Chicago. The WGN organ is still in service. Many outstanding church installations were done by Kimball, the most famous of which was the 1900–1901 rebuild of the Mormon Tabernacle organ in Salt Lake City.[56]

The last organ to leave the Kimball factory was one that had been ordered by Richard Simonton, noted organ enthusiast, for his residence. It was a small concert instrument, built from materials and pipes still in stock in the factory. Just after it was completed, the pipe organ division was liquidated. All organ consoles and large wooden pipes in stock were taken out into the factory lot and burned. Wallace Kimball, president, decided that the shortage of materials, due to the beginning of World War II and the low profit return, meant the end of Kimball's manufacture of pipe organs. The future, he believed, lay in the photoelectric cell organ. The year of this fateful decision was 1942.[57]

William H. Barnes and Edward Gammans in *Two Centuries of American Organ Building* wrote: "Their [Kimball's] pipe organs, theatre, church and concert, were some of the very best organs produced in that period. Their exit from the pipe organ building scene is greatly to be regretted."[58] Today the Kimball name lives on, since 1959 the property of the Jasper Corporation, which claims to be the largest producer of pianos and organs in the United States.[59]

MARR AND COLTON

The Marr and Colton Company had its origins in the Robert Hope-Jones and Wurlitzer companies. It was founded by David Marr, a native of London, England, who had emigrated to this country in 1904.[60] Marr had worked for seven years as an apprentice in a pipe organ company in Edinburgh, Scotland, where one of the other employees was Robert Hope-Jones, previously mentioned.

Upon arriving in this country, David Marr went to work for the Skinner Organ Company in Boston where he again encountered Robert Hope-Jones. When Hope-Jones left Skinner to open his own factory in Elmira, New York, in 1907, Marr accompanied him. It was here that he first met John J. Colton, who was to play a large part in his business affairs in the future. When Wurlitzer absorbed the Hope-Jones Company, Marr went along to North Tonawanda, eventually becoming factory superintendent for the firm.

In 1915, Marr opened his own pipe organ factory in Warsaw, New York. He had been invited to do so by various business interests in Warsaw who promised financial backing. He was joined by John J. Colton, who had by now studied tuning and voicing of pipe organs. Although the new firm was the Marr and Colton Company because of the long-standing friendship of these two men, John J. Colton was not an investor in the firm.

The company began in a garage (which is still standing) and later moved to a plant at the foot of Industrial Street in Warsaw. Here it was accessible to rail lines for the shipment of raw materials and finished organs. The company's first instrument was built for the Oatka Theatre in Warsaw. Not long thereafter, it began using the advertising slogan, "America's Finest Organ."

At its height in the mid-twenties, Marr and Colton had about 375 people on its payroll. David Marr served as president of the concern, and John J. Colton, known as "Jack," served as chief tuner and voicer. David Marr liked to give each organ its final test by personally playing "Just a Cottage Small By a Waterfall" or "Waltz of the Flowers" before the instrument in the erecting room was dismantled and shipped. The Marrs frequently went along for the opening of new theatre installations and sometimes David Marr would do the final tuning with Mrs. Marr holding down the proper keys.

The Marr and Colton Company built one of its largest theatre organs for the 4,000 seat Rochester Theatre in Rochester, New York. This was a five manual, twenty-four rank instrument which was opened in November 1927. Other notable installations included the three manual, seventeen rank instrument in the Oriole Theatre, Detroit; the organ in radio station WJR, Detroit; the three manual, twenty rank instrument in Keeney's Theatre, Elmira, New York; the four manual, twenty-eight rank instrument in the Piccadilly Theatre in New York (now in Warner's, Hollywood); the four manual, twenty rank instrument in the Rivoli Theatre, Toledo, Ohio; the four manual, seventeen rank instrument in the Capitol Theatre, Wheeling, West Virginia, the four manual instrument in the 2,000 seat Zaring's Egyptian Theatre, Indianapolis, and the four manual, eighteen rank organ in the Roosevelt Theatre, Buffalo.[61]

The Marr and Colton Company is particularly remembered for a very ingenious invention known as the "Symphonic Registrator." This was a device of presets which were controlled by a row of colored stop tablets at the console. Each was labeled for a particular mood or emotional tone. When the stop tablet was pressed, a preset combination of organ voices were engaged to spare the organist the trouble of trying to decide which stops combined together would sound best to produce a particular mood or effect. The Symphonic Registrator was not a part of every Marr and Colton, as its development came late in the theatre organ's golden age, but one such instrument included the following tabs:

1. Love, Mother
2. Love, Romantic
3. Love, Passion
4. Lullaby
5. Quietude
6. Jealousy
7. Hatred
8. Anger
9. Excitement
10. Agitation
11. Suspense
12. Garden
13. Water
14. Rural
15. Children
16. Happiness
17. Festival
18. Fox Trot (1)
19. Fox Trot (2)
20. Waltz (1)
21. Waltz (2)
22. March
23. Mysterious
24. Gruesome
25. Neutral (1)
26. Neutral (2)
27. Neutral (3)
28. Night
29. Fire
30. Storm
31. Chase
32. Chinese
33. Oriental
34. Spanish
35. Funeral
36. Sorrow
37. Pathetic
38. Cathedral
39. Full Organ[62]

Among well-known organists who worked with the Marr and Colton Company was one very colorful gentleman named C. Sharpe Minor. His first name was Charles and his mother's maiden name was Sharpe, which, when put together, made a perfect name for a musical personality. Minor made a few recordings for the Edison Company which give us a glimpse of his playing. He is particularly remembered as a showman and undoubtedly he helped to sell many Marr and Colton organs.

Like most theatre organ companies, Marr and Colton went bankrupt after the advent of sound films and the Depression of the thirties. It built approximately "500–600 organs for theatres, churches, auditoriums, radio stations and homes. Not one instrument was sold outside the continental United States."

The company ceased operations in 1932. John Colton went to work with the Kilgen Company in St. Louis and died shortly thereafter. David Marr carried on a small organ service and repair business, working out of his cellar and garage until his death in 1951.[63]

MÖLLER

The Möller Company of Hagerstown, Maryland, has for years billed itself as the "World's Largest Pipe Organ Builder." Mathias Peter Möller was born on the island of Bornholm, Denmark, in 1854. He emigrated to America in 1872, eventually working for the Felgemaker Organ Company of Erie, Pennsylvania. In 1880 he moved to Hagerstown to establish his pipe organ factory. By the time of his death in 1934 he had also engaged in the hotel and automobile business.[64] By 1982 the Möller Company had built approximately 11,600 pipe organs during its history, and of this total about 500 were theatre organs.[65]

Möller first installed an organ in a theatre in Montgomery, Alabama (Orpheum Theatre, Opus #1177), around 1913. This two manual, twelve register organ was a transplanted church instrument with a few percussions and special effects added. However, in 1927 Möller built its first fully unified theatre pipe organ. It was Opus #4777, a three manual, fifteen rank (157 register) instrument destined for the Allegheny Theatre, Philadelphia, Pennsylvania. It is estimated that after 1927 until the end of the theatre organ era, about one-quarter of the factory's total output was destined for theatres. Today, Möller is one of two companies still in business that built theatre organs in the "golden era" and is still able to build a theatre pipe organ on demand.

One of the outstanding installations built by Möller for a theatre was the four manual, thirty-nine rank organ for Stanley's Metropolitan Theatre in Philadelphia installed in 1928. As was true for the larger Möller theatre organs, the console was enormous—fully ten feet wide. The organ included a full complement of percussive effects.[66]

Another famous Möller theatre organ was the five manual, twenty-seven rank instrument built for world-famous theatre organist, Reginald Foort. This was Opus #6690, shipped from the factory October 22, 1938. Utterly unique in the annals of organ building, this thirty-ton instrument was built to be able—designed so that it could be set up within twenty-four hours, disassembled after a concert engagement, and trucked (via four large thirty-foot vans) to a new location to be reassembled again. "All in all, the organ was erected and dismantled a total of 187 times in the relatively short period it was in use from late 1938 until the involvement of Britain in the hostilities of World War II in 1940."[67] The complete story of this remarkable instrument is told by Reginald Foort in his illuminating book, *The Cinema Organ*.[68]

This organ was purchased by the BBC for broadcasting purposes during World War II and was sold to Radio Holland in the 1960s. In July 1973 it was removed and shipped back to the Möller factory to be rebuilt for a prospective purchaser, the owner of a pizza palace restaurant in San Diego, California.[69] On hand to try the instrument upon the arrival from Holland was its original owner, Reginald Foort, who reinaugurated the instrument in the Organ Power No. 2 (pizza restaurant), Pacific Beach, California, October 2, 1975.[70] This organ was moved once more and installed in the Civic Auditorium, Pasadena, California in 1980.

Perhaps the best-known of the Möller theatre organs in the United States is the four manual, forty-two rank instrument in the fabulous Fox Theatre, Atlanta, Georgia. The Fox, with just under 4,000 seats, is now the third largest theatre in the United States (after Radio City Music Hall and the Detroit and St. Louis Fox theatres). It opened Christmas Day (the first show was at 1:30 P.M.), 1929, "an enormous mosque, with great bronze domes, soaring parapets and towering minarets. . . ."[71] The theatre is an atmospheric house, where stars twinkle and clouds drift by on the ceiling. The organ in this stupendous temple of the film was and still is colossal. It was the largest theatre organ Möller ever built, and the Fox provides such an excellent acoustical setting that this is undoubtedly the finest sounding Möller ever. It is Opus #5566 and was one of the last theatre organs Möller built. It has been carefully and lovingly maintained by Joe Patten of Atlanta and beautifully recorded by organist Bob Van Camp.[72]

The Möller Company has produced one or two new theatre pipe organs in recent years for pizza palaces. It is well able to produce any size theatre organ to order even to this day. Only one other major builder in America—Wicks—is still able to do this.

ROBERT MORTON

Perhaps the most prolific of all the builders of theatre pipe organs was the Robert Morton firm of Van Nuys, California. The California Organ Company of Van Nuys was the descendant of the Murray M. Harris Company of Los Angeles, which had built a number of organs for theatres in 1911 and 1912 before it experienced financial failure. The Johnson Organ Company had been its immediate successor. Financial promoters for the newly laid-out community of Van Nuys lured Johnson there from Los Angeles. The company opened a new factory in 1913 but, in less than a year, the land developers who had brought him there took over the operation of his plant, renaming it the California Organ Company.

At the same time in Berkeley, California, another firm, the American Photo Player Company, was doing a very brisk business selling its "Fotoplayers"—a piano augmented by several ranks of pipes and assorted percussions, traps, and special effects. These instruments sold basically to theatres of under 2,000 seats, and they sold by the thousands. However, as larger theatres were built, sales leveled off. Larger instruments were needed.

In the California Organ Company was an employee named Stanley Williams, who had been an organ builder apprentice under none other than Robert Hope-Jones. When the company decided to expand into the theatre field, the executives got together with the head of the American Photo Player Company, and Williams was finally directed to build such an instrument at the California Theatre in Santa Barbara in 1917.

The name Robert Morton was chosen by Harold J. Werner, president of the American Photo Player Company. He had two sons named Robert and Morton. A new name was needed for the new instrument so Werner decided to put the two boys' names together—Robert Morton. The company was chartered to do business in California in 1917.[73]

One of the first organs to be built in 1917 was the three manual instrument in Miller's California Theatre, Los Angeles. One of the first organists to play it was Jesse Crawford—in the days before he moved to Chicago.[74]

Altogether, the company produced four five-manual organs. Three went to the theatres. The best remembered of these was the thirty rank instrument installed in the Kinema Theatre (later renamed the Criterion) in Los Angeles.[75]

A little known facet of Robert Morton history concerns a manufacturing and sales agreement made with the Wicks Organ Company of Highland, Illinois. Harold Werner negotiated with Wicks to produce Robert Morton theatre organs for sale in the midwestern and eastern portions of the United States. These organs built by Wicks were not identical to Robert Morton organs. They used Wicks's direct-electric action without pouches. "If the Morton salesman demonstrated one of the organs built in Van Nuys, and the buyer's theatre was located closer to Highland, Illinois, the instrument to be delivered was one of those built by Wicks."[76] This arrangement continued until 1924 when the Robert Morton Company temporarily ceased operations.[77]

The Robert Morton Company received a new lease on life when Mortimer Fleishacker brought the company out of bankruptcy. It went on to produce some of its finest organs before closing its doors for the last time at the end of the golden era of the theatre organ.

A controversy has raged for many years as to which builder of theatre organs made the most instruments. Wurlitzer was the best advertised and presumed by many to be the largest builder. Farny Wurlitzer put the figures of Wurlitzer's total output of theatre organs at around 3,000.[78] (Actual output numbered 2,238.)

In a copyrighted story from the *Los Angeles Times*, dated January 2, 1972, Paul Carlsted, former factory manager for the Robert Morton Company, claims that Robert Morton was the world's largest manufacturer of theatre pipe organs. He places their total output at just under 6,000 units.[79] It is assumed that this figure would include those built for Robert Morton by Wicks. It appears impossible to verify or deny this claim.

A notable Robert Morton installation included the four manual, sixty-one rank, two console instrument for the Elks Temple in Los Angeles. The largest ever built by Robert Morton was the four manual, eighty-five rank classical instrument installed in Bovard Auditorium, University of California at Los Angeles, in 1920–21.[80]

Alexander Pantages, head of the Pantages theatre chain, entered into an agreement with Robert Morton and installed Morton organs exclusively in his theatres. The Consolidated Theatres chain in Hawaii equipped most of it theatres with Mortons. The Robert Morton in the Princess Theatre in Honolulu was recorded by Don George, and the Robert Morton in the Waikiki Theatre in Honolulu was recorded by Edwin Sawtelle and in more recent years by John De Mello.

Perhaps the most famous of the Morton organs was the four manual, twenty rank instrument in the Saenger Theatre, New Orleans. Under the expert guidance of John Hammond, this instrument held the Saenger patrons enthralled. The Saenger Robert Morton held the same place for the Morton Company that the New York Paramount organ held for Wurlitzer. Due to a splendid acoustical setting, the Saenger was Robert Morton's finest sounding instrument, the one against which all other Robert Mortons were judged.[81] Fortunately this organ and theatre remain intact. Since restoration has been carried out, Saenger patrons can thrill once again to the sound of this remarkable instrument.

WICKS

The Wicks Pipe Organ Company was founded in 1906 by Louis Wick.[82] The factory was established in Highland, Illinois, just across the Mississippi River from St. Louis. In 1914 the Wicks Company introduced a direct-electric action, which involved a direct electric magnet under each pipe. This gave Wicks a great advantage in the building of its theatre pipe organs.[83]

The Wicks Company is presided over by Martin M. Wick, who is the son of the founder. The company does a large business in church and classical instruments but also has produced some theatre or unit organs in recent years for private homes and pizza palaces.

By arrangement with the Robert Morton Company of Van Nuys, California, many theatre organs were built and marketed by Wicks under the Robert Morton name (see above). Wicks also built quite a few theatre organs under its own name—mostly for smaller theatres. One Wicks theatre organ was installed as far away as Hawaii.[84] A Wicks theatre pipe organ was installed in the Grand Opera House, St. Louis, Missouri, and was inaugurated in March 1928 by Wolfram Schaeffer of Stuttgart, Germany. There is no list of Wicks installations extant or any reliable figures as to total theatre output.

PART II: LESSER-KNOWN MANUFACTURERS

AEOLIAN

The Aeolian Company was primarily a builder of residence organs. The company was first launched in the 1890's as a manufacturer of reed organs of considerable size and remarkable tone quality known as Orchestrelles with an automatic roll-playing mechanism in them. From this they graduated to the building of pipe organs with automatic roll players. They were not the only company manufacturing pipe organs with automatic roll-playing mechanisms. Austin, Estey, Kilgen, Kimball, Link, Möller, Skinner, Welte, Wicks, Wurlitzer, and others also built such instruments in the 1920s. The Aeolian Company, however, built up a much larger library of organ rolls than the others and was usually credited with having a superior roll-playing mechanism.

Aeolian pipe organs went into the residences of the wealthy in America. A particularly fine instrument was installed in Charles M. Schwab's New York residence, where it was played and recorded by Archer Gibson. Gibson is credited with having recorded about half of the organ rolls in Aeolian's extensive library.[85] He also made a number of recordings for the Victor Talking Machine Company on Schwab's organ.

Perhaps the most notable residence installation ever completed by Aeolian (and the largest pipe organ ever installed in a private residence in the United States) was the 10,000 pipe, 169 rank, four manual instrument built for M. Pierre S. duPont and installed in the ballroom of the estate called Longwood Gardens near Kennett Square, Pennsylvania. This organ included five thirty-two foot pedal stops, percussions, and a nine foot Weber concert grand piano. It featured a separate Duo-Art player mechanism console from which the organ could be played automatically.[86] This instrument was designed and played by Firmin Swinnen, who was a theatre and concert organist. The tremendous cost of building this organ is believed to have been a contributing factor in the demise of the old Aeolian Company. The company had its corporate headquarters at 689 Fifth Avenue, New York City. Frank Taft was head of the organ department for many years.[87] Leslie Leet was factory superintendent during the years of 1929–30 when the duPont organ was built.[88] The company merged with the Skinner Organ Company in 1931, and after that time, few residence organs were built.[89]

Aeolian did build a few theatre organs. Around 1929 one such instrument of unknown size was installed in the Keswick Theatre in Glenside, Pennsylvania. This organ is believed to have been of three manuals and definitely featured a horseshoe console.[90]

ARTCRAFT

Artcraft organs were built in Santa Monica, California. Little is known about the company except that it advertised itself in the twenties as "builders of theatre, residence and church organs."[91]

AUSTIN

Austin is still a respected name in the pipe organ world. Founded by John T. Austin in the early 1900s, the company soon showed great creativity. Basil G. Austin, brother of John, was also active in the firm. Barnes and Gammons credit these two brothers with "obtaining more patents on innovations in organ mechanisms than any organ builder before or since."[92] Among these are the well-known universal air chest, and the

Austin console of unique design.[93] Austin also built and perfected an automatic roll-playing mechanism and recording device used at the factory to produce organ rolls for residence installations.

Austin built some theatre organs. These were chiefly straight, romantically voiced instruments with some added percussions and effects. (Perhaps the most noted of these instruments was the organ that Austin built for the Eastman Theatre in Rochester, New York.) At the Eastman School, organ accompaniment of movies was taught as a separate, serious course of study. Both a Wurlitzer and a Marr and Colton were installed in the school and used as practice organs. However, the organ in the Eastman Theatre was a four manual, 155 rank instrument of classical design with some added percussions. It was installed backstage, and much of the sound was lost before it reached the audience. Thc reason for the backstage installation was Eastman's personal insistence that since the organ was to be used for silent picture accompaniment, the sound should come from behind the screen. Everyone, including Wurlitzer sales people who wanted the contract, and Harold Gleason, Eastman's private organist, tried to change his mind. Eastman remained intransigent. The result was that the finished organ was not much more than a distant rumble.[94] It remained intact until recently when it was removed.[95]

Austin installed about nine organs in Brooklyn theatres, seven in New York City; and six in Cleveland, in addition to others in theatres across the country. Barnes and Gammons estimated that Austin had produced about 2,500 instruments of all types from its inception until 1970.[96] More than one hundred organs were installed in theatres, and of these approximately twelve were unit instruments. None had horseshoe consoles.

BALCOM AND VAUGHN

Organized in 1929 in Seattle, Washington, by C. M. Balcom, formerly of the Kimball Company, Balcom and Vaughn did rebuild, install, and service theatre pipe organs. It did, on occasion, build consoles, chests, shutters, regulators, tremolos, and other parts for theatre organs but never manufactured a complete organ including making its own pipes. This was true of many of the smaller companies. Balcom and Vaughn produces classical instruments today, and most of its work is for churches.[97]

BEMAN

The Beman Organ Company began operations in 1884 and remained in business until 1942. Located in Binghamton, New York, the company produced church organs almost exclusively. Some Beman organs were installed in theatres in the Binghamton, New York, area, but none remain extant. By 1924 the company had produced a total of 317 organs, twenty-seven of which were installed within a few miles of the Eldridge Street factory.[98]

Famous theatre organist Fred Feibel recalled playing a Beman Symphonic organ in the Summit Theatre, Union City, New Jersey, early in his career:

> The elderly Mr. Beman, a really fine gentleman and a great organ technician, used to come to the theatre when installing major additions, which once included a new console. He enjoyed sitting beside me on the organ bench while I played for the silent movie.[99]

BENNETT

The Bennett Company was originally established as Bennett Brothers in Milwaukee around 1880.[100] Around the turn of the century Robert J. Bennett joined Octavius Marshall, formerly of Philadelphia, to form the Marshall-Bennett Company located in Rock Island, Illinois. By 1909 the company had reorganized as the Bennett Organ Company. The Bennett Company apparently did install some organs in theatres, although none are known to be extant.[101]

BUHL

Paul C. Buhl, founder of the firm, was born in Germany in 1878. After completing public school he was apprenticed for a period of four years to Wiegle, a famous organ builder. At the age of nineteen, he emigrated to America, first settling in

Springfield, Massachusetts, where he worked briefly with the J. W. Steere Organ Company, before making his permanent home in Utica, New York, in 1905. This same year he entered into partnership with Albert L. Barnes, a local organist, and established the Barnes and Buhl Organ Company located on Columbia Street near Schuyler. Albert Barnes died the next year, and Frank E. Blashfield from Boston took up the vacant partnership.[102] The company operated under the name of Buhl and Blashfield from 1914 to 1927, when it was renamed the Buhl Organ Company—the name under which it operated until the death of Buhl in 1950.

Paul Buhl was named vice president of the Rochester Organ Company in 1929, and Rochester organs were built in the Buhl factory. Altogether Paul Buhl had a part in building over 200 instruments, most of which went to churches. A few were installed in theatres including the Colonial Theatre in Utica, New York. In 1921 a Buhl and Blashfield theatre organ was shipped to the Honolulu Music Company for installation in the Peoples Theatre (renamed the Princess) in Honolulu. When it was decided that a larger instrument would be needed, it was installed instead in the Kaimuki Theatre, where it remained from 1922 to 1954. It was later removed to the Kailua Methodist Church where it remained for more than twenty years before being sold to a private individual.[103]

Buhl theatre organs were equipped with such features as double-touch, and some had roll playing mechanisms attached. Most Buhl theatre organs were three manual instruments.[104]

COZATT

The Cozatt Organ Company was established by Perry Cozatt in Danville, Illinois.[105] Cozatt, an immigrant to this country, was a man of many skills. A printer, engraver, and photographer, he was interested in pipe organs and calliopes. He built both in a factory attached to his residence outside Danville. Because of his ability in several areas he did the photography, designed, and printed his own advertising brochures for his pipe organs. Most of his installations were in churches and theatres in the Midwest. One of the most important was a three manual instrument installed in the Fine Arts Theatre in Monmouth, Illinois, with Lloyd Jones presiding at the console. A school for theatre organ was operated in conjunction with the company, which featured the use of a four manual instrument.

Perry Cozatt built and installed a four manual, eleven rank instrument in his own residence in 1921 and used it for demonstration purposes. After his death in 1960 the organ lay idle for a time before being purchased for installation in a private residence.

In later years, when pipe organ companies found themselves in competition with electronic organ companies such as Hammond, Cozatt built and marketed a single manual, two rank (Violin Diapason and Flute) organ with twenty-five note radiating pedal board called the "Organette." The console was detachable, and all the pipe work could be placed in its own cabinet under expression, or in a chamber. Chimes were optional. A remarkable fact is that Cozatt made the entire organ himself including the pipes.

Perry Cozatt's son, Perry, Jr., joined the firm and he continues a thriving business building calliopes.

FRAZEE

Leslie H. Frazee, founder of the company, was born in Saint John, New Brunswick, in 1870. At the tender age of fourteen he went to work for the F. A. Peters Organ Company in his hometown where he learned a great many basic organ-building skills. In 1894 he moved to Boston and went to work for Jesse Woodbury, organ builder, eventually becoming voicer for all the company's pipework. When Woodbury retired in 1910, Leslie Frazee, E. E. Smallman, and Henry D. Kimball (who was not related to W. W. Kimball) formed the firm of Kimball, Smallman, and Frazee. In 1915 Smallman retired, and the firm became the Kimball-Frazee Organ Company. Kimball died in 1920, and Leslie Frazee's son, H. Norman, took over the business, renaming it the Frazee Organ Company. The home office and factory were located in Boston. Later they built a plant in West Everett, Massachusetts, and after World War II moved to South Natick, Massachusetts. H. Norman Frazee conducted the business until his death at the age of sixty-three on May 17, 1969.[106]

Leslie H. Frazee had another son, Roy L. Frazee, who was the musician of the family. He attended the New England Conservatory of Music, became a church organist, and eventually got into the theatre organ field. He is especially remembered for his tenure at the Granada Theatre, Malden, Massachusetts, and Keith's Theatre, Boston.

Almost all of the Frazee Company's output was for churches. It did build several theatre organs including a three manual instrument for the Orpheum Theatre, Boston, and another instrument of unknown size for the State Theatre, Milford, Massachusetts. Barnes and Gammons commented on the high quality of the Frazee Company's work in their book, *Two Centuries of American Organ Building*.[107]

GOTTFRIED

Anton Gottfried arrived in the United States from Germany in 1888. Having worked for Walcker, Europe's largest organ builder, he had no difficulty finding a job in this country in his chosen field. He joined the Frank Roosevelt Organ Company of New York, later moving on to the C. S. Haskell Company in Philadelphia. Roosevelt then hired him to head its Philadelphia branch, and he began manufacturing organ parts and supplies for the parent firm. In 1894 he joined the Felgemaker Company in Erie, Pennsylvania, but it was not long before he went into business for himself. His greatest ability lay in manufacturing and voicing reed pipes although he manufactured pipes of all types for other organ builders—especially those that duplicated orchestral voices. His pipes were shipped to various places around the world.[108] Much of his output was for churches, but he also made pipes for theatre organs. Numbers of builders such as Link and Page bought most, if not all, of their metal pipework from Gottfried. Gottfried did manufacture at least one complete theatre pipe organ—a four manual horseshoe console instrument for the New Carmen Theatre in Philadelphia in 1928.

Gottfried was widely recognized for his expert work. Dr.

Osaker Walcker, his former employer in Germany, wrote him, "In my opinion there is no doubt that you are the greatest artist in the art of voicing and the leader of the world in organ pipe tone and production."[109] Barnes and Gammons called Gottfried "one of the best reed voicers in the country."[110] In 1950 after fifty years in business Gottfried sold out to Dr. Andrian Standaart of the famed Dutch family of organ builders, who was setting up an organ business in Suffolk, Virginia. Gottfried became vice president of the company.[111]

GUENTHER

The Guenther Organ Company of Portland, Oregon, assembled pipe organs, as did many companies, buying pipes and other components from Gottfried, Dennison, Pierce, and other builders. It is believed that a limited number of these instruments were installed in theatres.[112]

HALL

Harry Hall was born in Nottingham, England, in 1870 and was apprenticed to an organ builder at an early age. He came to the United States and established his own organ-building firm in New Haven, Connecticut, in 1895. His first organ was a three manual instrument built for the Mishkin Israel Synagogue in New Haven. This organ was a success and led to more business. The company grew rapidly and in 1912 built a much larger factory in West Haven, Connecticut.

With the coming of the theatre organ era, Hall built and installed a number of instruments to meet the growing demand. One of the most successful was a three manual organ built for Poli's Palace Theatre, Bridgeport—one of several built for the Poli's Theatrical Enterprises chain in Connecticut.

For a brief period the Hall Organ Company was affiliated with the Welte-Mignon Company, but in 1927 this relationship was severed by mutual consent. During the period when these companies were merged Hall built a two manual organ to Welte's specifications and installed it in the Welte-Mignon Studio, New York City. After the Depression, Harry Hall continued in business alone in a smaller way, rebuilding and caring for both church and theatre organs in the West Haven area until his death in 1945.[113]

HILLGREEN-LANE

Hillgreen-Lane of Alliance, Ohio, built organs for churches, homes, and theatres until its demise in the 1970s. This company produced a number of theatre instruments during the "golden era" of the theatre organ. Pitts Pipe Organs of Omaha, Nebraska, handled sales for the western half of the United States. The eastern territory was handled from the factory. Pitts must have done a good job of sales work, for there were many Hillgreen-Lane theatre organs in the Omaha, Nebraska, area.[114]

One of the Hillgreen-Lane theatre organs to receive recent publicity was the three manual, fourteen rank instrument installed in the Sunshine Theatre in Albuquerque, New Mexico, in 1928. Donated to the New Mexico Military Institute of Roswell, New Mexico, in 1940, it was restored in 1971–72 and rededicated in April 1973 by theatre organist Dennis James.[115]

The Hillgreen-Lane Company built a new theatre organ as late as 1948 for installation in the new Odeon Theatre in Toronto (now the Carlton Theatre). This three manual instrument was opened by theatre organist Al Bollington. The installation reflected more modern tonal design than the typical Hillgreen-Lane or other theatre installations of the theatre organ era.[116]

KOHL

The Kohl Organ Company of Rochester, New York, built several theatre organs which were installed in Rochester theatres. One was a three manual, horseshoe console instrument for the Monroe Theatre in Rochester. This organ was later removed and installed in a church in Connecticut before being relocated again—this time in a private home in Florida. Other Rochester theatres that had Kohl organs were the Arnett, Cameo, Clinton, Empress, Family, Jefferson, Plaza, Princess, Stahley, Sun, and World. These were small neighborhood houses, and the organs were mostly two manual instruments. The Kohl Company advertised as "Arthur A. Kohl, Organ

Builder, Rochester, New York" and remained in business until Kohl's retirement in the 1950s.[117]

HINNERS

The Hinners Organ Company was founded by John L. Hinners in Pekin, Illinois, in 1881. Hinners was born in Wheeling, Ohio, of German immigrant parents. His first experience in the organ business was as a reed organ builder for Mason and Hamlin. His first business partner was J. J. Fink whose share of the company was bought out in 1885 by U. J. Albertsen. About 1890 Hinners and Albertsen began mass producing small pipe organs, which were sold by direct mail to its customers. The company employed no salesmen but printed its catalogue in both German and English to reach the many communities of German immigrants established in the Midwest before the turn of the century.

Albertsen retired from the company in 1902, and four years later John L. Hinners died. His son Arthur became head of the company which continued in business until 1936.[118] During those years Hinners built several organs for theatres. A three manual tubular pneumatic instrument was installed in the American Theatre, Terre Haute, Indiana, for example. Other four or five rank organs installed in theatres included the following: Castle Theatre, Bloomington, Illinois; the Belasco Theatre, Quincy, Illinois; Pekin Theatre, Pekin, Illinois; a theatre in Muscatine, Iowa; and the Princess Theatre, Rushville, Illinois. Doubtless there were others. The largest and best remembered Hinners theatre organ was the three manual, eleven rank instrument in the Madison Theatre in downtown Peoria, Illinois. The organ, still intact in the theatre, has not been played since the early 1950s.[119]

HOLTKAMP

The Voettler, Holtkamp and Sparling Organ Company of Cleveland, Ohio, was formed by George F. Voettler, an organ builder from Cleveland in business as early as 1856. In 1903 Henry H. Holtkamp joined the firm and the third partner, Allen G. Sparling, entered the company in 1914. Walter Holtkamp, Sr., became a partner following World War I and eventually emerged as one of the most prominent leaders in the organ reform (an attempt to return to older classical organ building principles.)[120]

During the theatre organ era the company built a number of theatre organs. These include instruments in the Garner Theatre, Toledo Ohio; the Hippodrome Theatre, Youngstown, Ohio; the Westerville Theatre, Westerville, Ohio; and the Lincoln Theatre, Cleveland, Ohio.[121]

Henry H. Holtkamp died in 1931, and Walter Holtkamp, Sr., became company head. A. G. Sparling retired in 1943, and the company changed its name to the Holtkamp Organ Company. Walter Holtkamp, Jr., joined the firm sometime thereafter.[122]

HOOK AND HASTINGS

Hook and Hastings was a prestigious name in organ building for over a hundred years. Founded in Boston in 1827 by Elias and George G. Hook, the company went on to build over 2,000 organs, "including some of the largest and most important in the world at the time they were built."[123] Francis Hastings joined the firm about 1870. This firm built such notable organs as the instrument for the Cincinnati Music Hall in 1878 and the original organ in Riverside Church, New York, in 1927.[124] Before it ceased operations in 1936, it did build a few organs for theatres. One installation was in the Circle Theatre in Indianapolis which was later replaced by a Wurlitzer. It is not known to what extent this company engaged in the manufacture of organs for theatres, but probably it was on a very limited basis.

LINK

In Huntington, Indiana, in the early 1900s, the Shaff Brothers Piano Company was building and selling pianos to the Automatic Musical Company of Binghamton, New York. The Automatic Musical Company went bankrupt in 1910, and George Link's son, Edwin A. Link, was asked to go to Binghamton to operate the company. The Links had two sons, George T. Link and Edwin A. Link, Jr. Together the family moved to Binghamton, and Edwin, Sr., took over the company's affairs. In a few years he bought it outright and changed its name to the Link Piano Company and continued manufacturing automatic pianos called "nickelodeons" because they were coin-operated.[125]

In 1914 the company began building its first theatre organs—a piano with four ranks of pipes and special effects attached. By the 1920s the company was producing full-size pipe organs for churches, homes, and theatres. Of the 1,000 pipe organs that the company built, about 200 were installed in theatres.[126] Some of the two manual instruments were fitted with Link's own automatic roll-playing mechanism. About twelve three manual Link theatre organs were constructed and a five manual instrument was designed but never built.[127]

Link employed famed theatre organist C. Sharpe Minor for a time and used his name in advertising. The Link Company even designed a model named for Minor—the "C. Sharpe Minor Unit Organ."[128] Three organs of this model were installed, one in the Capitol Theatre, Binghamton, New York, another in the State Theatre, Ithaca, New York, and the third in the Holtnorth Theatre, Cleveland, Ohio. A three manual, twelve rank traveling organ was constructed by Link for C. Sharpe Minor who did some touring with it, but on a limited basis. Like many of the other lesser-known builders of theatre organs, Link purchased most of its pipe work from the Anton Gottfried Company of Erie, Pennsylvania. Link ceased manufacturing pipe organs at the time of the Depression.

Later, Link developed an aircraft trainer during World War II, which it continues to manufacture in contemporary versions for today's space age. The firm, now under the direction of Edwin Link, Jr., is also doing research and development of advanced underwater diving equipment.[129] In 1968 Link gave the three manual, eleven rank Link theatre organ formerly installed in the Capitol Theatre (1927) in Binghamton, New York, to the new Roberson Center for the Arts and Sciences in Binghamton. He completely refurbished, enlarged, and installed the organ as a gift to the people of Binghamton. Thus the Link theatre organ lives on for future generations to enjoy.[130]

LOUISVILLE

The Louisville Pipe Organ Company was founded by three former employees of the Bennett Pipe Organ Company in business for some time in Rock Island, Illinois. Louisville organs used the same magnets used by Bennett, and undoubtedly there were other examples of the carryover of Bennett technology. First established in Louisville, the company preserved its same name but moved to Terre Haute, Indiana, in 1929 before going bankrupt in 1932. Some of the employees returned to Louisville and operated an organ maintenance service known as the Louisville Organ Company for several years thereafter.[131]

Several theatre pipe organs were built by the Louisville Company during the silent film era. They were known as Louisville "uniphones" and featured horseshoe consoles and usual theatre pipe organ unification, and they were of excellent workmanship. The best-known of these organs was the three manual, eight rank instrument built in 1927 for the Louisville Labor Temple, a union hall-theatre. During the 1930s the United Hebrew Congregation Synagogue of Terre Haute, Indiana, purchased the organ, discarded the louder pipes, percussions, and effects, added a Dulciana and two Diapasons, and installed it for use in worship. In 1965 it was purchased by Thomas Ferree, now of the Heaston Pipe Organ Company, Indianapolis, and installed in the Rivoli Theatre, Indianapolis.

From the time of its opening in 1966 it began attracting national and international attention because of the outstanding series of guest artists who appeared there in concert and accompanied silent films. It has been recorded by several artists including Dessa Byrd and Tom Gnaster, the latter releasing a remarkable recording of the organ in quadraphonic sound. The organ was later closed and the process of dismantling began in 1974.[132] Parts of the organ (pipes, chests, and relay) were installed in the residence of Dr. John W. Landon in Lexington, Kentucky, by the Heaston Pipe Organ Company in 1976.

MEYER

Jerome B. Meyer of Milwaukee, Wisconsin, produced a few pipe organs, both classical and theatre. The firm's specialty was building pipe work for other builders, especially wooden pipes although they also manufactured metal pipes. Meyer did build a few complete organs in the Milwaukee area.[133]

MIDMER-LOSH

The Midmer-Losh Company built a number of outstanding organs in this country. Located at Merrick, Long Island, its origin can be traced back to 1860.[134] George Losh was owner of the Midmer-Losh Company. Born in Perry County, Pennsylvania, in 1892, George Losh worked for the Möller Company for several years, as did his brother Seibert, before they purchased the well-known organ-building firm of Reuben Midmer and Son Organ Company in 1920. Wanting to preserve continuity with the former firm, they preserved the name, calling it the Midmer-Losh Company.[135] Although they built some smaller organs for theatres and a notable concert instrument for the Atlantic City, New Jersey, high school auditorium, the Midmer-Losh Company will always be remembered for the remarkable seven manual, 455 rank instrument constructed and installed in the Atlantic City Municipal Auditorium, known to many as Convention Hall.

It is described as "the largest pipe organ in the world" by noted pipe organ authorities, Barnes and Gammons.[136] (For purposes of comparison the organ in the Wanamaker Store, Philadephia, has six manuals and 469 ranks. Which is the largest instrument depends upon whether one is comparing the number of manuals, the number of ranks of pipes, or the actual number of pipes.) The Atlantic City Convention Hall instrument was never fully completed, but a company brochure about the organ, published while it was nearing completion in 1930, stated that the finished organ would have "five hundred registers. . . .[and] the grand console will have seven manuals, seven octaves, and twelve hundred stop keys."[137] In addition, a five manual movable console was installed as was a five manual "second console."[138] The cost of this organ was reputed to be a half-million dollars. Senator Emerson Richards, noted organ architect, drew up the specifications and was responsible for convincing the city fathers to install such an organ in the first place. So unusual were the specifications that no other builder except Midmer-Losh bid on the work.[139] Seibert Losh moved ahead to build this unusual instrument for the auditorium, which seats 42,000 persons. Henry Vincent Willis, of the famed family of English organ builders, was on the Midmer-Losh staff at the time and was responsibile for some of the excellent pipe work that went into this organ.[140]

The organ was equipped with ten blowers totaling 500 horsepower, producing 100 inches of wind pressure for some stops. Some pipes had to be fastened in place, so that the tremendous wind pressure would not blow them out.[141] Barnes and Gammons write of this instrument: "When we played all of it one night, it was necessary to ask the power company to put on another generator so we could start all the blowers."[142] They believe that the principal reason for the tremendous size of this organ was to outdo the organ in Wanamaker's store in Philadelphia. The instrument was never fully completed, however. The Depression intervened. Midmer-Losh and Senator Richards went bankrupt, "the city went broke, and the bonding company which had guaranteed the completion of the organ went broke."[143] Yet enough of the organ was installed and playing that it really didn't matter a great deal. It is still operable today and is played on infrequent occasions.

Other famous Midmer-Losh installations include the old New York Hippodrome Theatre, which had a three manual instrument with one row of stop tablets. The number of ranks is unknown.[144] The Midmer-Losh Company probably built a total of nearly fifty pipe organs.[145]

PAGE

One very remarkable builder of theatre organs who installed less than one hundred instruments was the Page Organ Company of Lima, Ohio. This company might be lost to history were it not for the outstanding workmanship that went into its organs. Several of them are still intact in theatres or have been reinstalled in homes and are still playing.

In 1918 two Lima, Ohio, residents, Dode Lamson and Harry Page Maus, built a pipe organ (in the basement of Lamson's home at 514 South Metcalf Street) designed for accompanying silent films. The instrument featured a full keyboard, a roll-playing mechanism which accepted ordinary player piano rolls, and all sorts of sound effects. Finally they trundled their invention out of the basement to its new home—the Quilna Theatre on West Market Street, Lima.[146]

This was not Lamson's first experience with pipe organs. He had spent a few years installing and servicing them for a California firm. Maus knew little about pipe organs, but he had considerable business experience with musical instruments. He had operated a store in Lafayette, Ohio, which, among other things, sold pianos. When he moved to Lima, he sold furniture, pianos, and other musical items. He also sold automobiles for a period of time.

After selling the organ to the Quilna Theatre, Lamson and Maus decided to go into business officially. The base of operations was moved to the third floor of Maus' four-story building at 604 North Main Street in Lima. Orders began to come in and the partners decided to incorporate. The papers were signed April 27, 1923, setting up the Page Organ Company. Harry Page Maus was named president, treasurer and general manager.[147] The firm moved to Defiance, Ohio, briefly, keeping the Lima business address (523 North Jackson Street). Eventually it moved back to the same Main Street location to stay.

Two manual instruments became the mainstay of the company although many larger instruments were built. Page bought its pipe work from Anton Gottfried and from Schaap. The company used very elaborate consoles with much scroll work, and the instruments were more highly unified than most other theatre organs. One instrument of fifteen ranks had typical Page unification, which resulted in 203 stop tablets.

Several of the theatres that installed Page organs were designed by John Eberson, an architect known for his atmospheric theatres. In regard to one such installation, a three manual, seven rank instrument installed in Eberson's New Palace Theatre, Marion, Ohio, Eberson was quoted as saying, "I frankly admit that this is one of the slickest little installations I have seen, hence I shall have no hesitancy to call your product to the attention of my clients."[148] This he did in the case of several other theatres including the Paramount Theatre,

Anderson, Indiana. This theatre was to have been named the Palace Theatre, but was leased by Paramount-Publix and opened as the Paramount Theatre in 1929. This Eberson-designed house, built at the corner of 12th and Meridian streets, boasted 1,700 seats and cost about $800,000—a large sum even at that time.[149] The interior decor was that of a gracious Spanish villa with hanging vines, statues, porticos, arches, and lanterns.[150] The organ was a three manual, seven rank Page with console in green and gold, covered with glitter. In spite of its size, it was more than capable of filling the theatre with gorgeous sound. This organ was recorded by Dr. John W. Landon.

Another well-known Page installation is in the Embassy Theatre, Fort Wayne, Indiana—a four manual, fifteen rank instrument. This has become perhaps the most famous of all the Page theatre organs, since it has been played regularly by well-known theatre organist Buddy Nolan. Nolan has given a number of "Theatre Organ at Midnight" concerts at this organ, which have attracted listeners from several states, and has recorded two stereo discs here.[151] The beautiful Embassy Theatre, which dates from 1928, has closed as a motion picture theatre but has reopened under the direction of the Embassy Theatre Foundation.[152] Special shows and events are scheduled throughout the year.

A four manual, fifteen rank Page organ was installed in radio station WHT in the Wrigley Building in Chicago. *The American Organist*, commenting on this instrument, referred to the beautiful console by saying, "This console was built for the radio, to be heard, not seen; yet it was evidently also built to be seen for it is one of unusual ornamentation."[153] The finish is "polychrome of bright gold and rose."[154] This organ was designed for Al Carney of the radio team of "Al and Pat," *The American Organist* continued,

On Sundays the Page Company broadcasts its "Page Organ Hour," using a high type of music and well known players. As the signing off draws near, the famous Good Night salutation from WHT steals softly over the air as a lullaby—WHT at the Wrigley Building, Chicago, with Al and Pat and the Page organ are bidding you Good Night in their own original way so no matter where you are, or how you are when you hear "Home Sweet Home," chimes and taps, you will know it is WHT bidding Good Night—Good Night.[155]

This organ included a Pageophone stop to imitate the Vibraphone. Other Page innovations included reiterating cowbells among the special effects, and a Sousaphone stop. The WHT organ was eventually removed and installed in the Michigan Theatre in Flint. From there it went to a private home.

The largest Page organ ever built was the four manual, sixteen rank instrument installed in William Wrigley's famous Casino on Catalina Island off the California coast. This organ is still playable and is used regularly.

The well-known radio station WOWO in Fort Wayne, Indiana, had a Page pipe organ of about twelve ranks. The organ was actually owned by Main Auto Supply on the second floor at the rear of the same building in which the WOWO studios were located. It was played by Orville Foster, "Marguerite," Percy Robbins, and others. Eventually the organ was sold to the Fort Wayne Gospel Tabernacle.

The Page Company advertised widely in many trade journals such as *Motion Picture Exhibitor*. It ran a series of ads on its installations under the banner, "Another Page in History."[156] Page organs were appreciated in their own hometown. Every theatre in Lima that had an organ had a Page. (The one exception was the Ohio Theatre which had a Wurlitzer.) Harry Page Maus established Lima's first radio station, WOAC, installed an organ in it, and featured it on the air.

A significant portion of the Page Company's output went to churches, lodges, and residences. Perhaps fifty organs, half of the total, went to theatres. Thus Page might have stood a better chance of surviving the Depresssion than some companies whose organs were almost all installed in theatres. However, many churches that had purchased organs were hard hit by the Depression and could not pay for them. The coming of sound films affected all companies adversely, and Page was hard hit by a fire in 1931, which destroyed most of the factory.

In addition Maus' health was failing. The company filed for bankruptcy in Toledo, Ohio, August 4, 1934.[157] Maus retired in 1937 and died in West Palm Beach, Florida in 1942.[158]

PILCHER

A very respected builder of church organs was Henry Pilcher. The firm, Henry Pilcher's Sons, Inc., was first established in Dover, England, in 1820.[159] The Pilchers came to the United States in 1832, settled in Chicago until the Chicago fire in 1871, and eventually established themselves in Louisville, Kentucky, in 1874.[160] A number of Pilcher organs were installed in theatres. The Louisville *Times*, September 10, 1924, mentions a sizeable organ costing $30,000 that was then being installed in the Rialto Theatre, Louisville. Pilcher had a reputation for good solid work and many of the firm's church organs are still in regular service. In 1944 the Pilcher Company ceased doing business under its own name and was absorbed by the Möller Company.

REUTER

Reuter is another respected name in the church organ field. The Reuter Company was established in 1917 at Trenton, Illinois.[161] The founders included former Wicks Organ Company employees A. G. Sobol, Henry Yost, and A. C. Reuter, whose name the company bore. After building a few instruments, the company relocated in Lawrence, Kansas, where it continues to operate today. Located as it is, in the middle of the United States geographically, the company enjoyed a market in which there were few local competitors. During the 1920s Reuter did build a number of theatre organs, the first installed in 1919 and the last in 1929. All in all, about forty theatre instruments were produced—thirty installed in Texas, six in Kansas, three in California, and the balance (only a few) in western and midwestern states. It is estimated that the production of theatre instruments never represented more than one quarter of the company's total output at any one time.

Reuter used horseshoe consoles and even equipped one organ with a player unit—the two manual, seven rank Reuter installed in radio station KMA, Shenandoah, Iowa, in December 1927. The three manual, eight rank Reuter installed in the Varsity Theatre in Lawrence, Kansas, in September 1926 became the company's local show piece and demonstration instrument.

The Dent theatre chain in Texas installed a number of Reuter organs in its theatres. This accounts for a portion of the thirty theatre organs installed by Reuter in Texas. Some of these were on very low wind pressure (five to seven inches) versus eight to ten inches used elsewhere.[162]

The largest theatre organ built by Reuter was a four manual, fourteen rank instrument installed in the Arcadia Theatre, Dallas, Texas, in 1927. This was the only four manual theatre organ Reuter ever built.

SCHAEFER

The Schaefer Organ Company was established in Slinger, Wisconsin in 1875. Although the company produced church organs almost exclusively, two organs were installed in theatres. One instrument of about ten ranks was installed in the Opera House, Hartford, Wisconsin. When sound pictures arrived, this organ was removed, tonally revised, and installed in Our Savior's Lutheran Church, Oconomowoc, Wisconsin, and is still in operation with its original console. A second Schaefer pipe organ was installed in the Rainbow Theatre, Milwaukee, Wisconsin. (The exact size of the instrument is unknown, but it was believed to be larger than ten ranks.) This organ was also removed, tonally revised, and installed in Sacred Heart Sanitorium, Milwaukee. During the Depression when there was very little organ work to be done, the Schaefer Company did transfer several organs from theatres to churches.[163]

SCHUELKE

The William E. Schuelke Organ Company of Milwaukee, Wisconsin, built a number of organs for theatres. Reportedly they had contracts for more than twenty organs in Chicago theatres alone in the years 1912 to 1914. For unknown reasons the company went bankrupt in 1914. It is not known how many organs were built and installed prior to this date. Max Schuelke was president and manager of the firm.

E. M. SKINNER

Ernest M. Skinner was one of the great men of American organ building. Born in 1866, he lived a long and interesting life, becoming quite a controversial figure in church and concert organ circles. He began building pipe organs around 1900 after having worked for a few years with the Hutchings Votey Organ Company. He built organs for two of the most prominent churches in America, The Cathedral of St. John the Divine and St. Thomas Church, New York City. These instruments established his reputation.[164] An excellent E. M. Skinner organ was installed in the Scottish Rite Cathedral in Indianapolis (the largest building devoted to lodge activities in the world) and remains virtually unaltered to the present day.

Robert Hope-Jones became a vice president of the Skinner Company in 1905 for a brief period. Some sources believe that it was here that Hope-Jones designed the first horseshoe console, which was built to his specifications by Harry J. Carruthers in the E. M. Skinner factory, Boston. This organ, which attracted much public attention, was installed in the First Congregational Church, Elmira, New York.[165]

Other authorities, including organ builder J. Llelyn Haggart, point out that a semi-horseshoe console was used by Hope-Jones at least as early as 1896 in the Worcester Cathedral organ in England, and perhaps it was used previously. However, the first full horseshoe console was built in Robert Hope-Jones' factory at Elmira, New York, in 1907. Hope-Jones and James H. Nuttall (who had just emigrated from England at Hope-Jones' request) were discussing consoles one day. Nuttall (who had worked with Hope-Jones in England and was a master organ builder in his own right) said, "Why not follow the normal arc of the arms as you are seated at the console?" A sketch of Nuttall's idea was quickly made, and Hope-Jones told him to make the necessary drawings. The console department at the Elmira factory at that time was under the direction of Theodore Ilse, assisted by Fred Wood, H. Badger, and David Marr. Such a console was built.

Probably the first horseshoe console to be installed was the three manual, fourteen rank (not unified) organ for the Cleremont Congregational Church (near Pomona, California). This organ was installed and tonally finished by James H. Nuttall himself in 1907. Prior to his death Haggart had original photographs of this console in his possession dating from 1925 when he rebuilt the switchboard and relay of this organ for Mr. Nuttall.

Other early horseshoe console Hope-Jones organs include the instrument installed in the Baptist Temple, Philadelphia, June 6, 1911.

Joseph J. Carruthers, Sr., and Joseph J. Carruthers, Jr., had been employed at Hope-Jones' Birkenhead plant in England in supervisory capacities. Harry J. Carruthers began his organ-building career with Hope-Jones in the voicing room at the Elmira, New York, factory. He was perhaps seventeen years of age at the time. James Nuttall, on the other hand, was about thirty years of age and an experienced organ builder by 1907 when the full horseshoe console was born. Thus it is to him, no doubt, that the honor of fabricating the first such console belongs.[166]

The E. M. Skinner firm later changed its name to the Skinner Organ Company and in 1931 became the Aeolian-Skinner Company after it acquired control of the old Aeolian Company. Aeolian-Skinner was generally looked upon as the most prestigious organ builder in America until its demise in the early 1970s. Much of that reputation may be due to G. Donald Harrison who joined the firm in 1927 and was its guiding light until his death in 1955 just as he was completing the rebuilding of the St. Thomas Church organ in New York.

During the 1920s when the company was known as the Skinner Organ Company, it did manufacture theatre pipe organs on a limited basis. These were basically straight organs with little unification but with outstanding orchestral voices. E. M. Skinner was a pioneer in the development and use of orchestral voicing in church and concert hall instruments. Organists with classical training who became theatre organists particularly liked Skinner instruments.

One of Skinner's most notable theatre organs was installed

in the Colony Theatre at 53rd and Broadway, New York City. This instrument had a four manual console of classical design, the design that was found on all Skinner theatre organ consoles. The Colony Theatre Skinner, installed about 1925, enjoyed the distinction of being the third organ in New York City on a lift, "the first being the Möller in the Lexington, the second the Marr and Colton in the Piccadilly."[167]

E. M. Skinner built exactly twelve complete organs for theatres. A contract was signed for a thirteenth instrument, but it was never installed. Certainly, many were installed in larger private residences and some in studios and radio stations. Radio station WNAC in Boston had a Skinner organ of undetermined size, played by theatre organist John Kiley. Also, the original organ in the city's Metropolitan Theatre was a four manual Skinner. New York's NBC studios contained a Skinner pipe organ at one time. Herman Voss recorded two 78 rpm discs of hymns on this instrument.[168] Coolidge Auditorium on the first level of the Library of Congress, Washington, D.C., has a fine Skinner organ, which is still intact.

SMITH

Frederick Smith was one of the men trained under Hope-Jones who established his own company.[169] Smith organs were marketed under such names as Geneva, Seeburg, and Leathurby.[170] Smith, who is sometimes credited with having suggested the first horseshoe-shaped console, worked with Hope-Jones in England, later coming to the United States to work with E. M. Skinner. In 1912 he established his own company in North Tonawanda, New York. The organs built there were sold as "Smith Orchestral Organs." In 1917 Smith joined the J. (Justus) P. Seeburg Company in Chicago and for a time Seeburg-Smith organs were manufactured.[171] However, the company moved to Geneva, Illinois in 1922 when Seeburg's interest in the firm was bought by Harry Hogan and E. C. Hogan.[172] The organs made at Geneva were marketed as Geneva-Smith Unit Organs.

Smith left Geneva for Alameda, California, in 1923, and here he established another Smith Organ Company. He worked in conjunction with the Leathurby Company of San Francisco, and they marketed organs under the name of Leathurby-Smith. The company continued to manufacture theatre organs there until 1928. For the last four years of its operation, the firm was known as F. W. Smith and Son. The son was Charles F. Smith.

The Smith Company built organs that were quite similar in construction during all the changes of address and business associations.

> Pipes were never made by this firm, but were purchased from Gottfried (reeds) and from Samuel Pierce, Reading, Mass., (flues), now known as Dennison. Percussions were from Lyon and Healy of Chicago and Deagan and Kehler. Actually constructed, therefore, were the consoles, relays, chests, reservoirs, actions, and other appurtenances.[173]

Charles Smith estimated that about 1,000 organs were sold by all the Smith-related firms.

The Smith Company built everything from a pit organ to a four manual, seventeen rank instrument. This was its largest organ and was installed in the Forest Hill Theatre, Long Island City, New York.[174] The Smith Company got out of the pipe organ business in early 1928 and thus did not follow the usual pattern of theatre organ builders—being forced into bankruptcy due to the advent of sound films and the Depression. The Geneva Company was reestablished in 1974 by Vladimir Pech.[175]

SPENCER

Evan Spencer, superintendent of the Murray M. Harris Organ Company and later the American Photoplayer Company in Berkeley, California, built several theatre instruments before he left to found his own classical organ company in Pasadena, California. Spencer is remembered for the magnificent Tibia pipes he constructed from California redwood.[176]

TELLERS

The Tellers Pipe Organ Company was founded in Erie, Pennsylvania, in 1906 by brothers Henry and Ignatius Tellers and William Sommerhof, all of whom had worked with the

Felgemaker Pipe Organ Company. When Felgemaker went out of business in 1918, the Tellers-Sommerhof Company began filling its unfinished contracts. In the 1920s Tellers added a new partner and became the Tellers-Kent Company.[177] During these years the company installed some splendid classical instruments including the three manual organ (installed in 1928) in Schriner Auditorium, Taylor University, Upland, Indiana.

The Tellers Company eventually passed into the hands of Herman J. Tellers, son of the founder, who continued the business until his retirement in 1972, when it was sold to Lawrence Phelps and Associates.[178] During the sixty-six years of its operation the Tellers Company built about 1,000 pipe organs. Approximately twenty of these were installed in theatres.[179] A Tellers theatre organ which recently received national attention was the instrument installed around 1920 in Shea's Theatre, Erie, Pennsylvania. The three manual, twenty-four rank organ was saved from the wrecking ball in 1968 by Robert Luckey of that city who reinstalled the organ at Gannon College, Erie, in 1975.[180]

U.S. PIPE ORGAN

The United States Pipe Organ Company of Crum Lynne, Pennsylvania was well known in the Philadelphia area and the eastern United States. Remarkably the company is still in business at the same address as in the 1920s, although today it does largely maintenance work. An original brochure from 1928 shows an impressive list of installations in Pennsylvania, New Jersey, New York, Maryland, and Connecticut. Depicted is a two manual horseshoe console which looks very similar to the work of the nation's most advertised brand. The company advertised the "fastest action on the market," "unified just enough," and "patented cypherless devices." Among installations claimed in the brochure is an organ in Carnegie Hall, New York City.[181]

One of these organs is currently extant in regular use. Opened by organist Jesse Price, March 5, 1928, the three manual U.S. Pipe Organ in the Lansdale Theatre, Lansdale, Pennsylvania, was removed to the Phoenixville Baptist Church, Phoenixville, Pennsylvania, in 1942. After thirty years it was sold to Roger and Dorothy Bloom who installed it in their Downington, Pennsylvania residence. In 1978 it was moved to the Sunnybrook Ballroom in Pottstown, Pennsylvania. The name plate on the console is distinctive—an outline of the map of the United States in royal blue and gold, with Crum Lynne, Pennsylvania, marked by a star—the home of U.S. Pipe Organs. An additional name plate which was unearthed in a Lancaster, Pennsylvania flea market reads, "United States Pipe Organ Company—Builder of Kloehs' Unit Orchestra." Gus Kloehs of Crum Lynne was prominent in the history of the company.[182]

VOTEY

The Votey Company was affiliated with various other firms and builders throughout its history. Around 1900 it was known as the Hutchings-Votey Company, so named for George S. Hutchings, an established organ builder in the Boston area.[183] Some of the Hutchings-Votey personnel went to work for E. M. Skinner in later years.

Votey built a limited number of theatre organs in its own right. The extent of its work in this field is unknown. No known list of Votey theatre organ installations survives.

WEICKHARDT

The Weickhardt Organ Company built and installed a number of organs in theatres in the early days of silent films. In the Chicago area alone it installed instruments in the Crawford, LaSalle, Palm, Oakland, Biograph, and Vitagraph theatres.

WELTE

Welte is a proud old name in the music business. Founded in 1832, it continued in business until the end of World War II.[184] Freiburg, Germany, where the home plants were located, was almost completely destroyed by the bombing of the Allied powers.

The Welte Company first produced pipe organs in Germany around 1900 and sold them in other countries around the world.[185] Eventually, Welte built a salon or studio in New York which contained a fine pipe organ used for demonstration purposes.

Although Welte built many theatre organs in Germany, none employed the use of a horseshoe console. In 1914, Wurlitzer acquired 48 percent of the stock in the American Welte firm.[186] At the end of World War I, the balance of Welte's American stock was seized and sold under the Alien Property Act.[187]

The Welte name was associated over the period of its life with a great many other organ builders. For a time it was Welte-Mignon. There was a New York association with the Estey Corporation. A beautiful studio was built in 1927 at 695 Fifth Avenue, New York City, where a large three manual, thirty-three rank horseshoe console Welte organ was installed. From this organ, NBC radio broadcasts originated over WEAF.

In 1929 the company went into bankruptcy and became the Welte-Tripp Organ Corporation.[188] In 1931 there was another sale, and W. W. Kimball acquired Welte's assets.[189]

Welte's mainstay was the manufacture of pipe organs for residences. Over the years the company installed a good many fine residence organs in the homes of the wealthy. One such organ, still being heard, is the three manual, fifteen rank horseshoe console Welte in Death Valley Scotty's Castle in Nevada. Recently restored, it is the scene of regularly scheduled concerts by noted theatre organists today and has been recorded by Rex Koury.

Some other theatre-type installations by Welte included a three manual instrument in the Capitol Theatre, Port Chester, New York, and radio station KPO San Francisco. This organ was later sold to NBC Hollywood and installed in studios at Sunset and Vine.[190]

In 1928 the Welte Company lost its studios at 695 Fifth Avenue, New York. The three manual organ there had been recorded by Milton Charles, Marsh McCurdy, and Emil Velazco. It was finally sold to the Paul Rader Tabernacle in Chicago, which continues today as the Chicago Gospel Tabernacle.[191]

The Barker Brothers Home Furnishings Company of Los Angeles had the Los Angeles franchise for Welte. This store, advertised as the "World's Largest Home Furnishings Store," had three Welte organs installed for display and demonstration purposes—a four manual classical instrument, a three manual theatre model, and a two manual reproducing organ.[192]

Welte owned the patents on reproducing pianos, and even the major builders in this country such as Duo-Art and Ampico had to pay royalties to market their own pianos. After the sale of the Welte assets to Kimball in 1931, the name gradually disappeared from advertising in journals and magazines. There is no known list of Welte theatre organ installations in existence. Today the Welte name exists only in the remaining instruments which still sound forth their music in many places on the globe.

WOOD

The William Wood Pipe Organ Company was founded in Portland, Oregon, in 1922, with William Wood as president. Wood gained a great deal of experience working as an organ service man for the Jensen and Von Herberg theatre circuit in the Portland, Oregon, area. Many of these organs were Wurlitzers. In addition he maintained a Marr and Colton organ in Forest Grove, Oregon. When he began building his own instruments in 1922, the chestwork was much like Marr and Colton in design.

Wood manufactured most of his wooden pipes but purchased all his metal pipes from Anton Gottfried in Erie, Pennsylvania. Musical percussions came from J. C. Deagan, Chicago, and magnets and other electrical parts came from Reisner, Hagerstown, Maryland. The theatre consoles were attractive and horseshoe in design. Some Wood pipe organs were built for and installed in churches, but the bulk of the firm's output was for theatres.

The company sold more two manual, eight rank organs than any of its other available models. One of the outstanding installations was a three manual, nine rank instrument with piano in the Gellers Theatre, Portland. The largest was the four manual, thirteen rank instrument installed in the Roller Rink in the Oaks Amusement Park near Portland.

William Wood's brother, Darwin, was a popular theatre organist in the Portland area. He taught organ, broadcast over radio, and held the position of organist at the Blue Mouse, State, Oregon, and Gellers theatres consecutively.

The Wood Company went out of business in the early 1930s. William Wood installed one of his last organs in the Shrine Roller Rink in Los Angeles and became manager of this rink. He died in 1936. Darwin Wood lived until 1946.[193]

NOTES

1. Letter from British theatre organ researcher, Ian McIver, October 14, 1972.
2. Alexander Turner, "Father of the Theatre Organ," *The Tibia*, 1, no. 1 (Fall 1955): Part I, p. 6.
3. Ibid., p. 7.
4. William H. Barnes and Edward B. Gammons, *Two Centuries of American Organ Building* (Glen Rock, N.J.: J. Fischer and Bro., 1970), p. 51.
5. Alexander Turner, "Father of the Theatre Organ," *The Tibia*, 1, no. 2 (Summer 1956): Part II, p. 4.
6. Barnes and Gammons, *Two Centuries of American Organ Building*, p. 52.
7. Robert Hope-Jones, "Recent Developments of Organ Building," (a lecture delivered before the National Association of Organists at the Auditorium, Ocean Grove, N.J., August 6, 1910, also quoted in part in Orpha Ochse, *The History of the Organ in the United States* (Bloomington: Indiana University Press, 1975), pp. 335–37.
8. Robert Graw, "The Hope-Jones Unit Orchestra," *Modern Electronics*, 1914, pp. 131–32.
9. Reginald Foort, *The Cinema Organ*, 2d ed., revised (Vestal, N.Y.: Vestal Press, 1970), p. 87.
10. *Exhibitor's Herald-World*, October 25, 1930.
11. Ben M. Hall, *The Best Remaining Seats* (New York: Clarkson N. Potter, Inc., 1961), p. 183. (Used by permission.)
12. John Skolle, *The Lady of the Casa* (Santa Fe, N.M.: Rydal Press, 1959), p. 46.
13. Ibid., pp. 48–49.
14. Ibid., p. 50.
15. Ibid., p. 56.
16. Ibid., pp. 62–63.
17. Interview with Farny Wurlitzer, June 5, 1971.

18. Correspondence with Billy Nalle, September 1975.

19. Interview with Farny Wurlitzer, June 5, 1971.

20. Q. David Bowers, *Put Another Nickel In* (Vestal, N.Y.: Vestal Press, 1966), p. 84, quoting, "The U.S. Organ," *Fortune*, April 1931, n.p.

21. Interview with Richard C. Simonton, March 10, 1970; and *The Wurlitzer Unit Organ* (Cincinnati: The Rudolph Wurlitzer Company, 1926), p. 38; (reprint ed., Vestal, N.Y.: Vestal Press, n.d.).

22. Jesse Crawford's tape-recorded autobiography.

23. Hall, *The Best Remaining Seats*, p. 196.

24. Bowers, *Put Another Nickel In*, p. 32.

25. *Console*, February 1972, p. 12.

26. Interview with Eddy Hanson, April 4, 1971.

27. Richard Callahan, "Al Melgard at the Chicago Stadium Pipe Organ" (Record jacket notes from a long-playing record of this same title produced by Replica Records, Des Plaines, Ill., Record number 504), n.d.

28. Barnes and Gammons, *Two Centuries of American Organ Building*, p. 53.

29. Callahan, "Al Melgard at the Chicago Stadium Pipe Organ."

30. Ibid.

31. Correspondence with Helen M. Barton, May 1974.

32. "History of the Estey Company." (Special feature published by *Console* magazine), January 1972.

33. Ibid.

34. Barnes and Gammons, *Two Centuries of American Organ Building*, p. 28.

35. Ibid.

36. "History of the Estey Company."

37. Ibid.

38. Ibid. The complete correspondence and business papers of the Estey Company, now in the possession of the Library of the University of Vermont, Burlington, document the various additions to and changes in the Capitol Theatre organ over the years. Copies of some of these documents are in the author's possession.

39. See Chapter Five, "The Theatre Organ on Phonograph and Radio."

40. *The Kilgen Wonder Organ: The Voice of the Silent Drama* (1927 Kilgen catalog, reprint ed., Vestal, N.Y.: Vestal Press, n.d.), p. 4.

41. Ibid., p. 5.

42. Orpha Ochse, *The History of the Organ in the United States* (Bloomington, Indiana University Press, 1975), p. 367.

43. *Kilgen Wonder Organ*, p. 4.

44. Barnes and Gammons, *Two Centuries of American Organ Building*, p 68.

45. *Console*, March 1971, p. 10.

46. Van Allen Bradley, *Music for the Millions* (Chicago: Henry Regnery Company, 1957), p. 1.

47. Ibid., p. 70.

48. Ibid., p. 21.

49. Ibid., p. 181.

50. *Console*, November 1973, p. 27.

51. Hall, *Best Remaining Seats*, p. 192.

52. Bradley, *Music for the Millions*, p. 183.

53. Barnes and Gammons, *Two Centuries of American Organ Building*, p. 65.

54. *Console*, February 1971, p. 21.

55. Bradley, *Music for the Millions*, pp. 182, 188–89.

56. Ibid., p. 183.

57. Ibid., p. 181.

58. Barnes and Gammons, *Two Centuries of American Organ Building*, p. 65.

59. Correspondence with Lloyd Klos, 1976.

60. Lloyd Klos, "The Marr and Colton Company," *Theatre Organ*, Spring 1963, p. 18.

61. Ibid., p. 19.

62. Ibid., pp. 20–21.

63. Ibid., p. 22.

64. Dick Kline, "M. P. Möller, Builders of Classical Organs Who Applied Their Art to the Theatre Field," *Theatre Organ*, Winter 1965, pp. 4ff.

65. Correspondence with Peter Möller Daniels, Vice President of M. P. Möller, Inc., March 1982.

66. Kline, "M. P. Möller."

67. Ray Brubacher, "A Great Traveler Comes Home—Opus 6690," *Theatre Organ*, October 1973, pp. 5–10.

68. Reginald Foort, *The Cinema Organ*, 2d ed., revised (Vestal, N.Y.: Vestal Press, 1970).

69. Brubacher, "A Great Traveler Comes Home."

70. Stu Green, "Organ Power," *Theatre Organ*, December 1975-January 1976, pp. 23ff.

71. Ben M. Hall, "Here with the Wind," (Record jacket notes from a long-playing record of this same title featuring Bob Van Camp at the organ, produced by Concert Recordings, Lynwood, Calif., Record number CR-0023.)

72. Ibid.

73. Tom B'Hend, "The Robert Morton Unit Organ—A History," (Section III, part I), *Console*, September 1966, pp. 1–30.

74. Mention of this organ is made in the full-length biography of Jesse Crawford: John W. Landon, *Jesse Crawford, The Poet of The Organ; Wizard of the Mighty Wurlitzer* (Vestal, N.Y.: Vestal Press, 1974).

75. B'Hend, "The Robert Morton Unit Organ."

76. Ibid., p. 9.

77. Ibid., p. 23.

78. Interview with Farny Wurlitzer, June 5, 1971.

79. "Almost 6,000 Theatre Organs," *Theatre Organ*, June 1972, p. 20.

80. B'Hend, "The Robert Morton Unit Organ," p. 7.

81. Dolton McAlpin, "The Saenger and Its Robert Morton," *Console*, February 1973, pp. 12–20.

82. Ochse, *History of the Organ in the United States*, p. 368.

83. Barnes and Gammons, *Two Centuries of American Organ Building*, p. 98.

84. See Appendix 2, "Hawaii."

85. Barnes and Gammons, *Two Centuries of American Organ Building*.

86. "The Art of Firmin Swinnen" (Record jacket notes from a long-playing record of this same title, featuring Firmin Swinnen at the pipe organ of the DuPont estate, Longwood Gardens, produced by Swinnen Art, 1907 Veale Road, Wilmington, Del. 19810. Record number FS–1).

87. Barnes and Gammons, *Two Centuries of American Organ Building*, p. 67.

88. Ibid.

89. Ibid.

90. Advertisement in the author's possession. Source of its publication unknown.

91. Correspondence with Tom B'Hend, May 1974.

92. Barnes and Gammons, *Two Centuries of American Organ Building*, p. 80.

93. Ibid.

94. Correspondence with Lloyd Klos, 1976.

95. *Console*, March 1972, p. 14.

96. Barnes and Gammons, *Two Centuries of American Organ Building*, p. 82.

97. Correspondence with C. M. "Sandy" Balcom, February 1976.

98. Correspondence with Edwin P. Miller, Jr., Coordinator of Information Services, Binghamton Public Library, Binghamton, N.Y.

99. Lloyd Klos, "Fred Feibel," *Theatre Organ*, October 1971, p. 16.

100. Barnes and Gammons, *Two Centuries of American Organ Building*, p. 140.

101. Correspondence with Mrs. Marie Hoscheid, Librarian, Public Library, Moline, Ill., April 1975.

102. *Observor-Dispatch*, Utica, N.Y., July 23, 1922.

103. See Appendix 2, "Hawaii."

104. *Observor-Dispatch*, Utica, N.Y., July 23, 1922.

105. Most of the information about Cozatt pipe organs comes from correspondence with Victor Hyde (June 1976), owner of a four manual, eleven rank Cozatt theatre pipe organ, and advertising brochures in his collection, which he kindly loaned the author.

106. Much of the information appearing here on the Frazee Company comes from correspondence with Harry W. French, contributing editor of *Good Old Days Magazine*, but formerly Secretary of the Frazee Company for over forty years. For an excellent article on theatre pipe organs (including Frazee) and organists see: Harry W. French, "Looking Hollywood Way," *Good Old Days*, October 1972, pp. 22ff. Correspondence with Harry French dates from November 1973 to 1975.

107. Barnes and Gammons, *Two Centuries of American Organ Building*, p. 68.

108. Christopher Thorn, "Erie, Pennsylvania—America's Former Organ Capital," *Console*, March 1975, p. 26.

109. Ibid.

110. Barnes and Gammons, *Two Centuries of American Organ Building*, p. 36.

111. Thorn, "Erie, Pennsylvania."

112. Correspondence with C. M. "Sandy" Balcom, February 1976.

113. Correspondence with Mrs. Werner H. Kaufmann, daughter of Harry Hall, November 1974.

114. *Console*, March 1972, p. 27.

115. Robert C. MacNeur, "Theatre Organ Restored in New Mexico School," *Theatre Organ*, June 1973, pp. 28–29.

116. Stewart Duncan, "Toronto's Odeon-Carlton," *Theatre Organ*, August 1970, p. 16.

117. Correspondence with Lloyd Klos, April 1975.

118. Ochse, *History of the Organ in the United States*, pp. 299–301.

119. Correspondence with Bill Bartlow, March 1975; and Ken Michelson, March 1975.

120. Ochse, *History of the Organ in the United States*, p. 369, and Barnes and Gammons, *Two Centuries of American Organ Building*, pp. 69–72.

121. List compiled by Charles Powers.

122. Ochse, *History of the Organ in the United States*, and Barnes and Gammons, *Two Centuries of American Organ Building*.

123. Barnes and Gammons, *Two Centuries of American Organ Building*, p. 17.

124. Ibid., pp. 17–18.

125. "The Story of the Link Orchestral Organ." Privately printed by the Link Company, Binghamton, N.Y. (n.d.).

126. Duane Arey, "Pipe Organs and Pilot Trainers," *Theatre Organ*, Winter 1962–63, pp. 10ff.

127. Ibid.

128. "Link C. Sharpe-Minor Unit Organs," (Link sales brochure, reprint ed., Vestal, N.Y.: Vestal Press, n.d.).

129. Arey, "Pipe Organs and Pilot Trainers."

130. Billy Nalle, "Perspective in a Cultural Center," *Music*, January 1969, pp. 32ff.

131. Correspondence with Tom Ferree, owner of the Louisville Uniphone Theatre organ, formerly in the Rivoli Theatre, Indianapolis. Correspondence dates from July 1974.

132. Ibid.

133. Correspondence with Richard C. Simonton, February 1976.

134. "Under the Sassafras Tree"—Midmer-Losh brochure in the author's possession. The cover gives 1860 as the year the company was founded. No publication date is given for the brochure.

135. Andrew A. LaTorre, "Nunc Dimittis," *Diapason*, August 1975, p. 18.

136. Barnes and Gammons, *Two Centuries of American Organ Building*, p. 86.

137. "Under the Sassafras Tree."

138. *Console*, November 1972, p. 7.

139. Barnes and Gammons, *Two Centuries of American Organ Building*.

140. "Under the Sassafras Tree."

141. Barnes and Gammons, *Two Centuries of American Organ Building*, p. 88.

142. Ibid., p. 86.

143. Ibid., pp. 86–88.

144. Ibid., p. 88.

145. LaTorre, "Nunc Dimittis."

146. Correspondence with Buddy Nolan, 1975.

147. Eric M. Reeve, "A Brief Page History," *Console*, February 1970, p. 6.

148. Ibid., p. 7.

149. *Anderson Herald*, November 8, 1973, p. 26.

150. Ibid.

151. "The Embassy at Midnight," Concert Recording DR-0007 (released in 1966), and the later disc, "After Midnight," Concert Recording CR 0071. Concert Recordings, Lynwood, Calif.

152. *Console*, February 1974, p. 28.

153. *The American Organist*, 1928, p. 126. Photograph and description in the possession of the author.

154. Ibid.

155. *The American Organist*, p. 126.

156. Reeve, "A Brief Page History," p. 6.

157. *Diapason*, September 1934, n.p.

158. Nolan, Correspondence with the author.

159. Barnes and Gammons, *Two Centuries of American Organ Building*, p. 29.

160. Ibid.

161. Barnes and Gammons, *Two Centuries of American Organ Building*, p. 29.

162. Jack L. Sievert, "The Reuter Theatre Organ," *Theatre Organ*, Summer 1962, pp. 4–7.

163. Correspondence with Bernard J. Schaefer, President; Schaefer Organ Company, April 1975.

164. Barnes and Gammons, *Two Centuries of American Organ Building*, p. 74.

165. Harry J. Carruthers, "The Two Hope-Jones Corporations," *Console*, November 1969, p. 24, and correspondence with organ authority J. Llelyn Haggart, July 1976.

166. Ibid.

167. "New York Invites You," *The American Organist*, 1925, p. 202.

168. "Organ Favorites," Singspiration Album #24. Disc #1095—"Constantly Abiding"/"Close to Thee." Disc #1096—"Sunshine Medley"/"Stepping in the Light."

169. Barnes and Gammons, *Two Centuries of American Organ Building*, p. 53.

170. Ibid.

171. Douglas Marion, "The Smith Unit Organs," *Theatre Organ*, Winter 1960–61, pp. 5–7.

172. Ibid., and correspondence with Vladimir Pech, President, Geneva Organ Company, March 1975.

173. Marion, "The Smith Unit Organs," p. 5.

174. Ibid.

175. Pech, Correspondence with author.

176. B'Hend, "The Robert Morton Unit Organ."

177. Christopher Thorn, "One Man Saves Organ," *Theatre Organ*, December 1974, pp. 35–38.

178. Barnes and Gammons, *Two Centuries of American Organ Building*, pp. 88ff.

179. Thorn, "One Man Saves Organ," pp. 35–38.

180. Ibid.

181. 1928 advertising brochure of the U.S. Pipe Organ Company, Crum Lynn, Pennsylvania.

182. Correspondence with Roger and Dorothy Bloom, January 1976; and with Bill Tabor, November 1975.

183. Barnes and Gammons, *Two Centuries of American Organ Building*, p. 45.

184. "The Glory That Was Welte," *Console*, March 1972, p. 5.

185. Ibid., p. 7.

186. "Welte," *Console*, April 1972, p. 5.

187. Ibid., p. 6.

188. Ibid., p. 10.

189. Ibid., p. 11.

190. "Welte," *Console*, May 1972, p. 9.

191. The author played this Welte organ in the Chicago Gospel Tabernacle in 1961.

192. "Welte," *Console*, June 1972, p. 5.

193. Bill Peterson, "The William Wood Pipe Organ Company," *Theatre Organ*, Winter 1963–64, pp. 28–30.

1. Helen and Jesse Crawford, the famous husband and wife team, Paramount Theatre Studio Wurlitzer, Times Square, New York. (Courtesy Dr. John W. Landon.)

2. Silent film star Mary Pickford at the Wurlitzer organ, United Artist's Theatre, Los Angeles, 1928. (Courtesy *Console Magazine*, Tom B'Hend, Editor-Publisher.)

3. Kimball theatre pipe organ destined for the Forum Theatre, Los Angeles (later installed in the Wiltern Theatre, Los Angeles), shown here in the erecting room at the factory. (Courtesy *Console Magazine*, Tom B'Hend, Editor-Publisher.)

4. Kilgen theatre pipe organ, Piccadilly Theatre, Chicago, 1927. (Courtesy *Theatre Organ* magazine.)

5. Rosa Rio at the Brooklyn Fox Wurlitzer, 1933. (Courtesy Rosa Rio.)

6. Page theatre pipe organ, Paramount Theatre, Anderson, Indiana, installed in 1929. (Courtesy Dr. John W. Landon.)

7. Möller theatre pipe organ, Fox Theatre, Atlanta, Georgia. The theatre opened Christmas night 1929. (Courtesy *Theatre Organ* magazine.)

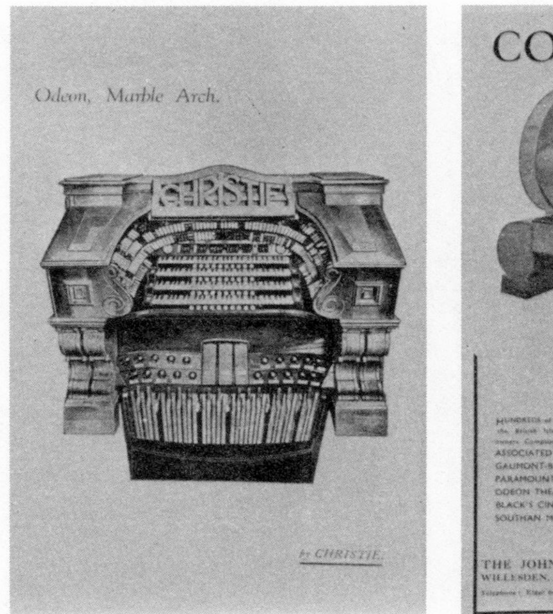

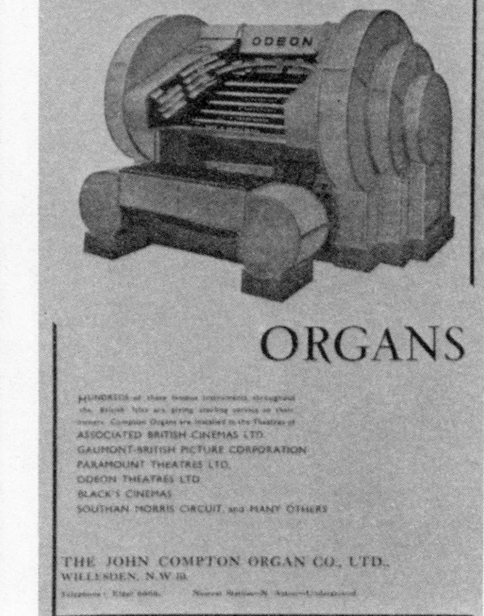

8. England's two major builders of theatre pipe organs. The Christie in the Odeon, Marble Arch, London, was a four manual, thirty-seven rank instrument, the largest theatre organ in Europe. The Compton organ pictured had multicolored lights at the ends of the console and in the bench, which could be set to cycle, changing colors. These were known as "fruit jelly surrounds." (Courtesy *Console Magazine*, Tom B'Hend, Editor-Publisher.)

FOUR
DEMISE AND REBIRTH

The Depression of the 1930s never has been equaled in American history. With 15 million people out of work there was less money to be spent even for necessities. This, coupled with the arrival of the "talkies" or sound pictures, signaled the demise of the theatre organ.

The professional theatre organists were in trouble. In 1927 when Warner Brothers starred Al Jolson in *The Jazz Singer*, some astute observers saw the handwriting on the wall and realized that it would be just a matter of time before theatre organists and all live musicians in theatres would be dismissed. Others felt this was undue pessimism. One such observer was Edward Benedict, theatre organist, who wrote an article in *Diapason* magazine in 1927 entitled "The Vitaphone, Friend or Foe?" He went out to hear a Vitaphone production and concluded:

> It is a question in my mind whether the human orchestra and organist will ever be supplanted by any device to accompany pictures. The real thing is always better than the imitation, but the threatened competition of the automatics will have a salutary effect on "movie" musicians in making them improve the quality of their work.[1]

Benedict was critical of the level of music in the sound film, calling it too "highbrow" for the average movie patron. Then he spoke words of comfort and assurance to organists and orchestra musicians in theatres:

> The great mission of the Vitaphone, in my opinion, is to bring the spoken word into the movie house. The human voice is hardly powerful enough to fill every nook and corner of a modern Cinema palace, but the words from the Vitaphone are distinctly audible at any distance from the stage. This means that Broadway's most capable performers can be brought to the hinterland in sight and sound.
>
> My deductions may be biased and faulty, but it is my humble opinion that the king of instruments and its competent manipulators are in no danger of being supplanted in the affections of the public by this clever mechanical suitor which has just entered the field.[2]

Benedict could not have foreseen the obliteration of live music in theatres, as there were a few years yet before the effects of sound pictures began to be widely felt.

In 1929 optimistic articles were still being written. Theatre organists were advised by Wade Hamilton, contributor to *The American Organist* magazine, to stay in the lead by never allowing a counter-attraction to pull ahead of the organ. Hamilton admitted that good "canned music" was probably superior to much mediocre live music being played by organists across the country, but he saw this as providing healthy competition which should spur the organist to upgrade his musical presentation.

Further advice that Hamilton gave was for the organist to play part of the picture accompaniment and allow the sound track on the film to accompany part. This strategy, he felt, should lead the public to "recognize that personal music is essential to its complete enjoyment of the motion picture."[3] Hamilton actually tried this at the Ritz Theatre in Tulsa, Oklahoma, where he then was organist. He felt that it introduced needed variety into the overall program.

Hamilton suggested that the theatre organist would do well to spend time and effort creating new ideas to vary the organ solo presentations. Variety, he felt, had good box office appeal. Further, he counseled the organist to avoid "red hot hokum." Leave jazz to the dance hall and instead, play more classical, semiclassical, and ballad-type numbers. He ended with this advice:

Let us try to give our patrons musical music, and if we can turn the threatened mechanical onslaught into a victory for ourselves, why not do it? We have been years building up the popularity of the organ until it has become part of our national life—let us continue until it becomes an indispensable part of our entertainment.[4]

Later in 1929 readers of *The American Organist* (which included large numbers of theatre organists) were encouraged to raise the level of their organ solo presentations and make them major attractions rather than "filler." The use of song slides was decried.[5] Then, whatever comfort might be derived from this word of encouragement surely was lost by reading the obituary, on the same page, of a theatre organist who committed suicide because of despondency over the loss of her job.

Despondent over the loss of her position as associate organist in Loews New York Theatre, New York City, where she had been playing for four years, Miss Moyer ended her life by jumping from her 12th story window at the Belvedere Hotel. According to friends, Miss Moyer grew increasingly despondent over the music situation in the theaters and when she and all other musicians of the theater were laid off by the Loew management, it was the dreaded climax and Miss Moyer took what she thought was the only way out. She was 29 years of age and came to New York some years ago from her home in Herkimer, N.Y.[6]

Again a humorous approach was tried by James E. Sheirer in "The Fall and Decline of the Tibia Tooter and What of It?" He suggested that a society of Ex-Tibia tooters ought to be organized with an official motto, "Toot the Tibia Quickly for the Wind is turned off," and the official song, he suggested, should be "The Lost Chord."[7] However, on the same page was a serious article quoted from *The National Exhibitor* to the effect that United Artists estimated sound devices would lose popularity in three to four months. Others in the business gave sound films no more than two or three years at most.[8]

By the end of the year, however, the situation obviously had changed for the worse. The editor of *The American Organist* had changed his mind and now was saying, "Perhaps the theatre organ will come back, but I am coming to the opinion that it will not. . . . The organ in the theatre seems dead. I do not expect it to revive."[9] The balance of his article is directed toward helping theatre organists look elsewhere for jobs.

> Crying because the theatre organ and theatre organist seem doomed to extinction, is not half so profitable as going out with a pair of binoculars and scanning the musical horizon to see if one cannot find some other opening in which to work.[10]

The author suggested jobs in radio, in funeral chapels, in wealthy homes that had organs, and Masonic lodges. Also possibilities existed with large insurance companies, such as American United Life in Indianapolis, which installed organs in its buildings. Concert organists, concert managers, and glee-club directors were also possibilities for employment.[11]

However, the suggestions seemed to be a rather "last-ditch" approach, as there simply were not enough positions for the five to six thousand persons who were theatre organists at the peak of the silent film era.[12]

In the early thirties, with a few large theatres still using organs, some writers saw sound pictures as a boon because the tiresome hours of picture accompaniment were gone, leaving the organist free to prepare a top-grade organ solo presentation. However, each week there was a decline in the number of theatres across the country employing organists. From time to time, the *Exhibitor's Herald-World* would feature an article on some organ specialty such as a dual-console program or a "stump the organist" novelty that seemed to attract a flicker of interest, but most of these ideas had little lasting value.

Early in 1932 the *Motion Picture Herald* ran an article that urged the theatre organist to "sell" his organ solo by using variety, imagination, the piano, soloists, and other variations and keeping the routine short. The article concluded that if an organist were willing to try something different and entertaining, he would greatly enhance the likelihood of his continued employment.[13]

A further encouraging word appeared in the February 1932 *Motion Picture Herald*, entitled "What About the Organ?" It was directed mainly at theatre managers. The writer told of being asked to secure organists for a number of large theatres across the country whose owners wanted to see whether live music would increase box office receipts. Furthermore, these were theatres with large, expensive pipe organs already installed and now simply lying idle. Their experiment reportedly was a success. One of the theatre owners was so pleased with the results that he planned to add organists to the payroll again in three of his other theatres. The other owners were reported as very pleased with the results.[14]

This may have encouraged some people, but there were noticeably few organ solos reviewed in the same issue of *Motion Picture Herald*. In the late 1920s such reviews filled several columns in each issue. Now there were scarcely any solos to review.

The last encouraging word to come from the *Motion Picture Herald* was in the form of an article (June 1933) entitled, "Use of Organists Rises 25 Percent." Such news was surely encouraging to the unemployed theatre organist. The article said:

> Despite the normal seasonal decline of summer and excessively warm weather prevailing virtually throughout the country at the moment, there has been an increase, during the past six weeks, at 25 percent in the employment of organists in theatres over the country, according to Harry Blair, president of the Noon-Day Club, a New York organization servicing organists in all states.[15]

The article went on to mention that the 25 percent increase was an indication that theatre managers and owners were rediscovering the box office appeal of the organ. It was felt that at least some of the impetus for this increase was coming from the demands of patrons for live entertainment. Stage show presentations likewise had declined until, in some places, the only live human being theatre patrons saw was the usher.

The reversal of this trend specifically is credited to Loews Theatres, Incorporated, which was reported to have recently added twenty theatre organists in its Eastern Division. For two years previously its entire staff of organists in the Eastern Division had totaled five or six. Theatre chains had determined that it cost less to employ an organist regularly than to pay the costs of refurbishing the instrument after it had stood idle for any length of time.

Radio was seen as having a positive effect. Theatre organ radio broadcasting was becoming quite popular with patrons permitted to sit in the audience while the organist was on the air. Sound films likewise featured "hit songs" which could be exploited by the theatre organist, both on the air and in the theatre, to stimulate patrons' interest.

The article went on to list a few organists who had signed new contracts within the last six weeks:

> . . . Mrs. Helen Crawford, New York Paramount; Bettye Lee Taylor at Loew's State, Syracuse; Bob West, Loew's Stanley, Baltimore; Adolph Goebel, RKO 86th Street, New York; Ted Crawford, Loew's, Norfolk, Virginia, and Al Curtis, Academy of Music, New York.
>
> Indicating the relative gain in employing an organist in lieu of maintaining an idle organ in the theatre, is an incident which occured recently at the RKO 86th Street theatre in New York. During the lengthy period of operation of a straight picture policy at the house, the organ was seriously damaged by rain. When, after persistent demands by regular patrons, the manager decided to reinstate the organ program, the instrument was found to be in an impossible condition. The re-establishment of the organ was delayed, but when demand continued, immediate action was taken.[16]

However, no reference to theatre organs appears in any issues of *Motion Picture Herald* following this. *The American Organist* stopped its "Photoplay" column for theatre organists by March 1930, and after 1931 scarcely a word about theatre organs appeared. *Jacob's Orchestra Monthly*, which had been a favorite publication for theatre musicians, had run a monthly column by a theatre organist, Lloyd G. Del Castillo. His column did not appear after December 1931. Likewise the advertisements for various schools of theatre organ playing all but vanished after June 1930.

Diapason magazine had featured a monthly column by Wesley Ray Burroughs entitled "With the Moving Picture Organist." The column was begun in 1916, but it died fourteen years later with the January 1930 issue.

Theatre organs went silent around the country, and organists sought other kinds of jobs. It was a difficult period for many who had served in theatres, perhaps for several years. One day they would open their weekly pay envelopes and find the feared "pink slips" signaling the end of their employment. A few found jobs playing the organ elsewhere. Most turned to other kinds of employment.

There was a certain optimism in the air in some quarters. The nation's new president, Franklin Roosevelt, had been inaugurated in March. Maybe he would be able to do something about the Depression. However, most theatre organists realized that a combination of factors—the Depression, sound motion pictures, and undeniably a great amount of undistinguished, uninspiring playing—had led to the demise of the theatre organ.

Some might argue that theatre attendance remained high in the 1930s. It did remain surprisingly high considering the financial straits in which many found themselves. In 1920 approximately 35 million people in this country went to the movies at least once per week.[17] By 1930 attendance peaked at 90 million.[18] It declined significantly in the early 1930s eventually building back to 85 million persons per week by 1947.[19] In view of the concurrent increase of population, the percentage of Americans attending movies weekly had declined significantly since 1930. The Depression saw unprecedented levels of unemployment, reaching nearly one-third of the total labor force by 1933.[20] Many people had little or no money with which to pay the lowest theatre admissions. Theatres turned to bank nights, giveaway programs, and other inducements to boost sagging revenues. Furthermore, many theatre properties were heavily mortgaged at the high interest rates prevailing when they were built. Many could not sustain the reduction of revenue, and nearly every major chain of motion picture theatres in the country went into receivership sometime during the 1930s. Even the Wurlitzer Company had to repossess a number of theatre pipe organs from theatres unable to continue paying for them.

Organists without work were plentiful, and many were willing to accept low wages to get jobs. However, the labor unions required that all live musicians be paid union scale. Theatres which did not comply would find themselves without projectionists and stage hands (to handle lighting and so on) because these men also were union members.

The assumption also can be made that a great many of the

patrons who continued attending the movies just did not care one way or another about organ music. They may have enjoyed hearing the organ but did not miss it enough to demand its reinstatement. Theatre managers probably would have found a way to finance and supply whatever the people wanted and were willing to pay for. Perhaps some people who thought of protesting the lack of live music in the theatre somehow never quite came around to doing it.

The Musicians' Union did not take this sort of thing without protest. Beginning in 1930, and for several years thereafter, the union ran a series of advertisements urging patrons of motion picture theatres to speak to the manager about reinstituting live music. Ads of this type, placed by the American Federation of Musicians, ran in popular magazines such as *Liberty*.[21] The union even went so far as to organize a Music Defense League to "oppose the elimination of Living Music from the Theatre."[22] A typical advertisement read:

> Is Modern Industrialism about to deal the Art of Music the saddest blow of its history?
>
> To blame Machinery as an Instrument of Decadence may seem startling, but it is true that Machinery in the form of Canned Music is elbowing Real Music out of motion picture theatres, thus denying to the masses the cultural influence of a Fine Art.
>
> Surely, if machine-made music displaces the artist in thousands of instances, the incentive for any individual to improve his talent—so necessary in all art—is minimized and music can no longer hold the cultural value that it has possessed. Any art is dependent for its progress upon the number of its enthusiastic executants.
>
> Do You, Mr. Reader, find the pleasure in Mechanical Music that you do in Real Music?
>
> AMERICANS PAY MORE GENEROUSLY FOR ENTERTAINMENT THAN ANY OTHER RACE ON EARTH. ARE THEY NOT, THEN, ENTITLED TO THE BEST?
>
> If you believe that Real Music should be saved to the masses who attend Motion Picture Theatres, make your opinion known to the manager of your favorite theatre. Very likely he will appreciate your frankness for he wants to please his patrons.[23]

By 1935 the theatre pipe organ manufacturers still left in business were trying to exploit other markets. The Wurlitzer

Company was placing ads for its church organs in various trade publications. No mention was made of the "Mighty Wurlitzers" that had thrilled theatre patrons.[24]

In April 1935 the first electric organ to be mass produced, the Hammond, was introduced to the public. It was to cause a revolution in the music world.[25] The Miller Theatre, Augusta, Georgia, installed a Hammond on a lift when the theatre opened in the thirties.[26] However, few theatres installed Hammonds because by this time there was little demand. Traveling artists, when they did appear, easily could travel with their own electric organs. Meanwhile, in thousands of orchestra pits from coast to coast, the "Mighty Wurlitzers" and other pipe organs slumbered in silence.

There were some bright spots, of course. Fine organ music continued to be heard daily at Radio City Music Hall where Dick Leibert held forth as chief organist, and with few gaps, live organ music continued at the New York Paramount, the Byrd Theatre in Richmond, the Fox Theatres in St. Louis, San Francisco, and Atlanta, and in other theatres scattered across the country. However, by the mid-thirties the number of organists employed full time to play in theatres had decreased to a mere handful. At the most famous theatres in the nation, the New York Paramount and Radio City Music Hall, the tradition continued.

PARAMOUNT THEATRE, NEW YORK CITY

Sound pictures had come to the New York Paramount Theatre in 1929. On August 4 of that year the Paramount ad proclaimed, "It's here! First Showing of Paramount Sound News." The sound newsreel had arrived. Jesse Crawford, chief organist of the Paramount at that time, already had left the organ accompaniment of the films to other staff organists. Crawford's solo productions continued as usual until he left the Paramount in 1933. After that, his wife Helen signed a separate contract with the theatre in 1933 and held the position of chief organist there for an unknown duration.[27] The organ remained silent (although Dan Papp, organ technician, kept it in repair as he did from its opening in 1926 until its closing in 1964) for about two years until Reginald Foort, one of the most famous of all theatre organists, came from England in early 1935 and played a ten-week engagement. So much interest was aroused in the organ that, following Foort's appearance, Don Baker, who had just returned from an English tour and now was organist of radio station WOR, was engaged as chief organist.[28] Baker held this post longer than any other organist, just under fourteen years, from 1935 to 1948. He was followed by a young organist from California named George Wright, who remained from 1949 until 1951.[29] During those years George Wright produced some eleven recordings, a few on the "Dowager Empress" as the main organ in the Paramount Theatre came to be called affectionately, and the rest on the upstairs broadcasting recording Wurlitzer.[30] These recordings not only served to keep interest in the theatre organ alive, but also were a forerunner of the later long-playing recordings of Wright on the HiFi label, which were to have such a significant part in the rebirth of interest in the theatre organ.

After George Wright left the New York Paramount, the organ was used only occasionally. Bob Mack (Robert R. McCombs) was available as organist when called until the time of the Paramount's closing in 1964.

The last occasional organist of the Paramount Theatre, New York, was Bill Floyd. Floyd assumed the post of organist in 1953 and remained available for the occasional use of the organ until 1964. In 1957 he recorded an album on the instrument for Emory Cook, high fidelity sound engineer. The album, recorded with a much wider audio range than previous such recordings, was enthusiastically received and likewise helped to foster interest once again in the theatre organ.

RADIO CITY MUSIC HALL

The fabulous Radio City Music Hall in Rockefeller Center opened as the International Music Hall, December 27, 1932, under the direction of Samuel Rothafel of Roxy Theatre fame. There were 6,200 seats, making it the largest presentation theatre in the world. The largest Wurlitzer ever produced went into the Music Hall, two four manual consoles and fifty-eight ranks, and since its opening, the organ has been featured on an average of eight times daily. On the organ staff when the theatre opened were Dick Leibert as chief organist, Arthur Gutow, Dr. C.A.J. Parmentier, and Betty Gould. However, neither Gutow nor Gould ever played at the Music Hall although Gould did play at the Center Theatre, also in Rockefeller Center. Leibert held this post until he retired September 6, 1973, thus setting a longevity record of over forty years of full-time service at one theatre, surpassed only by Eddie Weaver at the Loew's Richmond and Byrd Theatres, Richmond, Virginia.

A number of excellent musicians have served on the Music Hall staff over the years. Jack Ward was on the staff of Radio City Music Hall for over sixteen years until his death July 25, 1973, at seventy-five years of age. He previously had been a staff organist for NBC, playing for a wide variety of radio shows.[31] At one time he had traveled with the Wurlitzer company demonstrating its pipe organs.

One of the best-known Radio City Music Hall organists was Ashley Miller, whose tenure included a year and a half stint which began in the fall of 1946 and later a longer period from 1950 until January 1956.

Ray Bohr assumed the position of chief organist at Radio City Music Hall following the retirement of Dick Leibert in 1977.[32] He served more years on the staff than anyone other than Leibert. He became associate organist at Radio City Music Hall in 1947 and, at the same time, regularly played the Wurlitzer pipe organ in the Rainbow Room at the top of the RCA Building, Rockefeller Center. He continued at the Music Hall until the theatre closed in 1978. Since its reopening (reorganized as Radio City Music Hall Entertainment Center) a number of organists have held short-term, consecutive appointments at the instrument. The music hall and its organ continue to be among the top tourist attractions in New York City.

THEATRE ORGAN MAKES A COMEBACK

Out of the slumbering silence of the late thirties and forties came a renaissance of the theatre pipe organ in the 1950s. This surprising and unexpected "resurrection" occurred initially because of the invention and development of high fidelity sound recording and reproduction. High fidelity provided the perfect medium for the pipe organ. Its tonal range extends from 16 cycles per second in the bass to 16,000 cycles per second in the treble—in other words, the whole range of human hearing. No other single instrument covers the entire tonal spectrum in this way, not even the largest orchestras. Early high fidelity recordings of such artists as George Wright, Dick Leibert, Reginald Foort, and others sent "hi-fi bugs" into ecstacy as they listened to their "woofers" woof and their "tweeters" tweet. This led to a growing demand for theatre pipe organ recordings, a demand that has been sustained by the introduction of stereo recording and new quadrasonic sound.

On Tuesday, February 8, 1955, a hard core of theatre pipe organ enthusiasts responded to an invitation from Richard Simonton of Hollywood, California, to attend a meeting at which a national organization to promote their mutual interest was to be formed. There, in the large living room of Simonton's magnificent home, the American Association of Theatre Organ Enthusiasts was born.[33] The statement of purpose which was formulated read:

> . . . organized for the purpose of preserving the tradition of the theatre organ and to further the understanding of this instrument and its music through the exchange of information.[34]

Among those invited but unable to attend were Farny Wurlitzer and Jesse Crawford, who was out of town at the time. A partial list of those present included Dr. Orrin Hostetter, Ramona Gerhard Sutton, Judd Walton, Dr. Melvin Doner, "Tiny" James, Buddy Cole, Richard Vaughn, Bud Wittenburg, Paul Pease, Gordon Kibbee, Don George, Bob Jacobus, Frank Bindt, Dave Kelley, Harvey Heck, Jerry Sullivan, Gordon Blanchard, Archie March, Ray Booth, Ray Webber, Eddie Cleveland, Lloyd Darey, Marie Kibbee, Keith McCaleb, Kenny Wright, host and hostess Richard and Helena Simonton, and others.[35] From this group was elected the first slate of officers: Richard Simonton, president; Judd Walton, vice president; Paul

Pease, secretary-treasurer; and an Executive Committee: Buddy Cole, Dr. Orrin Hostetter, Gordon Kibbee, Richard Vaughn, and Bud Wittenberg.[36]

One of the most important results of this organizational meeting was the establishment of a publication known as the *Tibia* (named after the predominant flute voice of the theatre pipe organ), a quarterly journal to be devoted to the theatre pipe organ. Dr. Melvin H. Doner was chosen as first editor, with Ray Gorish as his assistant.[37]

The *Tibia* and its successor, *Theatre Organ* magazine, provide a continuing history of the theatre organ movement from 1955 to the present day. However, the *Tibia* was not the first theatre organ publication. Alden Miller of Minneapolis had authored and edited a number of newsletter-type publications variously known as the *Kinura, Ophicleide, Unit Orchestral Theatre Organ Magazine, Diaphone, Tibia*, and later the *Kinura Theatre Organ Digest*.[38]

Various clubs of theatre organ enthusiasts agreed to form a series of local chapters of the ATOE, renamed the American Theatre Organ Society, which now cover the nation from one end to the other. A surprisingly large number of enthusiasts have their own theatre pipe organ installations in homes and studios.

By 1962, *Time* magazine had recognized the growth and development of the theatre organ. Although the article did not bear the name of author Ben Hall, he wrote the following in the February 2 issue:

> There has never been anything to compare with the sound of a Mighty Wurlitzer in full cry. Its rumbling trumpeting majesty, its cooing, whimpering intimacy brought shivery pleasure to a generation of balcony sitters back in the golden age of the movie palace, saccharine with sentiment one moment, it was hell-for-leather Marine marching band the next, and for many a movie fan, when the Wurlitzer sank out of sight into the bowels of the orchestra pit, the best part of the show was over.
>
> Most cinemagoers today have forgotten the Mighty Wurlitzer along with the choruses of Sunkist Beauties, the personality bandleaders, and the bouncing ball—all victims of the talking picture. But there is one group that still remembers, a fiercely dedicated underground called

the American Association of Theatre Organ Enthusiasts. Like the electric trolley buffs, and the antique-auto fanciers, the Enthusiasts are a diehard coterie, with a single-minded mission to save those mighty relics of the recent past from the wrecker's hammer.

Some enthusiasts have been content to restore superannuated organs in movie theatres in return for the privilege of holding Sunday morning rallies, where everybody gets a chance to noodle before the house opens for business. But the real zealots remove complete organs from doomed movie palaces, from theatres where they have been neglected, unplayed and unloved, and install them in, under, and behind their homes.

Monster in the House. It is no small undertaking, for a Mighty Wurlitzer is like an iceberg, the largest portion of it is invisible. Hidden behind ornate grilles on either side of the stage in a theatre are a number of rooms, each bristling with ranks of pipes. One horn sounds like a flute, another a musical foghorn, a saxophone, a violin, a trumpet, or the percussion instruments, ranging from a grand piano to a castanet, which give the Wurlitzer its one-man-band versatility. These organ chambers must be duplicated in a home installation, and even the smallest organ needs more space than a kitchen for its hundreds of pipes, which vary in size from a pea shooter to a howitzer.

Restoring a wilted Wurlitzer can be both costly and time-consuming. Last year United Air Lines Captain Erwin Young installed an organ out of the Regent Theatre in Harrisburg, Pennsylvania, in his home near Mount Vernon in Virginia. Less mighty than most, Young's Wurlitzer has a two-manual console and seven ranks of pipes. But it has cost him more than $10,000 to purchase, ship, and install it in the new cinder-block and brick annex that he built for it behind his house. The work of wiring, releathering, tuning, and voicing took unnumbered hours. Sighs Young's wife: "I'm a Wurlitzer widow."

Rescued from Paramount. The American Association of Theatre Organ Enthusiasts was organized in 1955 in California by a group of Wurlitzer fans headed by Richard Simonton, who holds the Muzak franchise for Southern California (among his other interests: a 51% share of the Delta Queen, one of the last of the Mississippi River passenger steamers). Simonton, 45, was hooked on the Mighty Wurlitzer early in life, when he got a job in Seattle's Fifth Avenue Theatre. The lady organist played an all-request program every Saturday, but she had a poor memory for tunes. It was young Simonton's duty to stand beside the console and whistle the melodies for her as titles were yelled from the audience.

Simonton's own Wurlitzer is one of the largest home installations in the United States. Housed in a private 63-seat movie theatre in the basement of his Toluca Lake home in North Hollywood, the organ is a four-manual, 36-ranker, identical in size to the instruments in Manhattan's Paramount Theater, the Fox theaters in Detroit, St. Louis, Brooklyn and San Francisco.* Nucleus of Simonton's organ was a 19 rank job from Paramount Studios in Hollywood, to which he has added a new four manual console and ten additional tons of pipework.

Though he admits to being only a noodler himself, Simonton never lacks for live music. Famed Theater Organist Jesse Crawford, "The Poet of the Organ"—comes over to practice on the Wurlitzer three days a week. And when Simonton reels off a silent flicker in his basement Bijou, he always has on hand an old-time organist to accompany the picture with the requisite *mysteriosos* and *agitatos*.

The Giant Keepers. The American Association of Theatre Organ Enthusiasts numbers more than 1,500 devotees of the Mighty Wurlitzer and its cousins, the Silver Throated Barton, the Kilgen Wonder Organ, the Moller De Luxe, the Marr & Colton Symphonic Registrator. Among the cultists:

Humorist Herb Shriner, whose Larchmont, New York, home shelters a 14 rank Wurlitzer salvaged from the old Chicago Arena. Shriner is better known as a harmonica player (he recently played as soloist with the Cleveland Symphony) than as an organist. Says he: "All my life I wanted a mouth organ big enough to set down to and now I've got it. My wife calls it a mechanical mother-in-law;"

TV actor Joe Kearns ("Mr. Wilson" on Dennis the Menace), who literally built his Hollywood home around a 26-rank Wurlitzer;

Reinhold Delzer, Bismarck, North Dakota, contractor, who rescued the 20 rank Wurlitzer from the demolished Radio City Theater in Minneapolis. Delzer has carved out a grotto for his prize beneath his home after getting special permission from a nonplussed Bismark city commission to build organ chambers tangent to a city right of way;

Radio Red-Baiter, Fulton Lewis, Jr., who is not a card-carrying member of the A.T.O.E., has nonetheless gone underground with a theater organ in his basement—a modest three rank Robert Morton instrument salvaged from a Tampa movie house;

Richard Loderhose, Manhattan glue magnate, who bought the four manual, 21 rank Wurlitzer studio organ from the Paramount Theater

---

*Mightiest of all Wurlitzers: Radio City Music Hall's fifty eight rank monster with twin four manual consoles still in constant use after thirty years of intermissions.

building on Times Square, erected a 1,846 square foot outbuilding for it behind his suburban home. Since then, he has added 15 ranks of pipes, is currently wiring-in the giant five-manual Kimball organ console from the late lamented Roxy Theater in Manhattan. Says Loderhose, "If worse comes to worst, we can always live in it.[39]

By January 1970, the ATOE officially had changed its name to the American Theatre Organ Society. Its journal, the *Tibia*, had gone through several mergers and changes of name. Known as the *Tibia*, from 1955–58, it became *Theatre Organ* in 1959. Basically, this has remained its name ever since. Dr. Ralph Bell replaced Dr. Mel Doner as editor in the fall of 1957. He in turn was replaced by George Thompson who has been editor since the summer of 1961 and by Robert Gilbert in July 1981.[40] A separate publication, the *Bombarde*, edited by W. Stuart Green, was published from 1964 to 1966 when it merged with *Theatre Organ*. The combined magazine was known as *Theatre Organ Bombarde* until 1970 when the word "Bombarde" was removed from the masthead. W. Stuart Green, as editor emeritus, remains an active force in the magazine and Lloyd Klos, associate editor since 1967, has been one of its most prolific contributors.

The American Theatre Organ Society has grown remarkably in recent times. In some years there has been an increase of over 1,000 members. By 1981, nearly 6,000 persons belonged. More than 1,100 persons attended the national ATOS convention in Detroit in 1974.[41] This can be taken as an indication of the level of interest within the group. The American Theatre Organ Society has become international with chapters in New Zealand, Australia, and England.

The society now has its own national library and museum. It is important to maintain such archives if the tradition and history of the theatre organ are to be preserved.

While there is no other national organization of theatre pipe organ enthusiasts, there are other publications devoted to the theatre organ. Chief among them is *The Console* magazine. Published monthly, this journal is a voluntary, nonprofit enterprise of the International Theatre Organ Society, publishers.

Editor Tom B'Hend provides a "second voice" for the theatre organ movement in the United States.

In England, the Cinema Organ Society publishes a bimonthly journal, *Cinema Organ*. The Theatre Organ Club of Great Britain publishes *Theatre Organ Review*. In Australia, all five divisions of the Australian Theatre Organ Society publish their own monthly newsletters.

Some local chapters of the ATOS and local organ clubs own and maintain their own theatre pipe organs. Examples would include the Detroit Theater Organ Club, owning the Senate Theatre with its four manual, thirty-four rank Wurlitzer (from the Fisher Theatre). The Rochester Theater Organ Society has its four manual, twenty-two rank Wurlitzer now installed in the Auditorium Theatre, Rochester, New York. This society also has completed installation of a three manual, eight rank Wurlitzer in the 400-seat Eisenhart Auditorium, Rochester. Wichita Theatre Organ, Incorporated, in Wichita, Kansas is responsible for the installation of the famous New York Paramount Theatre Wurlitzer in Century II Center. The list is almost endless. Some chapters of ATOS have special working agreements with theatres including such things as restoration and maintenance of an organ in return for playing privileges.

In recent years a few companies have been established to market theatre organ records almost exclusively. For example, Doric Records of Alamo, California, has issued many recordings of theatre organ music including some reissues of original recordings from 78 rpm masters of famous organists of the past. Also, recordings are issued at intervals by the Detroit Theatre Organ Club, Detroit, Michigan; Rochester Theatre Organ Society, Rochester, New York; and Wichita Theatre Organ, Inc., Wichita, Kansas. The major recording companies such as RCA, Columbia, Capitol, and Decca have not shown much interest in theatre organ discs since the earlier years of high fidelity and stereo. One of the semimajor companies, Angel, has recorded a series of theatre organ discs, however.

There has been relatively little material on the theatre organ in printed form. Few books have been published that relate to this subject. The greatest milestone in the publication of theatre organ material was reached with the release of Ben M. Hall, *The Best Remaining Seats*, in 1961, now in a new edition and retitled, *Golden Age of the Movie Palace*. Although devoted to movie palace architecture and history, this book includes considerable material on the theatre organ.

In October 1974, Vestal Press of Vestal, New York, released the first full-length, hard cover biography of a theatre organist, *The Wizard of the Mighty Wurlitzer: Jesse Crawford, The Poet of the Organ* by Dr. John W. Landon. Earlier the publisher had reprinted organist Reginald Foort's autobiography, *The Cinema Organist*, published in England. Vestal Press remains the major publisher of theatre organ materials today, including reissues of historic catalogs and other reference works.[42] The Organ Literature Foundation (operated by Henry Karl Baker and Son), Braintree, Massachusetts, reissues out-of-print materials and markets a complete line of pamphlets, books, magazines, and recordings about both classical and theatre pipe organs.

The rebirth of the theatre organ drew new talent like a magnet. Some former theatre organists who had turned to other careers with the coming of sound pictures were now "rediscovered" and began making public appearances on rejuvenated theatre organs around the country. However, perhaps the most remarkable thing about the theatre organ's rebirth was the coming of a new, highly talented generation of organists who barely remembered the theatre organ of yesteryear, if at all. Many of this new generation were born in the 1950s or later.

The most recent chapter in the life of the theatre pipe organ is its emergence as an entertainment medium in pizza restaurants. A new level of popularity has been reached in the installation of organs in pizza "parlors" or "stores" as they are sometimes called. The first such instrument well may have been the Wurlitzer installed in "Ye Olde Pizza Joynt" in San Lorenzo, California.[43]

Carsten Henningsen, proprietor of this pizza palace, had the idea of installing an organ for the pleasure of his customers. A two manual, nine rank Wurlitzer from Fresno's State Theatre was installed and opened to the public July 25, 1962.[44] It was an instant success, leading to its enlargement to twelve ranks and the addition of a three manual console. It had far-reaching implications for the pizza parlor business. Other pizza parlor owners followed suit. Northern California may claim the most, but pizza and pipes can be found dotted here and there across the continent.

The Red Vest Pizza of Monterey, California, boasts the first pipe organ expressly built for a pizza parlor.[45] This instrument was built by the Wicks Organ Company of Highland, Illinois, and is a two manual, eight rank instrument of theatre organ voices, percussions, and traps.[46] In 1974 Wicks installed a second instrument, a two manual, six rank organ in the Pizza Machine, Pleasant Hill, California. The Wicks company and the Möller company both have the facilities to construct such instruments to order. They can be described as the only two major pipe organ builders still in business producing theatre-type instruments on demand.

RECENT DEVELOPMENTS

Just as the advent of high fidelity sound had a major part in the rebirth of the theatre pipe organ, and just as the advent of stereo helped sustain that interest, so one might hope that quadrasonic (four-channel) sound might encourage and enhance further interest. Much depends upon the degree of acceptance accorded quadrasonic sound by the public, for it means the purchase of additional expensive equipment and frequently results in discarding present record-playing components. Theatre organ records in quadrasonic sound are rare, but they could become the order of the day if there is a public demand. Billy Nalle recorded the first quadrasonic disc of theatre organ music in 1970. Tom Gnaster recorded a spectacular album on Tom Ferree's Louisville Uniphone theatre organ in the Rivoli Theatre, Indianapolis, in 1975. George Blackmore, a guest performer from England, had the honor of broadcasting (in quadrasonic sound) a part of the 1975 American Theatre Organ National Convention, a concert in the Orpheum Theatre, San Francisco. This historic broadcast was carried over radio station KKHI, San Francisco, and since has been released on quadrasonic disc by Doric Records. More such recordings may well be forthcoming. The newer technology of digital recording also may hold promise.

Another quadrasonic disc is of interest, " 'Two Loves Have I'—Jean and the Genii Computer Play the Lautzenheiser Wurlitzer." Genii is a special purpose computer which plays a Wurlitzer pipe organ from a musical score. It was developed by Marvin Lautzenheiser, a founder and computer systems analyst of Anagram Corporation, Springfield, Virginia.

> Unlike a reproducing player mechanism the computer reads the musical score (first translated into letters and numbers on punched cards) from a digital computer tape and gives a "live" performance. . . .Ten thousand signals per second are processed and sent to the proper organ circuit.[47]

Genii played her first official performance in 1972 for the National Convention of the American Theatre Organ Society.

Another digital computer device, under the direction of curator Gordon Belt, San Sylmar private museum, San Sylmar, California, records *and* reproduces its Wurlitzer theatre organ with uncanny realism that no audio recording system can hope to match: It replays the music by operation of the organ itself. At San Sylmar, noted theatre organists are asked to record some selections on this system for posterity.

Oral Roberts University of Tulsa, Oklahoma, a leader in innovation among America's private colleges, has installed what must be one of the world's most unusual pipe organs. Located in Christ's Chapel on the main campus is an instrument of 103 ranks built by Lawrence Phelps and Associates, Erie, Pennsylvania, which is actually two instruments in one—a four manual, seventy stop Phelps mechanical-action classical pipe organ, and a four manual, twenty-one rank theatre organ (basically Wurlitzer). The light oak console is horseshoe shaped, the top two rows of stop keys controlling the classical instrument and the balance controlling the theatre organ. The theatre organ is most adaptable to the playing of "evangelistic" gospel music while the classical instrument is for the sacred repertoire. The organ boasts 7,564 pipes.[48] Ray Bohr, formerly chief organist of Radio City Music Hall, New York, participated in a musical "first" when he gave the inaugural concert on this instrument on February 27, 1976.[49]

Century II Center in Wichita, Kansas, represents the growing edge of the theatre organ today. The former New York Paramount Wurlitzer (enlarged to thirty-nine ranks) is now located in a near-perfect acoustical setting in one of the four auditoriums in the complex. The center includes a 661-seat theatre for musical productions and drama and is the new home of the Wichita Community Theatre; a concert hall that seats over 2,000 persons, now the home of the Wichita Symphony; a 5,400-seat convention hall, and the great exhibition hall. There is no permanent seating in this latter hall but 4,000 seats can be provided, with 2,400 maximum in table seating for organ concerts.[50] The exhibition hall is the new home of the Wurlitzer theatre organ. This is the theatre organ so far ahead of its time when originally introduced in 1926 that it remains the tonal standard against which all others must be compared.

The organ is the property of Wichita Theatre Organ, Incorporated. It is presented in a variety of ways but each on a level calculated to win the respect and appreciation of thoughtful, serious music lovers. Neither is it presented so frequently as to satiate would-be patrons. Thus far the organ even has been utilized in several orchestral ensembles, including one concert with the Wichita Symphony. Guest theatre organists have presented concerts with audiences listening while seated at tables, and the organ has been used to accompany dancing (as has been done at Blackpool in England). Thus its use is creative and innovative. Those who are dedicated to its presentation see to it that they do not slip into a rut of similar, once-per-month presentations. Capable direction by Wichita Theatre Organ, Inc., involves artist-in-residence Billy Nalle who happily combines the educational credentials and artistic flexibility to be in the forefront of whatever lies in the future for this unique musical instrument.

The theatre pipe organ is anything but dead! Today in over 250 theatres, restaurants, pizza parlors, radio stations, and auditoriums across the country, theatre pipe organs are heard regularly, sometimes daily. Many silent films of Charlie Chaplin, Rudolph Valentino, Harold Lloyd, and others have been brought out of storage for authenic showings with pipe organ accompaniment in theatres and auditoriums. Organists from the old days such as John Muri, Gaylord Carter, and Lee Erwin, have dusted off their music and are back on the circuit again. More surprisingly, organist Lyn Larsen, who never even had heard a theatre pipe organ live until 1962, plays to capacity audiences wherever he appears, audiences in which the "under thirty" usually outnumber all others. Indiana University graduate Dennis James "packs them in" at Indiana University for his concerts and accompaniments to silent films. James' audiences are largely of college age proving that the superannuated have no corner on the appreciation of the theatre organ. Recently, James was appointed staff organist of the Ohio Theatre, Columbus, Ohio.

The theatre pipe organ has suffered through many vicissitudes since the early days of the "silents," but it has shown remarkable powers of endurance. Today, its future seems more secure than ever due to a growing coterie of dedicated enthusiasts and a growing public of all age levels.

Who knows what unenvisioned chapters remain yet to be written in the life of this wondrous instrument?

NOTES

1. Edward Benedict, "The Vitaphone, Friend or Foe," *Diapason*, April 1, 1927, p. 41.
2. Ibid.
3. Wade Hamilton, "Take Two Jumps Ahead—Stay There," *The American Organist*, 12 (1929): 162–64.
4. Ibid., p 163.
5. Malcolm Thompson, "Time to Take Stock," *The American Organist*, 12 (1929): 489.
6. Helen Jean Moyer, *The American Organist*, 12 (1929): 489.
7. James E. Scheirer, "The Fall and Decline of the Tibia Tooter and What of It?" *The American Organist*, 12 (1929): p. 33.
8. "Not a Funeral but a Gradual Fade-Out," *The American Organist*, 12 (1929): 33.
9. "What Next," *The American Organist*, 12 (1929): 738–40.
10. Ibid.
11. Ibid.

12. "Theatre Organs Enjoying Comeback," *The State Journal*, Lansing, Mich., September 22, 1971, p. D5.

13. Dan Daniels, "Merchandising the Organ Solo Today," *Motion Picture Herald*, 106 (January 16, 1932): 17ff.

14. "What About the Organ?" *Motion Picture Herald*, 106 (February 20, 1932): 68.

15. "Use of Organists Rises 25 Per Cent," *Motion Picture Herald*, 110 (June 17, 1933): 39.

16. Ibid.

17. Maitland Edey et al., eds., *This Fabulous Century*, vol. 3, *1920–1930* (New York: Time-Life Books, 1969), p. 228.

18. Ibid., p. 25.

19. Russel Nye, *The Unembarrassed Muse* (New York: Dial Press, 1970), p. 384.

20. William E. Leuchtenburg, *Franklin Roosevelt and the New Deal* (New York: Harper and Row, 1963), p. 139.

21. Richard Armour, ed., *Give Me Liberty* (New York: World Publishing Company, 1969), p. 120.

22. Ibid., p. 140.

23. Ibid., p. 120.

24. *The American Organist*, 18 (1935): 331, 445.

25. Ibid., p. 351. (The Hammond Organ was introduced to the public on April 13, 1935.)

26. Correspondence with Robert H. Clark, Jr., March 1976. (The Miller Theatre, Augusta, Ga., opened in 1939.)

27. "Use of Organists Rises 25 Per Cent," p. 39.

28. Ray Brubacher, "Farewell to the Famous New York Paramount," *Theatre Organ*, Fall 1964, pp. 4–6.

29. Ibid.

30. Lloyd Klos, "At the Crossroads of the World—The New York Paramount Theatre," *Theatre Organ*, April 1974, pp. 4–12.

31. "Closing Chord," *Theatre Organ*, August 1973, p. 51.

32. Ben M. Hall, "Twilight Reveries" (Record jacket notes from a long-playing, stereo record; part of a four-record collection, "Organ Memories," produced by Reader's Digest Records), and correspondence with Raymond F. Bohr, November 20, 1974. The author also interviewed Ray Bohr at Radio City Music Hall, March 5, 1976.

33. "Report of the Charter Meeting," *Tibia*, 1, no. 1 (Fall 1955): 5.

34. Ibid.

35. Ibid.

36. Ibid.

37. Ibid.

38. Melvin H. Doner, "The Editor Notes," *Tibia*, 1, no. 1 (Fall 1955): 2.

39. [Ben M. Hall], "Bigger Than Stereo," *Time*, February 2, 1962, p. 51.

40. Tom B'Hend, editor of *Console* magazine, served as editor of the 1964 Spring issue of *Theatre Organ* magazine but resigned to devote himself to publishing *Console* magazine.

41. July 12–17, 1974.

42. See "Bibliography" and "Notes on Sources."

43. Douglas Marion, "First Pizza Organ Built," *Theatre Organ*, June 1973, pp. 23–24.

44. Ibid.

45. Correspondence with Bill Langford, organist of Ye Olde Pizza Joynt, July 1976.

46. Ibid.

47. "Two Loves Have I: Jean & Genii" (Record jacket notes from a long-playing quadrasonic recording of the same title produced by Mark Custom Records. Recorded by Gerald Lewis Recording).

48. Promotional brochure from Oral Roberts University.

49. Interview with Ray Bohr at Radio City Music Hall, March 5, 1976.

50. Billy Nalle, "Century II," *Theatre Organ*, October 1974, pp. 9–11.

FIVE
THE THEATRE ORGAN ON PHONOGRAPH AND RADIO

Theatre organists became known to their audiences in other ways besides through live performances in theatres. One such means was phonograph records. The other was radio broadcasting.

Making records in the early days was a hit-or-miss affair. Before the mid–1920s, all recording was done acoustically before a horn. Microphones and electrical recording were not yet on the scene. Acoustical recording was cabable of capturing the human voice remarkably, but rarely did it succeed in capturing the full beauty and grandeur of a symphony orchestra, and never could it capture the full dynamic range of a pipe organ. Edison probably came the closest to perfection in his acoustical diamond discs (quarter-inch thick discs) in recording the pipe organ, but even his recordings were far surpassed by later electronic recording methods.

In the earliest days at Victor in Camden, New Jersey, discs were cut in a bare room located in a loft. The budding artist could only gain access to it by climbing a rickety ladder. For many years the recording crews kept check on the time and took a break at noon before the Campbell Soup Company across the street and down the block blew its noon whistle, lest that, too, be immortalized on disc.

Very few records of organ music of any type were issued in the early days. Sometimes a reed organ was used for accompaniment, but there were practically no studios available equipped with pipe organs. Portable recording equipment was available but was generally unsatisfactory in capturing the rich tones of the pipe organ.

Probably it was in the early 1920s that Victor purchased what was to be one of its finest recording studios. The congregation of the Camden (N.J.) Trinity Baptist Church was moving out and wanted to sell their old building. Victor bought the modified gothic brick structure which housed a three manual, twenty-one rank Estey pipe organ. By the mid-twenties the building had heavy use as a recording studio. All kinds of solo work and choral and symphonic recording were done here. The organ was used to accompany artists and occasionally for solo work. It was most frequently played by Mark Andrews, classical organist, who made many records of hymns and sacred music in the form of organ solos, accompanying vocalists such as Homer Rodeheaver and others; and the Trinity Choir composed of many famous Victor recording artists who were assembled together for choral work.

Other notable artists to record on this organ included Fats Waller who was billed as Thomas Waller at the Grand Organ. Fats made some of the most notable jazz solos of his entire career on this organ. Today these discs are eagerly sought by collectors. Fats recorded on this organ beginning November 17, 1926, and continued intermittently until January 1935. Sigmund Krumgold, Jesse Crawford's assistant at the New York Paramount Theatre for a time, also recorded organ accompaniments on this instrument.[1]

The organ was, of course, a church instrument, not designed for playing jazz, but an organist of Fats Waller's abilities was not dismayed. He put the organ through its paces, recording everything from fast, machine-gun fire staccatos to rich, rolling chords with equal ease. With Thomas Morris' Hot Babies jazz band the result was a relaxed, free-wheeling jazz sound. Although many numbers were rapidly played, they sounded so spontaneous that one wonders if they were using written arrangements and if they rehearsed at all.

The Trinity Baptist Church might still be in operation as a

recording studio today had not fate decreed otherwise. A high-speed subway line was installed nearby causing vibrations and background noises which made it impossible to do any further recording there. The church building then became a gymnasium for RCA Victor employees and headquarters for the RCA Athletic Association.[2] In the intervening years, the church has been torn down and today is a parking lot.[3]

A great many record companies had been experimenting with electrical processes. Orlando Marsh was one of the first, but he was not alone. Robert J. Callen, a young engineer at General Electric in Schenectady, New York, recalls that in 1926 the Gennett Record Company, part of the Starr Piano Company of Richmond, Indiana, was one of the first to offer commercial electric discs on the market. They leased electrical recording equipment from General Electric. After releasing a few electrical discs, they went back to the acoustical method of recording and the electrical recording equipment was leased to Brunswick, which had studios on the sixth and seventh floors of a building at 799 Seventh Avenue. Today, the same studios are in use by Columbia Records. The Columbia company experimented with electrical recording as well. One of the first of its offerings was of the blackface comedians Moran and Mack in the first of their "Two Black Crows" sketches.[4]

The Chicago *Sunday Tribune* for October 25, 1925, announced the development of a new Victor phonograph known as the "Orthophonic Victrola":

> In order to meet what is described as the development of tone consciousness by the American people during the last twenty-five years, and also to offset the inroads which the radio industry has made upon the phonograph business, the Victor Talking Machine Company, the Bell Laboratories of the American Telephone and Telegraph Company, and the Western Electric Company have cooperated in producing the new Orthophonic Victrola, which is engaging the attention of artists and music critics.
>
> This instrument, which is about twice the size of the ordinary cabinet phonograph, was given public demonstration for the first time last week at the luncheon of the Rotary Club at the Hotel Sherman.
>
> The Orthophonic Victrola, a home size instrument, has no electric

attachment and no loud speaker. It records instruments never before recorded. It reproduces sound vibrations of from 113 to 12,000 frequencies. . . .[5]

The major principle of the new machine was an S-shaped tone arm, lighter in weight than older machines, and a newly designed folded-horn type of acoustical tone chamber through which the sound emerged. Later, machines with electric rather than spring-wound motors appeared, and eventually acoustical reproducers were replaced with magnetic and crystal cartridges, and electrical amplifiers with volume and tone controls. All these machines bore the Orthophonic label. From the earliest Orthophonic machine described, the tone quality of the sound reproduced from phonograph records was greatly enhanced. Very shortly thereafter Victor introduced the Orthophonic record to accompany the phonograph.

For some time before this, electrical recording had been done. The only clue to the buyer was a tiny oval circle above the label with the letters "V.E." in it, imprinted in the record surface itself. This meant simply that this disc had been electrically recorded by Victor. Sometime in the late summer of 1926 Victor went to the Orthophonic, scroll seal record, which likewise was identified with the oval circle and the letters "V.E." but also which boasted a picturesque label with much fancy scrollwork on it.[6] Electrical recording more fully captured the sound of the pipe organ.

The advent of electrical recording made pipe organ recordings more practical. The results were much more satisfying to the ear than with the earlier acoustical methods. Quite a number of theatre organists made records in the late twenties. Portable electrical equipment made it possible to get good recordings in remote studios, especially if the studios were not excessively large. Large rooms seemed to swallow up the sound.

Victor's top name theatre organist was Jesse Crawford. Crawford recorded at the Chicago Wurlitzer showroom, the New York Wurlitzer showroom and especially at the studio Wurlitzer in the New York Paramount Building, ninth floor. Columbia recorded a number of organists in various theatres. They also recorded in smaller studios such as that of Emil Velazco who ran a school for budding theatre organists. Brunswick had two famous names on its label—Lew White and Eddie Dunstedter. Lew White was recorded on the rotunda organ in the Roxy Theatre, New York, on the Roxy Studio Kimball or the Kimball pipe organ in his own studio. White also recorded for the Banner, Victor, Melotone, Vocalian, and Okeh labels under his own name and such pseudonyms as Ken Wilson and Neil Allen. Dunstedter recorded on the organs of Kimball Hall, Chicago; the Barton organ of the Temple of Labor, Chicago; at the Wurlitzer in radio station WCCO in Minneapolis; and at the Wurlitzer of the Minnesota Theatre, Minneapolis. At this latter location he made two of the most remarkable theatre organ recordings ever produced. They were "The Parade of the Wooden Soldiers" (Brunswick Record 4293) and "That's How I Feel About You"/"If I Had You" (Brunswick Record 4320). Both of these recordings seemed to capture the full theatre sound because the natural reverberation of the building was evident. There was not the close deadness characteristic of so many other organ discs of this time.

Other notable artists recorded in the mid to late 1920s.[7] Milton Charles recorded for the Autograph, Conqueror, Gennett, Paramount, Silvertone, and Columbia labels at the Tivoli Theatre, the Chicago Theatre, radio station WENR and the Gunn School, all in the Chicago area. He recorded some selections under the pseudonym of Charles Dumas. Henri Keates recorded on the Broadway label at the Oriental Theatre in Chicago. Ralph Waldo Emerson recorded the Barton organ of radio station WLS for the Gennett label. Howard Peterson also recorded on this organ and on the Geneva organ at the Geneva Theatre in Geneva, Illinois, on the Columbia label. John Hammond (who appeared under the name of John Hassel on such labels as Diva, Clarion, Harmony, Velvet Tone, and Puritone) recorded on the Robert Morton organ of the Saenger Theatre, New Orleans.

Emil Velazco, who recorded under his own name for the Columbia label, also recorded under several pseudonyms for other labels. One such pseudonym was "Franklin Ferris." Another was "Carol Wynn." Unfortunately many of the master discs which he cut were pressed back to back with master discs by

John Hammond. Furthermore, they both recorded some of the same selections. Hence it is almost impossible to determine whether a particular organ solo on one of the minor record labels is actually Velazco or John Hammond. It most assuredly will be labeled as someone else. When Emil Velazco was interviewed in the late 1950s by theatre organ researcher Ben M. Hall, Velazco was unable to remember the many different pseudonyms under which he had recorded.[8]

The 1930s and 1940s were a time when the theatre organ seemed to fade in importance. Mighty Wurlitzers slumbered in silence in theatres from coast to coast. In their endless quest for the new and different, many people were attracted to the Hammond electronic keyboard instrument. Only a few artists continued turning out theatre organ records with any regularity—Jesse Crawford produced several albums for the Decca label on the Paramount Studio Wurlitzer before turning to Hammond. Don Baker, from his vantage point at the New York Paramount Theatre, recorded a number of sides for the Columbia and Continental labels, and Dick Leibert recording for RCA Victor turned out the largest number of albums of any of his contemporaries. After George Wright became organist of the New York Paramount Theatre, he recorded several sides for the King label. In California, Buddy Cole recorded for Capitol, and from England came some imports of Robinson Cleaver and other artists.

When the modern long-playing record was introduced by Columbia in 1948, many companies, old and new, jumped on the bandwagon. At first, long-playing discs were merely reissues of the 78 rpm material. The quality was often poor. However, with the coming of "high fidelity" in the 1950s and then stereophonic sound the picture changed. New high quality recordings by former BBC organist Reginald Foort, George Wright, Dick Leibert, and others captured the attention and respect of a whole new generation of listeners. At last it was possible to reproduce something near the full total range of the organ, and from woofer to tweeter the high fidelity or stereo systems proved that there was no instrument capable of such tonal compass as this. The use of audiotape for making the master recordings and the relatively low cost of vinyl made it possible for long-playing discs to be produced economically. The result was a great host of companies recording a great host of theatre pipe organs.

Meanwhile a new entertainment medium had arisen to challenge the preeminence of the phonograph. It was radio. The broadcasting of organ music caught on early when radio was still in its infancy. It was easy to fill several hours of broadcast time using one or two organists. The public liked it. Playing an organ always seemed, to the non-musician, to be more spectacular than playing a piano. Radio stations could exploit the public's considerable interest in organ music inexpensively. Organs in nearby theatres, homes, and auditoriums could be used.

It is not known when organ music was first heard over the airwaves. The two first radio stations in America, KDKA in Pittsburgh and WWJ (then known as WBL) in Detroit, both were inaugurated in 1920. Yet previous to this, Dr. Frank Conrad of Westinghouse was broadcasting in the evenings from his garage, reading the newspapers over the air. Someone, who was perhaps tired of this, suggested a change in programming. "Why don't you play some phonograph records?" he asked. Conrad complied, thus becoming the world's first disc jockey.[9] It is altogether possible that among the records played over the air were some of organ music.

At the start, radio broadcasting studios were primitive. From Dr. Frank Conrad's garage to a tent pitched on top of one of the Westinghouse factories, KDKA finally got its own studio room. Another early station, WOR New York, started in 1922 in a small makeshift space in the corner of the sporting goods section of a Newark department store.[10]

Usually there was a space only for a desk, a microphone, a phonograph and a piano. Certainly there was no room for a pipe organ, but arrangements could be made to use nearby organs via telephone hookups. Church services, including pipe organ music, were broadcast as early as 1921 over KDKA.[11] In November 1922 Westinghouse completed arrangements with the Estey Company to broadcast the pipe organ from the Estey Studio at 11 West 49th Street, New York, via a permanent wire connection to the Westinghouse broadcasting station, WJZ in

Newark, New Jersey. This organ was first broadcast on November 26, 1922.[12] Some claim that the Wanamaker organ in Philadelphia was the first to be broadcast. From 1922 to 1928, Wanamaker did operate its own radio station (WOO). The organ was featured from the start, and the broadcasts were heard in the United States, Canada, England, Europe, and as far away as Africa and Australia. Broadcasts from theatres began in the early twenties as well.

At the start, no one was paid for performing on radio. The first "commercial" on radio is believed to be a ten-minute talk by a Mr. Blackwell advertising a new apartment building in Jackson Heights, New York. The ten minutes of radio time on WEAF cost one dollar.[13] Artists who sang or played an instrument over the air were, in the minds of radio station owners, receiving free publicity for the theatres where they were appearing or the shows in which they performed. "John Smith" on the air playing the organ from the "Grand Theatre" was actually getting considerable free advertising for the "Grand Theatre." Samuel Rothafel (Roxy) took to the airwaves early with musicians and acts from New York's Capitol Theatre. Many other theatres followed suit. By 1924, Mr. and Mrs. Jesse Crawford could be heard live over WGN, Chicago, broadcasting their Sunday Noon Concerts direct from the Chicago Theatre.

Frequently the organ was used to fill in and "cover" for any broadcasting emergency. When a radio actress unexpectedly fainted, the organist, ever near his console, quickly gave out with some soothing organ music. Periods of silence simply were not permitted. The role of organ music on radio in the early days can be seen in a notice which appeared apologetically on the radio page of the *Chicago Tribune*, "Ruth Farley will be heard at the WGN Wurlitzer at 3:30 this afternoon provided that the football broadcast is finished at that hour."[14]

At NBC, New York, the organist or pianist was usually found in one of the smaller studios standing by from 8 A.M. to 1 A.M., seven days a week, to cover any emergency. For some of the more important radio broadcasts the standby was in Studio 3B (with a three manual organ).[15]

The newspapers of those infant days of radio were filled with the startling news that Mrs. Jones in Chicago had been able to "pull in" a station by using an outside antenna, or that Brand "X" was a superior radio because it had more tubes. A joke making the rounds at that time was: "Said one man to another, 'I put on a larger aerial and last night I got England.' Replied the other, 'Well, I opened my window last night and got Chile.' "[16]

In 1922 there were 20,000 radio sets in the Chicago area. By 1924 a similar survey indicated that the number of radio sets had jumped to more than 100,000.[17] By 1925 the Chicago area boasted 40 radio stations.[18] The same growth was occurring across the nation as a whole. By 1930 there were 618 radio stations, and a year later 2 million American families owned radios.[19]

When the radio networks were formed starting in 1926, New York seemed to be the logical headquarters.[20] New York had been considered the financial and cultural center of the United States for many years. Each of the networks was based in a New York "flagship" station. The CBS network was once based at WABC. NBC was divided into two networks—WJZ being the base of the Blue Network, and WEAF being the base of the Red Network.[21] Each of the important stations either had its own theatre pipe organ or had contractual agreements to broadcast from one. The New York Paramount Studio Wurlitzer was broadcast by Jesse Crawford over both Red and Blue NBC networks. Crawford also broadcast from the same studio for CBS for a time. Ann Leaf and other organists also played over the air on this organ. In fact, it was probably heard by more people than any other theatre organ on radio. Fred Feibel broadcast on it for more than seven years. Dr. C.A.J. Parmentier, Lew White, Winters and Weber, Don Baker, Fats Waller, and others broadcast on it. For a period of time Ann Leaf both opened and closed the CBS Network from this organ, morning and evening, with her broadcasts, "Ann Leaf at the Organ" and "Nocturne."[22]

From dawn to dark across the United States theatre pipe organ music was much in evidence on radio. Even after organs had gone silent in theatres, they were still heard on the air. A great many theatre organists, out of a job after the coming of sound pictures, drifted into radio. Until the end of World War II, theatre pipe organ music could be heard on the air frequently. Gradually the number of broadcasts declined. The organs needing serious repair for various reasons either could not be maintained due to war shortages, or simply were not. The public began clamoring for something new. Rock and roll music was just around the corner, and television was ready to become America's prime entertainment medium. Old time radio was dying and few live broadcasts of theatre organ music survived into the 1950s.

Other areas of the country besides New York had well-known radio stations broadcasting live theatre pipe organ music in the pre-World War II days. In Chicago Irma Glen played up to thirty-two shows per week as organist for WENR and WMAQ.[23] "Larry" Ambrose Larsen was organist of WGN and played the famous "Little Orphan Annie" theme on the network broadcast of the same name, which originated in Chicago.[24] Len Salvo was on the WGN organ staff, and until the mid–1970s Harold Turner played the WGN (Wurlitzer-Kimball) regularly over that station. Ralph Waldo Emerson (that was his real name) broadcast over WBBM.[25] Dean Fossler, Porter Heaps, Norm Sherr, Eddie House, Wilson Doty, and Preston and Edna Sellars are a few of the many other names which were associated with the broadcasting of pipe organs in Chicago in the early days. Well-known theatre organist Eddy Hanson had a distinguished career of radio broadcasting in Chicago during these years.

The CBS and NBC networks had their own organs in Hollywood and San Francisco. Station KNX broadcast from Columbia Square in Los Angeles. Radio station KMOX in St. Louis, WHAS in Louisville, WFDF in Flint, and KDKA in Pittsburgh are but a few of the many stations across America that carried live theatre organ broadcasts at least into the mid–1950s.

Radio station KDKA obtained its Wurlitzer pipe organ from a theatre in the vicinity of Uniontown, Pennsylvania. Originally inaugurated by Jesse Crawford, it was featured on many live broadcasts by Bernie Armstrong, Lois Miller, and Aneurin Bodycombe.[26] Aneurin ("Red") Bodycombe was perhaps the best known of the KDKA organists. For several years he played a series of weekly broadcasts for the Dairyman's Cooperative Sales Association entitled "DCSA Organ Melodies" and featuring Bill Nesbitt as announcer. These broadcasts were typical of the format of organ broadcasts across the country.

(Announcer)
Good evening, these are DCSA Organ Melodies.

Organ plays—"Somewhere Over the Rainbow"

(Announcer)
The fellow at the great big console tonight as usual, Aneurin Bodycombe. Dairymen's Cooperative Sales Association with its thousands of members in the tri-state area is very happy to tape this program for you this Saturday. This is Bill Nesbitt suggesting that you make sure that that family of yours gets lots of milk every day. Milk, you know, is the best bargain on your shopping list.

Organ plays—"Somewhere Over The Rainbow"

(Announcer)
My friend [garbled] I hope you like Cole Porter, I don't know what happened to me there. I do hope you like Cole Porter. The name of the tune that Aneurin is going to play is "Night and Day." It goes like this.

Organ plays—"Night and Day"

(Announcer)
One of the things we do on this program is talk about milk and muscle, and being overweight and underweight and stuff like that. And maybe you're overweight or maybe you're underweight, I don't know, either way, though you need milk. Milk builds muscle, not fat. Milk is the only natural food in the whole world that contains large quantities of proteins, minerals, and vitamins. So you see, milk helps maintain your pep and vitality, even when you are on a diet. If you are overweight, drink a glass of milk 15 minutes before you eat. This will dull your appetite. You'll eat less really fattening foods. You'll reduce calorie intake. Plump or slim, you never outgrow your need for milk. Drink three glasses every day. (Organ plays in background.)

(Announcer)
"Whatever Will Be, Will Be." It has a foreign title which I can't pronounce. It's a very popular tune. Aneurin plays it for you next.

Organ plays—"Whatever Will Be, Will Be"

(Announcer)
I thought that next week I would sing a chorus of that, but I don't think I really will. The "Wedding Of The Painted Doll," is another little thing that's been popular for a good many years. About 25, I believe. It has a lilt to it though, that I think you will enjoy as Aneurin Bodycombe plays it for you.

Organ plays—"Wedding Of The Painted Doll"

(Announcer)
Did you know that Congress has made available $75 million dollars for the supplying of milk to school children? Last year the government set aside $50 million dollars to provide this milk and more than 62,000 schools took advantage of it, but still much of this fund was unspent. The advantages of a milk break for school children cannot be overemphasized. It relieves nervousness and tension, keeps minds and bodies alert, helps children get the most from their lessons. If your child's school is participating in this special milk program for children which covers grades from kindergarten through high school, it's a real good thing but if not, contact your local principal or school board member and ask about the Special Milk Program for Children. They'll be very happy to answer any questions that you might have. (Organ plays in background.)

(Announcer)
Aneurin closes the show this evening with one of my favorite tunes. He seems to pick one of my favorites every night to close with though, and I hope it is one of yours. It's a very beautiful thing, "I Believe." Aneurin.

Organ plays—"I Believe"

(Announcer)
Every once in a while I think that I would like to take organ lessons, or maybe anyway, piano lessons, learn how to play things like that. Then I hear Aneurin Bodycombe play something like "I Believe" and I get discouraged. After all, I don't know why I should get discouraged about learning to play the organ, only takes about 75 years to learn to play it that way, but of course Aneurin did it much quicker. It only took him about 20. Oh well, I suppose that's life. I hope you enjoyed today's program of DCSA Organ Melodies. And would you like us to tape a tune for you? A very simple thing. All you do is send in the name of the song of which you are especially fond. We can't play everyone's selection right away, but we'll play as many as possible, just as soon as we can.

Organ plays—"Somewhere Over The Rainbow"

(Announcer)
Hope you'll join us again next Saturday evening for DCSA Organ Melodies with Aneurin Bodycombe at the console, brought to you by Dairymen's Cooperative Sales Association. This is Bill Nesbitt.

Organ plays—"Somewhere Over the Rainbow"[27]

Radio station WHAS installed a Kilgen three manual, twelve rank pipe organ in the early 1930s especially built for radio work. It was later enlarged to four manuals and eighteen ranks. Herbert Lee (Herbie) Koch had a voice in its design and played it regularly for over twenty years.

Koch broadcast coast to coast from the WHAS organ over CBS—a program entitled "Keyboard and Console," which was heard on Saturday afternoon. Another of his broadcasts, "Dream Serenade," was heard more than 5,000 times over a period of fifteen years. This program included music of a variety of types interspersed with poetry. With the coming of television, Koch continued to be featured at the organ until he retired in 1955.

Radio station KMOX in St. Louis installed a four manual, sixteen rank Kilgen pipe organ in its studios. Among the best known organists who played it over the years were Eddie Dunstedter and Ramona Gerhard. In the early 1930s a remarkable program was aired called, "Three Consoles." It featured Milton Charles at the two manual, eight rank Wurlitzer in the studios of WBBM, Chicago (formerly the organ of the Gunn School), Eddie Dunstedter at the KMOX organ, St. Louis, and Ann Leaf at the New York Paramount Studio Wurlitzer, playing simultaneously. From all accounts these three organists were able to synchronize their playing perfectly on these noon-hour broadcasts.[28]

Radio station WFDF in Flint, Michigan, featured a daily broadcast for many years on the Barton organ in the Capitol Theatre. Billy Geyer, well-known organist in the Flint area, was at the console five days a week for the early afternoon radio show. It included organ solos, accompaniment of vocalists, and exchanging patter with the announcer.

One of the most famous radio broadcasts of organ music was the "Moon River" show from WLW, Cincinnati. The program, which began in 1930, featured organist Fats Waller from 1932 to 1933 and Lee Erwin for a total of eleven years. It was used to close the broadcast day, coming on at 11:00 P.M. Included were organ solos, vocal numbers, and poetry read in a well-modulated voice. The opening words set the stage for a dreamy, peaceful music with timeless appeal: "Moon River, a lazy stream of dreams, where vain desires forget themselves in the loveliness of sleep. Moon River, enchanted white ribbon, twined in the hair of night, where nothing is but sleep."[29] The theme music was Fritz Kreisler's "Caprice Viennois."

Radio station WLW was owned by Powell Crosley, Jr. Crosley liked organ music and had an Aeolian pipe organ with roll-playing mechanism in his Cincinnati mansion. He saw to it that much good organ music was carried over WLW. Perhaps it was for this reason that the station owned three Wurlitzer pipe organs and featured quite a number of organists over the years.

North of the border, Canadians enjoyed their own broadcasts of theatre pipe organ music in addition to those originating in the United States. Organists Roland Todd and Katherine Stokes broadcast over CBL, Toronto.[30] Quentin Maclean broadcast over the same station from Shea's Theatre in Toronto. The organ, a three manual, fifteen rank Wurlitzer, has since been installed in Toronto's Casa Loma. Maclean is remembered for his Wednesday evening broadcast, "Nocturne," which featured organ solos interspersed with poetry.

Many people who never heard a live theatre organ performance in a real theatre became acquainted with the organ by means of radio. One might hear transcriptions of Dick Leibert at the Radio City Music Hall Studio, or Lew White live from the RKO Center Theatre, Rockefeller Center, New York early Sunday morning. However, a real thrill for many listeners was to hear the pipe organ theme music for network radio broadcasts. Among the most famous broadcasts featuring live theatre pipe organ music were "Amos and Andy," featuring Gaylord Carter at the pipe organ from 1935–42; "One Man's Family" with Paul Carson at the NBC Wurlitzer, 1932–51; "I Love a a Mystery," also featuring Carson;[31] "Ma Perkins," "Backstage Wife," "The Guiding Light," "Lum and Abner," "Doctor I.Q.," "The Canary Pet Show," starring the Master Radio Canaries, "The Carters of Elm Street," "Kay Fairchild, Stepmother," "Through the Garden Gate," and "Woman in My House." This list is far from complete. There were many other broadcasts featuring pipe organ music. Such organists as Rosa Rio, Ann Leaf, Jack Ward, Dick Leibert, Fred Feibel and Jesse and Helen Crawford did considerable organ work over network radio. After the introduction of the Hammond organ in 1935 and the subsequent development of soap operas, the use of organ music increased. Almost no serial drama was without it.

One of the theatre organists who did a great deal of radio work was Rosa Rio. Rosa Rio attended both the Oberlin Conservatory and the Eastman School of Music in Rochester. Eventually she married her teacher, well-known theatre organist John Hammond.[32] In the late 1930s after a number of years of theatre organ experience, she became staff organist for NBC and later for ABC and CBS. She played as many as thirteen shows per week including "Cavalcade of America," "Front Page Farrell," "Lorenzo Jones," "Myrt and Marge," "The Shadow," and "Town Hall Tonight." Her longest running show was "My True Story." She also had her own coast-to-coast radio show, "Rosa Rio Rhythms," which was broadcast over the Armed Forces Radio Service during World War II.[33]

John Winters, an experienced theatre organist, came to radio in the mid-thirties. Like Rosa Rio he played for three major networks and alternated with Rosa Rio as organist for some of the same shows. Other well-known radio shows with which he was associated included "Mr. Keene, Tracer of Lost Persons," "Backstage Wife," and "Young Doctor Malone." Earlier, Winters had broadcast from the New York Paramount Studio Wurlitzer dual console as a part of a team with Leo Weber. Weber and Winters also did duet arrangements at the twin console Wurlitzer in the Staten Island Paramount.

Organist John Gart also developed quite a career as a broadcasting organist beginning in 1934. He furnished music for a number of daily radio shows including "Valiant Lady," "The Guiding Light," and for Eleanor Roosevelt's show, "My Day."

Some organists successfully made the transition to television following World War II. Rosa Rio played the organ for "Appointment with Adventure," "Brighter Day," "The Today Show," and many others. John Winters played for several television shows on CBS and ABC, and John Gart did considerable television work. The programs with which he was associated include: "Truth or Consequences" with Ralph Edwards, "The Robert Montgomery Show," "The Paul Winchell Show," and "Casey, Crime Photographer," to name a few.[34] In later years Ashley Miller supplied organ background music for the television soap opera, "Search for Tomorrow." Rex Koury provided the music for "Gunsmoke," Billy Nalle played for "I Remember Mama," and George Wright supplied organ music for ABC West Coast. Ken Griffin did some television work on the electric organ before his untimely death, and organist Jerry Burke and now Bob Ralston have been featured on the popular weekly "Lawrence Welk Show."

We do not know what is in store for the entertainment world in the future. Instead of recordings and radio and television broadcasts, will it be some other media form? It is clear that the organ has proven to be a durable instrument which evokes much public interest. The number of organs being installed in private homes, restaurants, pizza parlors, and auditoriums today leads to the inevitable conclusion that whatever the entertainment medium of the future, the organ will find a place in it.

NOTES

1. Charles Hayles, "Fats Waller—Organist," *Cinema Organ*, 18, no. 8 (December 1970): 12–14, and Ron Mace "The Pipe Organ Records of Thomas 'Fats' Waller," *Cinema Organ*, 18, no. 8 (December 1970): 20–22.

2. Clipping from unidentified Camden, N.J., daily newspaper, January 8, 1940, in possession of Public Library, Camden, N.J., "RCA Victor" file.

3. Author visited Camden, N.J., August 26, 1970, and with an old plat book from the Public Library, checked out the location of the former Trinity Baptist Church.

4. Robert J. Callen, "The Education and Tribulations of a Precur-

sory Disc Recording Engineer" (New York: Audio Engineering Society, 1971), pp. 1–8.

5. *Chicago Tribune*, October 25, 1925.

6. Brian Rust, *The Victor Master Book*, vol. 2, 1925–1936 (Stanhope, N.J.: Walter C. Allen 1970), p. 3.

7. The most complete reference work on theatre organists who recorded on phonograph records is: Melvin H. Doner and R. G. Mander, *Theatre Organ Discs of the World* (Winona, Minn.: privately printed, 1958). (See "Notes on Sources.")

8. Interview with Ben M. Hall, August 1958.

9. Ben Gross, *I Looked and I Listened* (New York: Arlington House, 1970), pp. 51–53.

10. Ibid., p. 54.

11. Ibid.

12. Orpha Ochse, *The History of the Organ in the United States* (Bloomington: Indiana University Press, 1975), p. 333.

13. Gross, *I Looked and I Listened*, p. 61.

14. *Chicago Tribune*, October 17, 1926.

15. Correspondence with Dr. C.A.J. Parmentier, April 1976.

16. As told to the author by theatre organ researcher, Lloyd Klos.

17. L. R. Clarke, "Pipe Dreams, Chicago, U.S.A.," *Theatre Organ*, June 1969, pp. 16ff.

18. Ibid.

19. Irving Settel, *A Pictorial History of Radio* (New York: Grosset and Dunlap, 1967), p. 79.

20. Gross, *I Looked and I Listened*, pp. 102, 110.

21. Mary Jane Higby, *Tune in Tomorrow* (New York: Cowles Educational Corporation, 1968), p. viii.

22. Lloyd Klos, "Theatre Organists on Radio," *Theatre Organ*, December 1973, pp. 26–30.

23. Clarke, "Pipe Dreams."

24. Klos, "Theatre Organists on Radio."

25. Clarke, "Pipe Dreams."

26. Correspondence with Miss Gundla Johnson, former staff member of radio station KDKA, April 25, 1974.

27. Transcript of KDKA radio broadcast from 1954. (Used by permission.)

28. Melvin H. Doner, "Mr. Pipe Organ," *Theatre Organ*, Fall 1963, p. 7.

29. Klos, "Theatre Organists on Radio." (A Mr. Clarke, official at WLW, stated in later years that Fats Waller's organ music was all anybody could wish for, but he never quite adjusted to the idea of Fats

throwing his empty gin bottles into the organ loft. See Ed Kirkeby et al., *Ain't Misbehavin'* (New York: Dodd, Mead and Company, 1966), p. 163.

30. Klos, "Theatre Organists on Radio."

31. Ibid.

32. Lloyd Klos, "The Story of Rosa Rio," *Theatre Organ*, February 1970, pp. 8–11.

33. Ibid.

34. Ibid.

APPENDIX 1
BIOGRAPHICAL NOTES

AYARS, LOWELL Ayars attended Philadelphia Musical Academy, Clarke Conservatory, University of Pennsylvania, and Trinity College, London, England. While obtaining his classical training in organ, he studied under Leonard MacClain and Edward Shippen Barnes. He also studied voice under Marguerite Barr. He began in the profession of accompanying silent films; after the introduction of sound, he was organist at the Stanley Theatre in his native Bridgeton, New Jersey, the Broadway Theatre in Pitman, New Jersey, and the Uptown Theatre in Philadelphia, where he broadcast over radio station WHAT. He also played some of the last silent films and spotlight solos, and he accompanied vaudeville acts, short subjects, newsreels, and sing-alongs. Later he played a series of daily broadcasts from his home over radio station WSNJ, Bridgeton.

Ayars went on to complete a master of science degree in education, and for approximately twenty years he taught choral music at Vineland, New Jersey, high school. He retired from teaching in 1975.

Ayars has performed for many American Theatre Organ Society chapters and organ clubs in the East and Midwest. In his home he has a two manual, eight rank Wurlitzer pipe organ. He has made a

---

The author has exercised the greatest care in proofreading, editing, and otherwise handling the biographical data used herein. Notwithstanding the best efforts, errors may occur. Neither the author nor publisher can accept responsibility for these errors other than taking reasonable steps to correct such mistakes called to our attention in succeeding editions of this publication.

number of recordings and has played for some of the National Conventions of the American Theatre Organ Society. He is a charter member of the American Theatre Organ Society and was official organist of the New York State Fair in 1975.

Ayars is one of the few organists trained to sing while playing the organ.

BAGA, ENA Positions held include the Strand, Southland (orchestral organist); the New Gallery, London (solo organist); the Tivoli, London, for eight years; three years touring with Gaumont British; and she was the last organist to play the BBC Compton before it was destroyed by incendiary bombs. She substituted for Reginald Dixon at the Tower Ballroom, Blackpool, during the war years and played at the Odeon, Blackpool; the Granada, Harrow; the Palladium, Copenhagen, Denmark; a three-year engagement on an electronic organ for J. Lyon's Corner House Restaurants; and the Lou Morris Circuit, freelance, from 1949–1952. After five years as hostess of the Public House, she traveled abroad playing electronic organs in Rhodesia, Libya, and South Africa. She served as organist on the *Queen Mary* from 1961 to 1962, then four years as demonstrator for Hammond Organ. For the past several years, she has taught and demonstrated on electronic organs, makes frequent appearances accompanying silent films, and plays frequent theatre pipe organ concerts throughout Great Britain—a very popular concert artist who has made many records and hundreds of broadcasts. Her signature tune is "Smoke Gets in Your Eyes." She is the sister of theatre organist Florence De Jong.

BAKER, DON (1903-) Don Baker is one of the best known of the theatre organists of the "golden era" still performing today. Born in St. Thomas, Ontario, Canada, in 1903, he began studying piano at age eight. He attended the Toronto Conservatory of Music and before he was sixteen became a member of the American Federation of Musicians, Calgary, Alberta, branch. By age twenty he had moved to New York where he took a position as pianist at the Flushing Theatre, Long Island. He soon applied for and received United States citizenship.

Baker's theatre organ career began unexpectedly one evening when the organist of the Flushing Theatre didn't appear and the manager asked Baker to fill in. He did so and became so fascinated with the organ that he started coming in early in the morning to practice. Within two months he was named chief organist.

From 1923 to 1929, Don Baker played at the Rivoli and Rialto theatres in New York City. When the Brooklyn Paramount opened, he joined the staff there. Two years were spent at the Staten Island Paramount, after which Baker went to England for a year and a half. There he played at several London theatres including the Granada, Tooting.

After Baker returned to the United States, he became staff organist at radio station WOR in New York City, and in 1935 he began almost fourteen years as chief organist of the New York Paramount, Times Square. He has done a great deal of recording, has had numbers of his musical arrangements published and has made about fifty films for Columbia Pictures.

In 1948 Baker moved West and played at such places as Lake Tahoe, Reno, and Las Vegas. He toured for the Conn Organ Company for several years but now has retired from that position. He has served on the staff of more than one organ-equipped pizza parlor and he continues to give concerts.

BLACKMORE, GEORGE (FRCO) (1921-) Born on January 24, 1921, in Chatham, England, at the age of nine he had become a chorister in Rochester Cathedral. He was educated at the Cathedral Choir School and studied music under Percy Whitlock and later under H. A. Bennett. At age twelve, after six months of instruction on organ, he won an organ scholarship to Kings School, Rochester, the youngest person to attain this honor. At the age of sixteen he was given the opportunity to play theatre organ at the Palace, Chatham, through the interest of Peter Kilby. He later did occasional substituting at the Majestic Theatre in Rochester. His full-time theatre organ positions include the Majestic, Rochester (1939–41); War Service; the Gaumont, Birmingham, also touring for Gaumont-British; Capitol and Astoria, Aberdeen (1950–57); and free-lance work thereafter. He worked for London Music Publishers, played concerts in Australia and the United States in 1967, and has been musical advisor and chief demonstrator for Hammond Organ (UK) since 1968. He has broadcast many times since 1941 and has made many long-playing recordings on theatre and electronic organs. He played a series of concerts in the United States in recent years. His signature tune is "Cock O' the North."

BOHR, RAY (1919-) Ray Bohr assumed the position of chief organist at Radio City Music Hall following the retirement of Dick Leibert. He served more years on the staff than anyone other than Leibert.

Bohr was born in Nyack, New York, November 2, 1919. He started studying piano at age six, and although he never took a degree in music, he was fortunate in having some excellent private instruction. Before World War II he studied with Robert Morse at St. John's Church in Greenwich Village, New York City. After the war he studied with Harold Friedell at Calvary Episcopal Church, New York City.

At age fourteen Bohr took a job with M. A. Clark and Sons, who built and maintained pipe organs. He convinced the manager of the Rockland Theatre near his home that the two manual, seven rank Wurlitzer in the theatre needed restoration. Bohr did most of the work himself, and once his ability as a musician became evident, the theatre manager hired him as regular organist.

Bohr also held church organ posts in Haverstraw and Pearl River, New York, before going into the army in World War II. The only time he touched an organ during the war years was when he played a memorial service at Iwo Jima for the late President Franklin D. Roosevelt.

After World War II Ray Bohr took a position as organ demonstrator for Wurlitzer and continued his classical organ studies. He became associate organist at Radio City Music Hall in 1947 while continuing to demonstrate for Wurlitzer. He began playing the pipe organ in the Rainbow Room at the top of the RCA Building in Rockefeller Center. During these years he also became organist for the television show "Bride and Groom," a post he was to hold for a year. He continued as associate organist at the Music Hall until he was advanced to chief organist in 1973, a position he held until the Music Hall closed and reorganized in 1978.

BOLLINGTON, AL (1904-) Born December 8, 1904, in Normanton, in 1914 he received the ALCM (Associate of the London College of Music), the youngest person to receive this award up to this time. Bollington also studied at the Royal Academy in London. In 1920 he began playing for silent films in his hometown. In 1922 he played piano on board an Atlantic ocean liner bound for New York. While in New York, he heard a theatre organ for the first time. Two years later he himself became orchestral organist at the Palace Theatre, Blackpool. Other theatres where he appeared include the Kilburn Grange Theatre, North London (1927), the Regal, Marble Arch (1928) as assistant to Quentin Maclean; the Brixton, Astoria (1928), as assistant to George Pattman; the Streatham Astoria; the Plaza, Piccadilly Circus (1935); the Paramount, Tottenham Court Road, London (1937).

Bollington did a number of BBC broadcasts, and after a stint in the armed forces as a pilot in World War II he took the position of organist at the Odeon Swiss Cottage Theatre and then the Paramount (Odeon) London. In 1948 he opened the new Odeon Theatre, Toronto. He later appeared at the Victoria Theatre and Shea's, Toronto, and broadcast over CBC. In the mid-fifties Bollington moved to California where he did some film studio work, television broadcasting, and touring for the Conn and Wurlitzer companies.

BROWN, JACKIE (1928-) Born in 1928, Brown began his career with the Granada Theatre chain. After leaving Granada, he had short engagements at the Gaumont, Watford, and the Dominion, Tottenham Court Road, London. Soon his talents of composing, arranging, and conducting came to the fore. He appeared regularly over the years with bands and as an electronic organist on television. He also made frequent appearances for organ society concerts. In his later years he was musical director for an electronic organ store. He broadcast many times on the BBC and recorded a number of phonograph records.

BYRD, DESSA (1898–1977) Born in Robinson, Illinois, Dessa Byrd won a scholarship to the Indianapolis Conservatory of Music. Her first job upon graduation in 1918 was playing the piano at the Alhambra Theatre, Indianapolis, Indiana. She left the Alhambra after six weeks to play the organ at the Rialto Theatre. Her only experience at the organ had been playing for church in her hometown.

Byrd accepted the position of relief organist when it became available, and later she became lead organist. Later a Wurlitzer pipe organ was installed at the Circle, replacing the original Hook and Hastings instrument, and Byrd was featured soloist on this fine instrument until 1929 when she moved to the Indiana Theatre, Indianapolis, where she served as solo organist until 1934.

She played with orchestras, accompanied films, played organ overtures, sing-alongs, stage shows, and organ solo spots. Byrd began playing at the Circle Theatre again in 1931 and remained there until 1939. She holds the distinction of being the first organist to broadcast over the radio (WFBM) in Indiana. The year was 1926. Byrd also played the Marr and Colton organ in the Fountain Square Theatre in Indianapolis, on radio. Over the years she broadcast on virtually every radio and television station in the Indianapolis area.

In 1935 the Hammond organ had just been introduced. Byrd had left the Indiana Theatre the year before, was continuing at the Circle Theatre, and was also hired by Pearson Music Company to be the first Hammond demonstrator in Indiana.

By all accounts she was the best-known and most famous theatre organist from the Indianapolis area.

Dessa Byrd died in May 1977.

CARTER, GAYLORD (1905-) Gaylord Carter is among the best-known of the theatre organists on the concert circuit. Born in Weisbaden, Germany, in 1905, he spent his boyhood in Wichita, Kansas. His family had come to this country to open a conservatory of music in Wichita, and his father took a post as church organist.

When Gaylord Carter was sixteen years of age, the family moved to Los Angeles. Carter soon obtained an after-school job playing the organ for silent pictures. In 1926 he took his first important post as organist for Grauman's Million Dollar Theatre in Los Angeles. Carter played other theatre engagements at the downtown Paramount, United Artists, Warner's Hollywood, and Egyptian theatres in the Los Angeles-Hollywood area. He also played the Seattle Paramount Theatre. By 1935 he was becoming deeply involved in radio broadcasting. He played for such radio shows as "California Melodies," "Hollywood Hotel," "The Packard Show," "The Second Mrs. Burton," and "Breakfast in Hollywood." He will always be associated in the public mind with the "Amos and Andy Show." For seven years he introduced the show playing "The Perfect Song," which was its theme.

Carter was on active duty during World War II in the navy. Since then, he has been busy with radio and television work. He has been associated with each of the major networks, CBS, NBC, and ABC in such programs as "Bride and Groom," "The Hal Sawyer Show," "The Big Payoff," and "Glamour Girl." The very popular Pinky Lee Television Show also featured Carter's artistry. In addition Carter has found time to do some church organ work.

In recent years Carter has toured the country accompanying silent films in his famous "Flicker Fingers" presentations of Buster Keaton, Harold Lloyd, Douglas Fairbanks, and others, a series of top-flight, action-packed movies, and they continue at present. He began these presentations in 1961.

Carter has played at several American Theatre Organ Society conventions and has an increasing number of long-playing and stereo records to his credit.

CASEY, TERANCE (1900-) Born in 1900, Casey has served as organist of the Regent, Brighton; the Tivoli, Strand, London (1928); the Regent, Brighton (1929–34); the Gaumont, Chelsea; the Gaumont, Haymarket, London; the Trocadero, Elephant and Castle; the State,

Kilburn; the Gaumont, Hammersmith (left there in 1949). He did free-lance work on the Hammond organ including serving as organist for a period of time on the *Queen Mary*. He played the Gaumont, Hay-market, until 1958. He also broadcast frequently and made many records.

CHARLES, MILTON Born in San Jose, California, Charles first studied classical organ before beginning his theatre organ career. His first theatre position was at the Jewel Theatre in San Francisco.

Milton Charles went on tour for Turner and Denkin theatres in Fresno and Stockton. Eventually he went to Grauman's Million Dollar Theatre in Los Angeles as assistant to C. Sharpe Minor.

Charles followed Jesse Crawford to Miller's California Theatre and then followed him on to Chicago where he worked at various Balaban and Katz theatres. He held forth at the Tivoli and worked a relief shift at the Chicago Theatre, occasionally doing the Sunday Noon Concerts. He also played the Uptown Theatre there.

When the Metropolitan Theatre in Los Angeles was reopened as the Paramount, Milton Charles went back as chief organist. The year was 1929. After a year and a half, he returned East to Philadelphia's Mastbaum Theatre. By 1936 he was becoming deeply involved as a broadcasting organist over CBS, Chicago. After the beginning of World War II Charles moved to Los Angeles, remaining with CBS. One of the many radio shows with which Charles was associated over the years was the "Dr. Christian Show." For ten years, until it finally went off the air, he furnished the organ music. After this he began doing free-lance work and for a period of about twenty years he played the organ nightly at the King's Arms restaurant in Los Angeles.

CLEAVER, H. ROBINSON (ARCO) (1906-   ) Born May 25, 1906, in Derbyshire, England, Cleaver won the Meadowcroft Exhibition for Organ Playing at the Royal Manchester College of Music and passed his Royal College of Organists exam at the age of twenty-one. He was solo organist at the Piccadilly Theatre in Manchester for over four years (1927–32) and broadcast from there. He served as organist at the Albert Hall, Sheffield; the Lonsdale Cinema, Carlisle (1932–35); the Regal, Bexleyheath (1935–36); Union Theatres; ABC Theatres; and Granada Theatres. He opened the Granada, Welling, in 1938 and remained with Granada Theatres until the mid–1950s. He also appeared at the Palladium Theatre, Copenhagen (1938).

Cleaver remains a popular concert artist. He has recorded a considerable number of records. He and his wife Molly had many personal appearances to their credit. Cleaver was the first organist to broadcast organ music on television in England (with Mrs. Cleaver, July 20, 1946). He is known for his composing and arranging. His signature tune is "An Earful of Music."

Molly Cleaver died November 27, 1977.

COLE, BUDDY (1917–1965) Buddy Cole, like many theatre organists, started in his chosen profession at an early age. His first job at the age of fourteen was as organist of the Figueroa Theatre in Los Angeles. It was his task to play for the vaudeville acts, talent shows, and community sings. Born a decade or two later than most theatre organists who were active in the "golden age" of the theatre organ, Cole launched his career as a professional musician at a time when the theatre organ was going into eclipse. There were plenty of fine instruments still in theatres, but few of them were being used. Hence, Buddy Cole found his niche chiefly as an accompanist, more often than not on the piano. He is particularly remembered as accompanist for Bing Crosby on record, as well as on radio broadcasts. However, he accompanied many other notable show business personalities including such luminaries as Tommy Dorsey, Marlene Dietrich, Nat King Cole, Rosemary Clooney, and Al Jolson.

During the years when Cole worked as an accompanist, his love for the theatre organ was undiminished. He recorded some 78 rpm discs for Capitol Records in the early post-World War II era on a nine rank Robert Morton pipe organ installed in his garage in North Hollywood. With the advent of high fidelity sound, Cole turned more of his attention and energies to completing the installation of a much larger organ in a new studio at his home. The organ eventually totaled twenty-seven ranks (three manuals) the main part of which was an eighteen rank Wurlitzer organ from the United Artists Theatre in Los Angeles.

Cole suffered from a heart condition for some time before his death in 1965. He is remembered as one of the "greats," responsible in part for the resurgence of interest in the theatre pipe organ in more recent times.

CRAWFORD, JESSE (1895–1962) and **HELEN CRAWFORD** (1899–1943) Jesse Crawford was born in Woodland, California, December 2, 1895. He was placed in an orphanage by his poverty-stricken mother after his father's death, and it was here that his musical ability was first recognized. After some early experience as a pianist for silent films, his first theatre organ position was at the Gem Theatre, Spokane. From here he moved to the Clemmer Theatre, Spokane.

Crawford's big break came when he was hired by Sid Gauman to play at the Million Dollar Theatre, Los Angeles. Early in 1921 Crawford was hired as chief organist of the Chicago Theatre, Chicago, a post he was to hold for five years. In early 1923 he met and married Helen Anderson, organist from the Roosevelt Theatre across the street. Shortly thereafter a second console was added at the Chicago, and Mr. and Mrs. Crawford began to appear in tandem. This captivated the public and their fame increased.

In 1926 the Crawfords opened the Paramount Theatre, Times Square, where they were to attain their greatest fame from personal appearances, radio broadcasts, and recordings. Crawford left the Paramount in March 1933, and after a few months' tour of English theatres returned to play at the Chicago World's Fair. He accepted a position with NBC, Chicago. In 1937 Mr. and Mrs. Crawford toured the country with an orchestra playing duets on the twin Hammond Organs.

In 1938 Jesse Crawford returned to NBC, New York, and began studying composition and arranging with Joseph Schillinger. He did solo work on NBC and with his wife played organ music for various soap operas and dramatic broadcasts.

Helen Crawford died January 15, 1943, as the result of an automobile accident. Jesse Crawford continued his broadcasting career. In 1944 Jesse met and married Lucy Peace. After a few years teaching on the Hammond organ at Steinway Hall in New York City, Jesse and Lucy moved to Los Angeles where he began teaching at the Penny-Owsley store. Jesse Crawford is the only American theatre organist to be the subject of a full-length biography, *Jesse Crawford, The Poet of the Organ; Wizard of the Mighty Wurlitzer* by John W. Landon.

Crawford died of a cerebral hemorrhage, May 27, 1962.

CROUDSON, HENRY (1898–1971) Born in 1898, Croudson worked originally as a bank clerk in the Midland Bank, Leeds. He spent seven years as organist of the Majestic Theatre, Leeds, from 1925 to 1932, and also worked at the Paramount, Leeds (1932 to 1935); the Paramount, Manchester (1935 to 1939); the Paramount, Glasgow (1939); the Curzon, Liverpool; the Plaza, Birkenhead; the Ritz, Birkenhead; the Majestic, Leeds; the Paramount, Leeds (1941 to 1945); the Gaumont, Haymarket, London (1945 to ?); the Plaza, Piccadilly, London (late 1950s); the Empire, Leicester Square (1959); the Ritz, Leicester Square (electronic organ) (1960). He made about 600 broadcasts from 1934 to 1960 and recorded 19 solo discs at the Paramount, Manchester, plus a number of other recordings as an accompanist at the EMI Studio in 1941. Croudson died in 1971.

D'ANTALFFY, DEZSO von Dezso von D'Antalffy spent most of his professional life on the East Coast. He was organist of the Eastman Theatre in Rochester, New York, in the early 1920s and on the staff of the Roxy Theatre in New York City when it opened. From there he joined the staff of Radio City Music Hall in New York.

DAVIES, WILLIAM Born in Lancashire, Davies studied piano, organ, composition, choral arranging, and conducting. He served in the RAF during World War II. While in service he broadcast programs of organ and piano music both in Great Britain and on Ceylon Radio. Following the war he joined the Gaumont British circuit and appeared as organ soloist across England until 1950 when he became associated with the Jack Hylton organization as organist and musical director in several London theatres. In 1955 he joined the BBC as staff organist and pianist. Since 1965 Davies has concentrated on recital work, lectures, and the composition of film scores. He is organist and master of music at Sutton Baptist Church, Surrey.

DE JONG, FLORENCE The eldest of three musical sisters who very early showed definite musical promise, Florence De Jong was a member of her father's orchestra at the Angel, Islington, in her early teens. Her first theatre appointment as organist was at this theatre. She was the first lady organist at the New Gallery when it was opened by Jack Courtnay. Subsequently she became soloist and remained there for thirteen years, during which time she played at many important premieres, under royal patronage. She has broadcast, recorded, made many personal appearances on films, and free-lanced as a guest organist both in England and on the Continent. Incidentally, it should be mentioned that she was the first British lady organist to broadcast. She played an engagement in Holland for AVRO, later the L. Morris Circuit.

For a number of years Florence De Jong has been musical director of the National Film Theatre in London where she continues to provide musical accompaniment to silent films.

DEL CASTILLO, LLOYD G. (1893-) Lloyd G. Del Castillo has had a long and remarkable musical career. He first studied organ at Harvard University and was co-founder of the *Harvard Musical Review* and conductor of the Harvard University orchestra.

He began his theatre organ career at Boston's Fenway Theatre in 1917. He was drafted, but by the time he arrived at the front, World

War I was over. In a matter of months Del Castillo was back at the Fenway Theatre. From there he went to the Boston Theatre, Shea's Buffalo, the Rialto in New York, the State in Boston, and finally the Metropolitan in Boston.

In 1927 Del Castillo opened his own theatre organ school, but two years later sound pictures had put a stop to the whole enterprise. Casting about for new opportunities, he became organist, conductor, and arranger for CBS (WEEI in Boston). At the beginning of World War II he moved to California, doing further radio work for CBS through station KNX and later the show "You Asked for It," on ABC-TV. A year's vacation in Europe followed. Upon his return Del Castillo became head of the organ department of the Sherman School of Music in Hollywood. Today he continues concertizing, composing, arranging, and recording. He has free-lanced for all the major television networks. In the late 1920s he wrote a monthly column, "Photoplaying," in *The American Organist* as well as writing for *Jacob's Orchestra Monthly*. As a writer with a genuine flair for humor, he created a mythical elevator operator—an uneducated but lovable character named Dinny Timmins who was always commenting on organists, organ music, and music in general. This column has been revived in recent years in *Theatre Organ* magazine.

DIXON, REGINALD (1904-) Born in Sheffield, England, in 1904, Dixon played the organ in church and various cinemas during his youth. In 1930 he won the prestigious post of resident organist of the Blackpool Tower Ballroom and remained there until his retirement in 1970. After his first records came out in 1932, the Blackpool management decided to give him the finest possible instrument and installed a three manual, fourteen rank Wurlitzer in the ballroom. During World War II Dixon's career was interrupted by service in the Royal Air Force. In 1957 the season was a silent one, because fire had destroyed the ballroom and the Wurlitzer organ had to be rebuilt. In 1958 another crisis occurred when Dixon had to undergo surgery—a delicate nerve operation on his right arm—but a few weeks later he was back at the ballroom on a regular basis. Dixon is known as "Mr. Blackpool." He may be the most prolific recording artist among British theatre organists. Many of his recordings have also been released in the United States where he is perhaps the best-known British theatre organist. He was elected to the American Theatre Organ Society Hall of Fame.

Dixon has been busy in his retirement playing theatre organ engagements and continuing to broadcast occasionally for the BBC.

DUNSTEDTER, EDDIE (1897–1974) Born in Edwardsville, Illinois, and christened Edward Jacob shortly after the turn of the century, Dunstedter first gave evidence of musical aptitude at a tender age when he sat down at the old reed organ in the family attic and played by ear the hymns that he had heard at church. By age nine Eddie was playing piano in a small vaudeville house. On one occasion when the acts were getting ready to rehearse, someone asked the whereabouts of the pianist. "He's out shooting marbles," said the theatre manager. This theatre, the Edwardsville Widley Theatre, had a three rank pit organ. By the time he had attained the age of eleven years, Eddie was playing the organ here regularly for the magnificent salary of eight dollars per week. On Sundays he played the organ at church while his brother Carl pumped the air.

Eddie Dunstedter went to work for the Kilgen Organ Company in St. Louis when he was about twenty years old. In 1917 he married Viva Drummond. Two children, Eddie, Jr., and Dodie, were born to them.

Dunstedter moved to St. Paul, Minnesota, a few years after his marriage. Here he opened the four manual Kilgen organ at the Capitol Theatre, later moving on to St. Louis to the Missouri Theatre where a four manual Wurlitzer was installed. Then it was back to the Capitol Theatre in St. Paul, to the Garrick in Minneapolis, and then to the State Theatre, Minneapolis. Just around the corner, the Minnesota Theatre was being constructed and a four manual Wurlitzer installed. It was here that Dunstedter was to make some of the most memorable recordings of theatre organ music that have ever been issued such as "The Parade of the Wooden Soldiers" (Brunswick record 4293) and "If I Had You" (Brunswick record 4320).

While at the Minnesota Theatre, Dunstedter had been busy with radio work on station WCCO. His playing was heard nationwide over CBS on the famed "Fast Freight" popular organ broadcasts. His theme song for many years was his own composition, "Open Your Eyes." In mid–1929 he was conducting a twenty-one-piece band broadcasting coast to coast.

In 1933 Dunstedter moved back to St. Louis where he became organist and musical director for radio station KMOX, where he broadcast from the four manual, sixteen rank Kilgen.

By 1937 Dunstedter was in California doing radio work over CBS Hollywood and at the MGM studios. Radio shows such as "Johnny Dollar," "The Lineup," and "Suspense" were followed by television shows such as "Playhouse 90" and "Romance."

In his later years Dunstedter gave occasional theatre organ programs and appeared at restaurants and supper clubs in the California area.

Dunstedter died July 30, 1974, just three days short of his seventy-seventh birthday.

ERWIN, LEE For more than a decade it was organist Lee Erwin who "took listeners nightly down the valley of a thousand yesterdays, to the bright waters of *Moon River*—that lazy stream of dreams—where nothing is—but sleep." This was the spoken introduction to one of the most famous radio broadcasts in the Midwest, "Moon River" (WLW, Cincinnati), and while these words were being read by an announcer with a mellifluous voice, Erwin played the haunting melody by Fritz Kreisler "Caprice Vennois."

Erwin began his musical career in Huntsville, Alabama, his birth place, at the age of twelve. His instrument was the piano. Awarded a scholarship to the Conservatory of Music in Cincinnati, he left piano for organ, which was to be his first love. He supported himself in part by playing the organ in a theatre nearby seven nights a week, for twenty dollars weekly. After completing his degree in organ, he went on to France for study with André Marchal, famed organist. Erwin spent several years studying in Europe, becoming assistant organist at the American Cathedral in Paris. In 1932 he returned home and became full-time organist at the Alabama Theatre, Birmingham. The next year he returned to Cincinnati as organist of the RKO Albee Theatre. Shortly thereafter, in 1933, he became staff organist at WLW (Cincinnati) and began an eleven-year association with the "Moon River" radio broadcast.

In 1944 he left Cincinnati for New York where he became organist for Arthur Godfrey's top-rated radio show on CBS—a position Erwin was to hold for twenty years.

He has since played for literally thousands of radio and television shows and is considered one of the best-trained and most experienced broadcasting artists available. He has written original scores for a number of silent films including "The Eagle" starring Rudolph Valentino, "Queen Kelley" starring Gloria Swanson, "My Best Girl" starring Mary Pickford, and "Irene" starring Colleen Moore, and has toured the country with them. Erwin has taught at New York's Lehman College, has spent much time composing and arranging music for the theatre organ, and still finds time to concertize across the country each year. In more recent years he has continued silent film accompaniment and spotlight solos as chief organist of the Carnegie Hall Cinema, New York.

FLOYD, BILL (1914-) Born in Elmira, New York, in 1914, Floyd was exposed to both church and theatre organ music from the time he was small. His mother had played various instruments in theatre orchestras including the drum and the organ in the Majestic Theatre in Elmira. At an early age he was able to begin practicing on the Marr and Colton organ in the theatre and also the Hope-Jones instrument in the Park Congregational Church.

Floyd was orphaned in the depth of the Depression. He made his way to New York City and applied for a job as organist of Radio City Music Hall, which was just opening. He was turned down, but in the long run it aided his career because he went on for further musical study, eventually becoming organist of the Beacon Theatre at Broadway and 74th Street. Later he became organist of the Staten Island Paramount as well, playing regularly at both theatres. Other theatres where Floyd appeared include: Paramount Theatres in Minneapolis, Minnesota, and Middleton, New York; Hammerstein Opera House, New York; and RKO Theatres: Palace, Akron; Keiths, Flushing, Long Island; and the Kenmore, Brooklyn.

After a few years out for army service and further study, Bill Floyd assumed the post of chief organist of the Paramount Theatre, Times Square, in 1953. Here he remained as long as the organ was used before its removal to California in 1964. While organist of the Paramount Theatre, Floyd also found time to fulfill all the duties of church organist at St. Rocco's Church, Newark. More recently Floyd has served as organist and choirmaster of St. Benedict's Catholic Church in Richmond, Virginia. He has continued to play supper club engagements in the area.

FOORT, REGINALD (1894–1980) Foort received a solid education in classical music in Britain (his home) at the Royal College of Music in London. He studied piano under Leschetitzky, a highly celebrated teacher of the day.

Foort's career as a theatre organist began in the mid 1920s. In 1926 he became chief organist of the newly remodeled New Gallery Cinema, Regent Street, London. The organ was the first successful Wurlitzer in England.

Foort recorded some of the top-selling 78 rpm discs of theatre organ music at this theatre. His renditions of "In a Monastery Garden" and "In a Chinese Temple Garden" each sold in the millions.

Foort moved on to some of the top theatre organ posts in Great Britain. He was organist at the Empire Theatre, London, previous to Jesse Crawford's English tour in 1933. Foort was president that year of the Theatre Organists' Association, which included nearly every theatre organist in Britain. In 1935 it was Foort's turn to come to the United States for an engagement at the New York Paramount Theatre.

In 1937 Foort was chosen as staff organist for the BBC. He became immensely popular as a radio artist because of his musical ability as well as his cheerful, friendly manner on microphone. During his professional life he opened forty-three new theatres and played over 2,000 radio and television programs in twelve different countries.

Just before World War II Foort went on tour with his own five manual, twenty-four-ton Möller theatre organ. The organ required a fleet of five thirty-foot vans and a crew of fourteen persons to move it from place to place. This organ was later sold to the BBC.

In 1951 Foort moved to the United States permanently. He held several positions as demonstrator for organ companies, played concerts across the country while at the same time holding church organist's positions. He was a prolific recording artist.

Foort died at his Florida home in 1980.

GLEN, IRMA (?–1982) Glen began her musical career at the age of fourteen when she made her concert debut as a young pianist. In Chicago she became featured organist at one of the large theatres and from this stepped up to a position as staff organist for the National Broadcasting Company. During the next twelve years, Irma Glen appeared in as many as twenty-three broadcasts a week and was regarded by her fans as one of the nation's top women organists. One of the programs that featured Irma Glen was "Lovable Music."

One person who listened to Irma Glen over radio station WENR in Chicago in the late 1920s was so impressed with her playing that he went to the station and anonymously sponsored an Irma Glen broadcast to be heard for fifteen minutes one night a week. Only Irma Glen knew who the sponsor was, and a part of the arrangement was that at no time would the sponsor's name be made public. This went on for two years.

The first family radio broadcast on the air was "The Smith Family," who broadcast from WENR. Irma Glen played the part of Betty the daughter and doubled at the organ for music bridges. In 1933 Glen taught at the American Conservatory of Music in Chicago. In later years, Irma Glen lived in Escondido, California. She continued composing music, playing the organ, writing, lecturing, and traveling.

Irma Glen died December 15, 1982.

GOULD, BETTY Born in Michigan, she began playing the piano at a very young age. Her first theatre organ experience was playing a

Bartola in an Ohio theatre. She then heard of a position at the Oxford Theatre, Minneapolis-St. Paul. This was the first full-size theatre organ that she played professionally. While on the staff of the Oxford Theatre, she also played the relief shift at the Tower Theatre in Minneapolis. Eventually she moved to Chicago where she presided over a Wurlitzer in the Lakeside Theatre. She moved to the post of assistant organist at the new Harding Theatre in Chicago and later joined the staff of the Oriental Theatre.

Gould also appeared at the McVickers, the Roosevelt, the Oriental, and the Chicago, all theatres in Chicago's Loop. Gould also played at the Tivoli Theatre, the Uptown Theatre, and the Norshore Theatre, Chicago. She went to St. Louis to open the Fox Theatre in early 1929.

In the fall of 1930 Gould opened the Stapleton Paramount Theatre (twin console Wurlitzer) on Staten Island. The other organist was Priscilla Holbrook, who called herself Jean. Betty Gould and Priscilla Holbrook were billed on the theatre marquee as Betty and Jean. Gould left the Stapleton Theatre in June 1931 due to illness.

After the coming of the Depression, Gould played here and there as jobs were available such as the Beacon Theatre, New York. In late 1932 she was hired by Samuel Rothafel (Roxy) to open the Center Theatre at Rockefeller Center. She broadcast from this theatre over NBC.

In the late 1930's she began demonstrating Hammond organs for the organ department of the Knabe Company. She appeared at various hotels around the country on the Hammond organ.

GRIERSON, TOM (1891–1966) Grierson was of Scottish descent and became an orphan at an early age. He studied under Sydney Nicholsen, who later became organist at Westminster Abbey.

While he was still a young man, he was hired as a pianist on a steamship coming to the United States, and when he became ill, he was left in Brooklyn, New York. This was the silent picture era, and he began playing organ accompaniment for silent films. In 1921 after a theatre engagement in Toledo, Ohio, he moved to Rochester, New York.

Grierson became musical director of the Irondequoit High School in addition to holding church and theatre positions. He became organist of the Regent Theatre, the Strand Theatre, and also played the relief shift in other theatres. It was at the RKO Palace Theatre that he became best known. Grierson spent fifteen years as chief organist of the RKO Palace Theatre, and during that time he broadcast both morning and evening over radio station WHAM in Rochester. It is estimated that he made over 10,000 performances.

In 1953 he retired to Florida for his health, but in 1959 he moved back to Rochester, New York, to supervise the piano and organ department of the Music Lovers Shop. He also played engagements in the Rochester area for special events.

Grierson was probably Rochester, New York's, best-known theatre organist. He died in 1966.

GRIFFIN, KEN Griffin was a theatre organist in the silent picture days in the Rocky Mountain states. His first musical instruction was on the violin. He later taught himself how to play the organ. After the invention of the Hammond organ in the mid–1930s, Griffin played this instrument in club appearances and hotels throughout the West and Midwest. After a term of military service in World War II, he began touring again in the East and Midwest, and in 1948 he produced the hit record "You Can't Be True Dear." His organ style was very simple, and the melody was always predominant. He did some radio and television broadcasting including a program entitled "67 Melody Lane."

GUSTARD, SYDNEY (1893–1977) Gustard was born in Tynemouth, England, March 22, 1893. His first cinema organ appointment was Christmas in 1919 as assistant organist in the New Pavilion Theatre, Newcastle-on-Tyne. In 1927 he opened the first Wurlitzer organ in Lancashire, the Trocodero, Liverpool. He moved to the new Gaumont Palace, Chester, in 1931 where he remained until 1936. He was invited to broadcast in 1932 by the BBC and from then until April 1933 he broadcast regularly, twice weekly, programs of forty-five and sixty minutes each. His signature tune was "In an Old Fashioned Town." He moved to the Plaza Theatre, Birkenhead, in 1937 and broadcast from there; he opened the organ at Curzon, Liverpool. Christmas 1938 he opened the new Compton organ in the Apollo Theatre in Manchester and continued broadcasting from there until 1940. He spent five and one-half years of service in the army in World War II, and following his service he rejoined the Gaumont British circuit and was appointed resident organist at the Gaumont Cinema, Camden Town, in 1945. He broadcast from there as well as from the Gaumont State, Kilburn, and the Gaumont, Watford. As recently as the 1950s he was still broadcasting over the BBC. However, he died November 14, 1977.

HAINES, CHAUNCEY (1900–1981) Haines was born in Detroit in 1900. His theatre organ career began in 1917 at the Deluxe Theatre (Wurlitzer) in Los Angeles. After a short stint in Chicago Haines moved back to California in 1924, playing at the Egyptian Theatre in Long Beach and the Forum Theatre in Los Angeles a year later. Before another year passed, he was bound for Chicago once more to become organist of the Norshore Theatre. Later he served on the organ staff at the Chicago Theatre.

With the coming of sound pictures Haines returned home to Los Angeles where he became musical director for radio stations KFAC and KMPC. He formed his own orchestra and began a careful study of classical music. Later he moved to Warner Brothers as an organist and remained in that position for ten years. In 1967 Haines became organist for the Los Angeles Dodgers and an instructor at the University of California at Los Angeles in film, music history, and related subjects. He continued to do considerable accompaniment of silent films until his death on April 25, 1981.

HAMMETT, CECIL V. ("VIC") (1918–1974) Born in Windsor, England, January 19, 1918, his first cinema organ position was at the Palace in Slough. At the same time he was organist of the Congregational church there. He moved to the Plaza, Iver, and then became assistant to well-known cinema organist Leslie James at Mme Tussaud's. He joined the Gaumont British circuit in 1935 and left them a year later to play the Regent, Leamington Spa. He joined the Shipman and King circuit and played all their theatres between 1936 and 1939. He left them to join Doorlay's Revue, "The Wonder Rocket," booked for a world tour starting June 1, 1939, beginning in the Scala Opera House, Berlin. He played the Hammond organ in this show. Being in Germany during the outbreak of the war, he was interned as a prisoner of war from September 11, 1939, to May 1945. He rejoined the Gaumont British circuit, July 16, 1945. He recorded organ solos at the Lewisham Town Hall organ, broadcast from the Scala, Berlin, from the Operetten Theatre, Leipzig, in 1939, and was organist at the Broadway Cinema, Stratford. Hammett was chosen to succeed theatre organist Sydney Torch at the Regal Cinema in Edmonton. In more recent years Hammett has toured New Zealand, Australia, Hong Kong, Tokyo, and the United States. He appeared at the Avenue Theatre in San Francisco, the Wiltern Theatre in Los Angeles, and the National Association of Music Merchants Trade Show in Chicago. He played frequent concerts on instruments maintained by England's organ clubs, including the three manual, ten rank Wurlitzer in Buckingham Town Hall.

Hammett died December 29, 1974, in a hospital near his home in Maldon, Essex, England.

HAMMOND, JOHN F. (1894–1972) Following his musical education, he was organist of Brooklyn's Strand Theatre, and while there, served as president of the New York Society of Theatre Organists. In 1922 he was appointed to the faculty of the Eastman School of Music in Rochester, New York. In 1924 he became organist of New York's Piccadilly Theatre, and about a year later he was featured in Warner's Theatre in New York City. When the Saenger Theatre was built in New Orleans in 1927 at a cost of $2 million, John Hammond was made chief organist of the Robert Morton instrument. He remained at that post for three years. Hammond eventually moved to Bogalusa, Louisiana, where he lived for twenty-eight years and served as church organist and choir director. He died at age seventy-eight on October 16, 1972.

HANSON, EDDY (1898-) Born in New London, Wisconsin, August 1, 1898, his first theatre organ position was on a Bartola pit organ in the Doty Theatre, Neenah, Wisconsin. This was the Barton Organ Company's first instrument. Hanson studied music at Lawrence University, Appleton, Wisconsin, before going to the Crystal Theatre, Chicago, to play another Bartola.

During World War I Hanson played saxophone with John Philip Sousa's band before returning to Chicago as a theatre organist. He worked for the Ascher Theatre chain and later several of the theatres in the Balaban and Katz chain including the Century (Diversey) and Paradise theatres.

In 1923 Hanson became one of the first organists in Chicago to perform on radio. He began on WDAP, predecessor of WGN, and later worked for WBBM, WLS, WLJ, and WCFL. As a prolific composer he has written more than three hundred songs, all of which are listed by the American Society of Composers, Authors and Publishers (ASCAP). His first notable radio hit was "At the End of the Sunset Trail."

In later years Hanson has appeared on the Hammond organ in restaurants and night clubs near his home in Waupaca, Wisconsin.

JAMES, DENNIS (1950-) Born September 12, 1950, in Philadelphia, Pennsylvania, he began music lessons at age seven on the accordian. In 1962 he began organ study with George Van Os in Audubon, New Jersey. Later James studied under Leonard MacClain in Philadelphia. In 1967 MacClain was scheduled to play a concert for the American Theatre Organ Society National Convention at the Senate Theatre, Detroit. At the last minute he suffered a heart attack and sent Dennis James in his place. The program was a success and catapulted James to national fame.

James studied organ at Indiana University and began to play concerts at various locations around the country. He was named organist in residence at the Ohio Theatre of the Performing Arts in Columbus. There he continues to give concerts, silent film presentations, and organ interludes during regular theatrical and motion picture presentations. His concert tours take him across the country and to other nations, including several appearances in England.

KEATES, HENRI A. (1887-) Born in Liverpool, England, February 15, 1887, the son of Mary Gee and Alfred Keates, he received his education at Brown High School. He married Maybelle Gilmore. Keates was a versatile musician, competent on the violin, cello, French horn, drums, piano, and organ. He traveled with various vaudeville acts throughout the country and by 1930 had already amassed twenty-two years of experience as organist, playing for silent pictures in quite a number of states. Keates was particularly well known in the Chicago area where he played at various theatres over several years' time. He appeared at McVickers Theatre in Chicago, the Liberty Theatre in Portland, Oregon, the Oriental Theatre, and the New Isis Theatre in Denver, Colorado.

KOURY, REX (1912-) Rex Koury was born in London, England, in 1912, moving with his parents to Cranford, New Jersey, the following year. About the same time that he began the usual piano lessons, he also began as a boy soprano in the local Episcopal church choir. Koury's parents provided organ lessons, and after a year's grounding in the classical method, Koury went to the Regent Theatre in Elizabeth, New Jersey, to hear William Meeder, a theatre organist of considerable reputation. Meeder was willing to accept Koury as a pupil. This was to open the door to the profession for him.

After playing in several neighborhood theatres in the New Jersey area near his home, Koury was hired by Meeder as assistant at the Regent. In late 1929 he joined the RKO Circuit, playing at the Proctor Theatre in Troy, New York. He was billed as "The World's Youngest Theatre Organist" and sometimes as "The Boy with Miles of Smiles." Then it was on to the Palace Theatre, Albany, before touring RKO Theatres in the New York metropolitan area. As the Depression made inroads in the entertainment industry, Koury went to San Diego and began fronting his first dance band.

Koury was able to line up a job as solo organist for NBC, Hollywood, for a year before enlisting in the armed forces. After being discharged in 1946, he returned to his post at NBC doing radio themes for some shows and solo organ broadcasts on pipes and the Hammond organ. When ABC was formed from NBC's Blue Network, Koury became its musical director for the West Coast. As television began to come in, he moved to that medium to score various programs including, "Gunsmoke," "The Fugitive," and the game show "You Don't Say" hosted by Tom Kennedy. As a musical director for NBC he composed and directed music for some of its prime programming. In most recent years Koury has become involved in the new theatre organ circuit, touring the various major theatre organ installations across the country.

KRUMGOLD, SIGMUND (1896-) Sigmund Krumgold was an organist of great ability and often substituted for the Crawfords at the New York Paramount Theatre when they were absent. In 1928 his name ran in the Paramount Theatre ads for a number of weeks as the featured soloist.

However, it was as an accompanist to silent films that Krumgold is best remembered. This was his primary function at the New York Paramount, for by this time, Crawford had given up playing the pictures. Krumgold's ability to accompany the "silents" is legendary. Many believe him to be one of the world's best at this art. Other organists would come just to experience his tasteful and flawless performances.

After leaving the New York Paramount, Krumgold moved to California where he worked with the major Hollywood producers of sound films.

LARSEN, LYN (1945-) Lyn Larsen is one of the brightest stars among the younger generation of theatre organists. Larsen was born in Long Beach, California, in 1945. At age three he began to show an interest in playing the piano in his parents' Santa Ana home. At age five he had a chance to sit at a pipe organ for the first time—the instrument in the First Methodist Church, Santa Ana, California. He knew at once that the organ would one day be "his" instrument.

By the time he was ten years of age, he had begun formal lessons on the organ. Two years later he played for a convention at the Embassy Auditorium in Los Angeles. For a year and a half thereafter he held a position as church organist, and by age fifteen he was playing the organ regularly in a restaurant.

Two years after he first heard a theatre organ, he gave his first theatre organ concert at the Los Angeles Wiltern Theatre for the Los Angeles Chapter of the American Theatre Organ Society.

Lyn Larsen's name has become synonymous with the best in current theatre organ entertainment. He has appeared in concert at almost every major theatre organ in the country, has an impressive list of theatre organ recordings to his credit, and has appeared on radio and television in the United States and Australia. He has also appeared with symphony orchestras both as organ soloist and guest conductor and has many compositions to his credit including the score for an Australian film. Larsen is at home at the theatre organ, concert organ, or piano. Most recently he has held the position of chief organist of the Organ Stop Pizza, Phoenix, Arizona. In addition he finds time for an extensive annual concert tour.

LEAF, ANN Ann Leaf was probably the most unusual of the Paramount Theatre staffers. She started at Sid Grauman's Million Dollar Theatre in Los Angeles at the tender age of seventeen. She was known as "The Mitey Mite of the Mighty Wurlitzer," as she was under five feet tall. In 1929 she began a radio career from the Paramount studio organ—a daily broadcast entitled "Nocturne," which came at the close of the broadcast day for the CBS Network. For a time she also opened the network in the morning with an organ broadcast "Ann Leaf at the Organ." She so impressed Jesse Crawford during her audition that he hired her on the spot. She likewise made some sound films and played live performances in the Paramount Theatre itself.

Ann Leaf also created the organ music for such familiar radio broadcasts as "Stella Dallas," "Woman of Courage," "Nora Drake," "Lorenzo Jones," "Mr. Keene," "Front Page Farrell," and "Kitty Kelly." She appeared as guest artist on a number of important network shows. On the Fred Allen Show she sat at the Paramount Studio organ and played via remote control with an orchestra located several blocks away in a CBS studio.

Ann Leaf frequently had to dash from one studio to another to keep her heavy schedule of radio broadcasting. Often she went on foot. Once she got stopped by a policeman on St. Patrick's Day for running through the parade. When she told him why, he replied, "Well, you should have started earlier."

Ann Leaf played a three-year engagement at the Rainbow Room in Rockefeller Center. Today she does concert touring, composing, and recording.

LEIBERT, DICK (1904–1976) Born April 29, 1904, at Bethlehem, Pennsylvania, Leibert was educated at Moravian Preparatory School where he played for chapel services and was nearly expelled for playing a jazzy version of "Onward Christian Soldiers" on one occasion.

At the age of fourteen he ran away to Washington, D.C., where he tried to find a way to make a living. He was given permission to practice on the organ at Loew's Palace Theatre at night, and eventually he became familiar with the theatre organ. It was at this theatre that he finally got his first chance as relief organist. He happened to hear of a scholarship at the Peabody Conservatory of Music at Baltimore, and being a determined individual, he hopped on the train and actually got there in time to win a five-year course. While holding the relief job at Loew's Palace Theatre in Washington, D.C., Leibert became interested in dance orchestras and organized his own band which played at the Washington Roof Gardens in the summer and at various night clubs during the winter. He appeared at the White House during these years to lead orchestras in preview showings of films for Mrs. Coolidge and her friends in the East Room, which had two portable movie projectors used for that purpose. He directed the orchestra and played the famous golden Steinway piano.

Loew's built a new deluxe theatre—the Penn Theatre in Pittsburgh—and Leibert was engaged as solo organist there. His biggest opportunity came when he was engaged in 1932 as chief organist of Radio City Music Hall, a post which he held until his retirement September 6, 1973, thus setting an unequaled record of over forty years of full-time service at one theatre. It may well be that more people heard him in person at Radio City Music Hall than any other organist playing in a theatre. Upon his retirement he moved to Fort Myers, Florida, where he died in October 1976.

McABEE, KAY McAbee was born in Illinois and still makes his home there. Although usually known for his extensive theatre organ work, McAbee holds the position of choirmaster and organist of St. Peter's Church, Frankfort, Illinois. He also heads the organ department at Sochan Music Center, Joliet, Illinois. In addition to these responsibilities, he finds time for appearances at various theatre organs around the country. He has concertized frequently at local and national American Theatre Organ Society events. In 1956 McAbee served as official organist for the Democratic National Convention.

McAbee has been featured at such theatre organs as the four manual, sixteen rank Barton in the Coronado Theatre, Rockford, Illinois, and the three manual, fourteen rank Wurlitzer in the Paramount Theatre, Aurora, Illinois. Perhaps he has been most closely associated with the four manual, twenty-one rank Barton in the Rialto Theatre, Joliet, Illinois.

At one time McAbee served as staff organist of Kimball Hall, Chicago. He has held the post of organist at several churches in the Chicago area. He has appeared with such artists as Count Basie, Phil Ford, Mimi Hines, and John Gary and has played hundreds of concerts across the United States.

MacCLAIN, LEONARD (1899–1967) Leonard MacClain was born in Philadelphia, September 8, 1899. His first theatre organ job was at the Jefferson Theatre. The regular house organist had been snowed in one wintry evening. MacClain and his girl friend and her mother arrived at the theatre. MacClain inquired as to why the organ was silent. When the reason was given, he volunteered to play, and for the next year it was his regular post.

In 1918 MacClain moved on to the Egyptian Theatre, then to the Family Theatre, on to Segal's Apollo Theatre, to the 56th Street Theatre, and the Leader Theatre from April 1920 until September 1927.

MacClain then moved on to the Strand Theatre where he stayed for four years. He began to get involved in radio broadcasting during these years when sound pictures first appeared. In 1932 he moved to the Commodore Theatre, near the campus of the University of Pennsylvania and in 1934 to the Tower Theatre, which boasted an exceptionally fine Wurlitzer. Although always associated with the records he cut there, MacClain was not there long before transferring to the newly opened State Theatre and finally to the Fox Theatre. The Fox was the last theatre in Philadelphia to use its pipe organ, and MacClain played there until 1941.

MacClain did radio work on a number of stations over the years. He broadcast over WIP, WPEN, WHAT, WCAU, and WIBG. He held the distinction of playing the first electronic organ broadcast coast to coast. The date was April 6, 1935, and the instrument, invented by Ivan Eremeef, was called a Photona.

MacClain found time to compose and arrange music, make children's records, teach organ, and play for all sorts of events and activities. He sometimes substituted at the Wanamaker organ and wrote a number of popular compositions for which he is remembered, including "Smile, Darn Ya, Smile" and "Yearning." He wrote music for television commercials and television series such as the theme song for "Martin Kane, Private Eye."

MacClain died on September 5, 1967.

MACK, BOB (ROBERT R. McCOMBS) (1914-) Mack was born in Perry, Iowa, in 1914. At five years of age he began piano lessons from a friend of the family who was a professor at Drake University, Des Moines, Iowa. His first instruction on a theatre organ was from

Mary Davis, house organist of the two manual, four rank Wurlitzer in the Regent Theatre in Winfield, Kansas. In later years Mack studied under Pietro Yon, organist of St. Patrick's Cathedral, and took some private instruction in the Schillinger method from Jesse Crawford and Rudolph Schramm.

Mack has appeared as organist of an impressive list of theatres. Some of the more famous are: the Criterion Theatre, Oklahoma City; the Ritz Theatre, Tulsa; the Malco Theatre, Memphis; the Palace Theatre, Dallas; the Byrd Theatre, Richmond; the Palace, Rochester, New York; Loew's Ohio, Columbus; The Saenger, New Orleans; Loew's Valencia Theatre, Long Island; Loew's Kings Theatre, Brooklyn; and the Fox Theatre, Brooklyn. Mack began playing for the Paramount chain in 1932. He is particulary remembered for his appearances at the Brooklyn Paramount for a period of sixteen years. In the 1950s and early 1960s he discovered that even teenagers could appreciate the theatre pipe organ if he played tunes they knew. When he played rock and roll tunes, they applauded in rhythm.

Mack played the New York Paramount Studio Wurlitzer off and on from 1938 until it was sold in 1955 (with the exception of the years during World War II when the studio was used by the government). In additon he played the big organ in the main auditorium on a contingency basis until the Paramount closed in 1964.

MACLEAN, QUENTIN MORVAREN (1896–1962) Born in London in 1896, Maclean began his organ studies at the age of eight. When he was only thirteen, he gave a public organ performance at John Sebastian Bach's Church in Leipzig, where he studied at the conservatory under Carl Straube for organ and Max Reger (himself a pupil of Brahms) for musical composition. He was in Leipzig when World War I broke out, and he was interned there. Returning to England following the war, he was honorary assistant organist at Westminster Cathedral, following which he became associated with the motion picture industry beginning about 1920 and made many appearances in British theatres as an organist. Three of the most notable positions that Maclean held were that of organist at the Trocadero, Elephant and Castle, at the Shepherd's Bush, Pavilion, and at the Regal Marble Arch. Here he designed the four manual, thirty-six rank Christie—largest theatre organ in Europe. Maclean is believed to be the first theatre organist to broadcast over the BBC. The year was 1925. In 1940 he immigrated to Toronto, Canada, where he broadcast regularly over the CBC. He was featured at Shea's Theatre in Toronto for eight years and at the Victoria Theatre, Toronto, where for two years he appeared nightly. For twenty years he was organist of the Holy Rosary Roman Catholic Church. When Shea's Theatre Wurlitzer was reinstalled in the huge Maple Leaf Gardens Arena, Maclean presided there. Maclean was perhaps the most famous of all British theatre organists and was a man of remarkable technical ability.

Maclean died July 9, 1962, in Toronto, Canada—his adopted home of twenty-three years.

MacPHERSON, SANDY (RODERICK HALLOWELL MacPHERSON) (1897–1975) Born March 3, 1897, in Paris, Ontario, a small Canadian town. In 1910 the family moved to Amherst, Nova Scotia. It was here that Sandy MacPherson began organ lessons in the First Baptist Church. He kept up his piano study as well, and at the age of fourteen he took his first job in the theatre in Amherst. Later he enrolled in the Conservatory of Music, Hamilton, Ontario. In 1921 he became organist of Loew's Theatre, Hamilton. Other theatres where MacPherson appeared included Shea's Hippodrome Theatre, Buffalo, and Loew's State, Buffalo, where he was first nicknamed "Sandy." He became an instructor in the Elmwood School of Music in Buffalo, teaching theatre organ students.

On vacation in England in 1927 MacPherson indicated his interest in appearing at the theatre organ there. He was later invited to open the Empire Theatre, Leicester Square, along with Reginald Foort. Over the years he completed a total of fifteen years service at the Empire.

MacPherson did considerable radio broadcasting over the BBC where he held a position as staff organist for twenty-five years. His frequent broadcasts during the height of the war, in the absence of other radio broadcasting, are well remembered in England.

MacPherson retired a few years prior to his death March 3, 1975, on his seventy-eighth birthday.

MAURO-COTTONE, MELCHIORRE (DR.) On October 24, 1919, the Capitol Theatre in New York City opened at the corner of 51st and Broadway. At the time of its opening it was the largest motion picture theatre in the world. The organ was a four manual Estey with luminous touch stop controls. Chief organist of this theatre for a number of years was Dr. Mauro-Cottone. He is remembered for his fine work accompanying films and particularly for his repertoire of classical and semiclassical music. In 1927 a new console of horseshoe design was added, and fifteen ranks of pipes were also added to the organ including complete sets of percussions and traps which the original instrument did not have. In 1928 Dr. Mauro-Cottone joined the organ staff of the New York Roxy Theatre. The Roxy, like the Capitol Theatre, had as its impressario Samuel L. Rothafel—"Roxy" who followed Major Edward Bowes in that position at the Capitol.

Dr. Mauro-Cottone was active in the New York Society of Theatre Organists, which he served as both trustee and director at various times. In the late 1930s he was affiliated with the Philharmonic Symphony Society of New York City.

MEEDER, WILLIAM H. (1901–1969) Born in South Orange, New Jersey, July 14, 1901, to Mary Chandler and Henry Meeder. He received his education at Columbia High School in South Orange, New Jersey. He married Dorothy Powell. From 1921 to 1922 he served as organist of the Lyceum Theatre, East Orange, New Jersey. From 1922 to 1928 he was organist of the Regent Theatre in Elizabeth, New Jersey. From 1928 until 1930 he was organist of the E. F. Albee Theatre in Brooklyn, New York. He also played the three manual Robert Morton organ at the RKO Richmond Hill Theatre and did considerable radio broadcasting and recording. In 1935 he was broadcasting over radio station WJZ, New York. He became staff organist at the National Broadcasting Company in New York and did organ work for the radio show "Search for Tomorrow." In 1946 he recorded twelve twelve-inch 78 rpm recordings for the Summit Sound System Company on the CBS studio organ, New York, which was formerly Lew White's studio organ (Kimball three manual, nine rank). These recordings were converted to long-playing discs in 1950.

MELGARD, AL, (1890–1977) Al Melgard was the musical director and organist of the Chicago Stadium for over forty years, achieving that position shortly after the stadium opened. (Organist Ralph Waldo Emerson did the honors on opening night.) Until his retirement in 1974, Melgard presided over what has been described as the "world's largest unit pipe organ," the huge six manual, sixty-two rank Barton pipe organ.

Melgard was born in Denmark. At the age of six he was brought to the United States by his parents. He began piano lessons at age seven, and at age twelve he graduated to the pipe organ. While he pursued studies at the American Conservatory of Music in Chicago, he played piano in a small silent film theatre. He went on to become organist of the Lincoln Dixie Theatre in Chicago where he also conducted the orchestra. Interestingly enough, one of his trumpet players was James C. Petrillo, later to become president of the American Federation of Musicians. A close associate of Dan Barton, organ builder, Melgard headed the Barton Organ School for some years. Melgard played both piano and organ as a member of the staff of station WGN and also broadcast over radio stations WLS and WBBM, Chicago, in the late 1920s.

Melgard died July 8, 1977.

MILLER, ASHLEY Ashley Miller was born in Brooklyn, New York. His first opportunity to try a theatre organ came when he was granted permission to practice on the organ in the Leonia Theatre, Leonia, New Jersey. He played for "kiddie" shows and occasional intermissions. He also appeared at the three manual Welte-Mignon organ in the Plaza Theatre, Englewood, New Jersey.

Miller furthered his musical education by studying abroad. He was fortunate to be taken as a pupil by Tobias Matthay of London, England—the last pupil of Franz Lizst. He returned to New York, entered the Juilliard School and spent four years studying organ with Gaston Dethier and three years study conducting with Albert Stoessel.

It was in 1939 that he launched his career with a series of Sunday morning organ concerts on the Aeolian-Skinner pipe organ in the Fifth Avenue studios of station WQXR. He also went to work for station WBNX playing programs of popular music from the pipe organ in their studios. The same year, at the New York World's Fair, he played an early model Hammond for the IBM exhibit.

In 1946, after completing military service, he was appointed organist of the New York Society of Ethnical Culture playing an original Hope-Jones installation. Miller also joined the Radio City Music Hall staff as organist in the fall of 1946. He remained a year and a half before leaving to form his own trio (guitar, drums, and organ), which was featured at the Park-Sheraton Hotel, New York City. In 1950 Miller returned to the Music Hall as organist remaining there until January 1956.

In 1966 he began a new facet of his career by turning to television, furnishing organ music for "Love of Life," "The Secret Storm," and "Search For Tomorrow." William Meeder died suddenly in January 1969 and an organist was needed for "Search For Tomorrow." Miller remained with "Search For Tomorrow" from 1969, until May 1974..

Today Miller teaches and makes personal appearances across the country.

MILLER, DON (F. DONALD) (1896–1971) Don Miller was born in Slater, Iowa, September 17, 1896. His mother was a teacher of piano and organ and he received his very early musical instruction from her. He showed a longing for theatrical life at the age of twelve and followed it thereafter. His first important engagement was at the Des Moines Theatre in Des Moines, Iowa.

He also appeared at the Broadway Strand Theatre in Detroit and the Madison Theatre in Peoria, Illinois, before he went to the Butterfield circuit in Michigan, and then went to the Olympia Theatre in Miami, Florida. During the winter season in 1926 he was organist at the Hollywood Beach Hotel in Hollywood, Florida, where he gave daily organ recitals and worked in conjunction with Arnold Johnson on several concerts. His big break came when he was given a contract with Kunsky Theatres in Detroit, where he played all their deluxe houses including the State, Capitol, Fisher, Riviera, and Fox theatres. In 1930 Miller played the Paramount Theatre in Detroit. In 1933 he went to Chicago to play at the Southtown and State-Lake theatres. An offer came for him to return to the Fisher Theatre, which he accepted gladly. He remained at the Fisher Theatre until his retirement.

During his professional career, Miller broadcast over radio stations WJR, WXYZ, WMUZ, and WMUZ-FM, Detroit, and radio station KRNT, Des Moines, Iowa. Prior to his retirement in 1962 he was organist at Henry Ford's famous Dearborn Inn in Dearborn, Michigan, for eleven years.

Miller died on December 1, 1971.

MINOR, C. SHARPE Charles Minor was as colorful a personality as the theatre organ profession ever produced. He was by all accounts a showman who knew how to attract and hold the attention of his audiences. His mother's maiden name was Sharpe and, seeing an opportunity for an eye-catcher on theatre marquees, he began billing himself as C. Sharpe Minor.

Minor appeared in a great many states of the union. In the early 1920s he played the Rialto and Rivoli theatres in New York. In mid–1925 he made an appearance at the Palace Theatre in Dallas, Texas. In 1926 he was at the Metropolitan Theatre in Boston, and later that same year at the Mosque Theatre, Newark. Early 1927 found him at the Regent Theatre, Grand Rapids, Michigan. He opened the four manual, twenty-four rank Marr and Colton organ in the Rochester Theatre, Rochester, New York, the same year.

In 1925 Minor had become affiliated with the Link Piano Company of Binghamton, New York, manufacturers of the Link Orchestral Pipe Organs. Thereafter, the company produced what were called Link-C. Sharpe Minor unit organs for theatres, advertised as available in two to five manual sizes. It is not known how long this business arrangement continued nor how many such organs were built.

In January 1929 Minor moved to Los Angeles where he opened his own studio and broadcasting room featuring a three manual Robert Morton organ. He also joined the staff of the United Artists' theatre in Los Angeles and began broadcasting over radio station KMTR.

Minor is also believed to be one of the very first organists to tour with his own pipe organ—a three manual, eight rank Link. Among the places where he appeared with this instrument was Buffalo, New York, in the middle to late 1920s.

In the 1940s C. Sharpe Minor was back in the Dallas, Texas, area. He appeared at the Palace Theatre again as part of a new policy of live entertainment there, and he also took a few students and coached them in showmanship. After this, the thread of his story is lost.

MURI, JOHN (1906-) John Muri was born in Hammond, Indiana, October 4, 1906. He began his musical education with three years of piano study at the Clifford Conservatory of Music in Hammond. Muri's theatre organ career began when he was seventeen. He played at the Temple Theatre in Hammond for a few months before moving to the Hoosier Theatre in Whiting, Indiana. The same year he had spent three months studying theatre organ with well-known Chicago organist, Claude B. Ball.

Muri remained at the Hoosier Theatre for three years, meanwhile beginning classical organ instruction with Arthur Dunham of the prestigious Chicago Temple. From the Hoosier Theatre Muri moved on to a seven-year stint at the Indiana Theatre, Indiana Harbor. During this time he completed a five-year period of study with Dunham.

In 1933, after theatre organs began to fall into disuse, Muri became musical director for radio station WWAE in Hammond, Indiana. He also did some radio work for radio station WIND in Gary, Indiana, and the ABC Radio Network. In 1937 he left his full-time career as musician and went into public school teaching. He continued to play for wrestling events, circuses, flower shows, high school basketball games, political rallies, and the like in the Hammond area from the mid–1930s until he moved to Detroit in 1968. Muri had become chairman of the English Department of Gavit High School in Hammond and was doing some university teaching at the Northwest Campus of Indiana University. In 1968 he joined the faculty of Wayne State University in Detroit.

Beginning in the early 1960s, with the revival of interest in the theatre pipe organ, Muri began presenting concerts across the country. He has appeared at many of the major theatre organ installations in the United States playing for silent films and giving concerts. For several years Muri wrote a bimonthly column in *Theatre Organ* magazine.

MURTAGH, HENRY Henry B. Murtagh played an important part in the life of Oliver Wallace, Jesse Crawford, Stuart Barrie, and other noted organists. Born in Springfield, Massachusetts, he was advised by Robert Hope-Jones to seek his fortune in the West. He took this advice to heart.

Murtagh holds the distinction of being the organist who played the first Wurlitzer Hope-Jones instrument ever heard by Oliver Wallace, Jesse Crawford, and Stuart Barrie. This occurred at Seattle's Liberty Theatre in 1914. The organ was a three manual, seventeen rank instrument (with a thirty-seven note solo manual). Murtagh created quite a sensation. He was, perhaps, the first to gave noon concerts attended by large crowds who numbered among them many organists and theatre managers and owners from the West Coast. All were anxious to hear and see this much advertised new "Unit Orchestra." Murtagh, advertised as the "Master of the Organ," gave ample evidence of his mastery of it—a mastery he owed in part to the helpful instruction of Robert Hope-Jones himself.

Murtagh moved on to Los Angeles where he followed Jesse Crawford as organ soloist at Grauman's Million Dollar Theatre. Later he followed Crawford as chief organist of the Chicago Theatre, Chicago, and in 1927 he moved to the Capitol Theatre, New York. He also played at the New York Rivoli Theatre, at Shea's Buffalo Theatre and the Lafayette Theatre in Buffalo. He did some traveling for the Loew's chain in 1928 including opening Loew's Ohio Theatre in Columbus that year. He also appeared for a short time at the New York Paramount Theatre in August 1928 to replace the vacationing Crawfords. In late 1928 he moved to the Brooklyn Paramount where he entertained the patrons along with organist George A. Johnson and others at the twin-console Wurlitzer.

NALLE, BILLY Billy Nalle was born in Fort Myers, Florida. By the 1940s he was playing piano with a local dance orchestra and had been heard on radio station WFTM (now WINK). His first organ lessons were from Eddie Ford, well-known organist of the Tampa Theatre, Tampa. After a few lessons he played a few organ solo intermissions at the Tampa Theatre and later at the Florida Theatre, Jacksonville.

In the 1950s Nalle went to the Juilliard School in New York to further his musical abilities. There he studied classical organ with Gaston Dethier and piano and popular music performances with Teddy Wilson. In 1950, Nalle also embarked upon a fifteen-year career in television which resulted in over 5,000 network telecasts on both NBC and CBS. Some of the television programs included "Studio One," "Hallmark Hall of Fame," "Kraft Theatre," "I Remember Mama," and "The Ed Sullivan Show."

In 1966 Nalle played the first official theatre organ concert to be offered as a part of a national convention of the American Guild of Organists. This event was held in the Fox Theatre, Atlanta.

Nalle was first to make a television commercial (for the Shell Oil Company) utilizing a theatre pipe organ. In 1971 he made the first quadrasonic recording of a theatre pipe organ to be released commercially.

Nalle has appeared in concert at such places as Roberson Center for the Arts and Sciences, Binghamton, New York; Auditorium Theatre, Rochester, New York; Senate Theatre (Detroit Theatre Organ Club), Detroit, Michigan; Longwood Gardens (former estate of Pierre DuPont), near Kennett Square, Pennsylvania; Cleveland-Akron-Canton Festival of the Arts, Palace Theatre, Cleveland; Strand Theatre, Plattsburg, New York, with the first theatre pipe organ light show, and the Cathedral of St. John the Divine, New York, on a specially installed Rodgers theatre organ.

In 1975 Nalle left New York to take up residence in Wichita, Kansas, to become the official artist in residence for Wichita Theatre Organ, Incorporated, at Century II Center, home of the former New York Paramount Theatre Wurlitzer. He is not only a performing artist but a writer whose articles have appeared in various publications including a monthly column of theatre organ news which appeared for four years (beginning in April 1972) in *Music* magazine, the official publication of the American Guild of Organists. He is a composer of several dozen compositions in the field of popular music.

NEW, REGINALD (1902–1958) New was born in Brockley, South East London, in 1902. His first solo cinema appointment was at Kings Cross Cinema on a "straight" (with traps) Hill, Norman and Beard, and his first modern unit organ appointment was on the little Wurlitzer of the Rink, Sydenham, in 1927. He moved to the Beaufort Theatre, Washwood Heath, Birmingham, in November 1929 and between then and 1933 gave 458 broadcasts on the two manual, eight rank Compton there. The instrument was later rebuilt as a three manual, eight rank organ in the EMI Recording Studios.

In 1932 New returned to his hometown as guest to open the dual purpose Compton in Lewisham Town Hall. In the summer of 1933 he succeeded Reginald Foort at the Famous Regal, Kingston-on-Thames. In 1935, he appeared at the State, Dartford, and associated theatres (1ater taken over by Granada). In 1939, he played at the Regal Beckenham and in 1944 at the Regal (Odeon) Marble Arch until a flying bomb damaged the theatre and he returned to Beckenham. In 1948, he played the Regal, Old Kent Road, London; in 1949, he began touring for ABC Theatres until 1956. For the last two years of his life, he played summer season engagements on Hammonds at Morecambe and Lowestoft and Ice Palace, Manchester during the winter of 1956–57. He died in 1958.

NOLAN, BUDDY Buddy Nolan is an organist who has attained national and international fame playing an unusual brand of theatre pipe organ—a Page pipe organ manufactured at Lima, Ohio. Like many theatre organists, Nolan was introduced to music very early. His mother, organist, pianist, and vocalist in her own right, saw to it that he received music lessons and much encouragement. In addition to the piano, Nolan took lessons on the accordian, becoming accomplished enough to appear on radio and in vaudeville as an accordian artist. He also studied classical organ with noted teacher Catherine Morgan.

Nolan, born in the Philadelphia area, discovered the Embassy Theatre and its magnificent Page organ when he moved to Fort Wayne, Indiana. He began playing there regularly, which meant a taxing schedule of five and six shows per day, seven days per week. Thereafter, when he went on tour playing electronic organs, he always managed to spend part of the year at the Embassy.

From 1952 to 1960 Nolan lived in California, but he returned to Fort Wayne, settling there permanently. Once more he began a regular schedule of appearances at the Embassy, as well as entertaining at the organ in some of the better-known restaurants in Fort Wayne and broadcasting organ music over a local FM radio station. In the early 1960s Nolan instituted midnight concerts called "The Embassy at Midnight" because they began after the regular daily film schedule had finished. These were greeted by large, enthusiastic audiences including persons who traveled from out of state to hear Nolan play the four manual, fifteen rank organ.

Nolan continues to appear occasionally at the Embassy Theatre which has since passed into the hands of a local group—the Fort Wayne Embassy Foundation. He also continues his personal appearances at one of Fort Wayne's quality restaurants.

NOURSE, EVERETT (1911-   ) Everett Nourse has been well known in the San Francisco Bay Area for many years. He served as staff organist at the San Francisco Fox Theatre from November 1944 until February 16, 1963, when the theatre closed. Sing-alongs were very popular at the 5,000-seat house during his tenure as organist.

Nourse's fame spread nationally with the release of the "Farewell to the Fox" series of three long-playing discs featuring himself and organist Tiny James at the San Francisco Fox Wurlitzer.

Nourse was born in Chico, California, June 8, 1911, spending his early years in Oakland. He graduated from Oakland High School and went on to attend the University of California at Berkeley. He began piano lessons at age seven, and by age eleven he was already composing his own music. Soon he turned to the organ, and it became a major interest in his life.

Theatre pipe organs where he has been featured include the Orpheum Theatre, the Warfield Theatre, and El Capitan Theatre in the San Francisco area; and the Paramount, the Fox, and the Grand Lake theatres in Oakland. When George Wright left San Francisco for New York in 1944, he recommended Nourse as his replacement at the Fox Theatre. This proved to be Nourse's big break. Radio broadcasting and personal appearances have kept this organist quite busy. He has played for numerous major events in California and has given concerts across the state. He has appeared at the California State Fair on several occasions and has played at many county fairs. He has performed for statewide conventions of Rotary International; California State Farm Bureau, and other groups. Nourse counts among the highlights of his life being chosen to play for the Republican National Convention in San Francisco in 1956.

PAGE, MILTON (DR.) (1921–1966) Born in Texas, Page became best known for his theatre organ work in New York City. In 1947 he became solo organist of the Roxy Theatre.

In 1949 he received an honorary doctorate of music from the Southern College of Fine Arts in Houston, Texas. After 1959 he toured for the Hammond Organ Company, presenting workshops and pop concerts in the United States and also in Europe. In more recent years he played a Conn theatre organ in a deluxe cocktail lounge at the Kennedy International Airport. He had once toured with the Milt Page Trio and was considering reviving the trio and going on tour again at the time of his death on March 26, 1966.

PARMENTIER, DR. C.A.J. (?–1981) Dr. C.A.J. Parmentier was one of the original organists on the staff of the New York Roxy Theatre when it opened March 11, 1927. He had come a long way from his birthplace in Belgium. His father had been a church organist for fifty years, and his brother was a well-known Belgian organist. Parmentier received a doctorate in music at the Université Philotechnique in Brussels and had appeared professionally in several countries before arriving in the United States in 1916. He worked at various times for the Loew's, Fox, and B. S. Moss theatre circuits. One of his most outstanding posts was as chief organist of the famous Capitol Theatre in New York City, at its time one of the most remarkable and luxurious theatres in the world.

Parmentier opened the Fox Theatre in Philadelphia in 1923. In 1924 he played the Century Theatre, Colony Theatre, and Cameo Theatre, all in New York City, and opened the rebuilt Broadway Strand Theatre in Detroit. In 1925 he appeared at the Academy of Music (three manual Möller) and in 1926 at William Brandt's Carlton Theatre in Brooklyn.

Parmentier is best remembered for his work on the staff of the New York Roxy Theatre with organist Lew White and others. He was one of the three organists who played this instrument on opening night, March 11, 1927, for the 6,200 luminaries and guests present.

At the grand opening of the Radio City Music Hall in Rockefeller Center, December 27, 1932, Parmentier and Dick Leibert presided at the twin-console Wurlitzer. Shortly thereafter Parmentier became organist of the RKO Center Theatre in Rockefeller Center. Eventually he returned to the Music Hall where he remained for several years.

During the early 1930s Parmentier played numerous broadcasts over CBS from the New York Paramount Studio. He was staff organist for NBC for three years. He performed at such notable organs as the instruments in Carnegie Hall, Wanamaker Auditorium, St. Patrick's Cathedral, and at Town Hall, New York. Parmentier has written and published a number of original organ compositions. In more recent years he served as organist for the hotels Waldorf-Astoria, Americana, and Hilton in New York. He did considerable free-lance work and concertized extensively prior to his death on February 21, 1981.

PORTER-BROWN, REGINALD (?–1982) Born near Barnsley, Yorkshire, Porter-Brown was soon into music; at the age of twelve he played the organ for a performance of Handel's *Messiah*. A year later he was organist and choirmaster at the local church and conducted a massed choir and band festival.

Recommended to the BBC by the late Sir Dan Godfrey, then conductor of Bournemouth Municipal Orchestra, he made over a thousand broadcasts. He was the youngest of four organists to open the original BBC Theatre Organ at St. George's Hall (the others being Quentin Maclean, Reginald Foort, and Harold Ramsay) and also opened the new BBC Theatre Organ in November 1970.

He has given many straight organ recitals up and down the country in concert halls and churches playing the "legitimate" works of Bach, Widor, and Franck.

Known by fellow organists as the "organist with the three hands" because of his unusual technique, he demonstrated it admirably by once giving a broadcast using only his left hand because he had broken his right wrist.

He has played before royalty on many occasions and traveled the world widely. He was an established composer of light music, and his works have been published in Germany and the USA and recorded in many other countries.

Porter-Brown died in December of 1982.

RAMSEY, HAROLD (1902–1976) Born in Great Yarmouth, England. Ramsey's parents moved to western Canada when he was nine years of age. After some classical instruction he became the first Canadian broadcasting organist. He studied with well-known organist Lynnwood Farnam in New York City and was appointed chief organist of the Rivoli Theatre on Broadway in 1923. From 1926 to 1932 he toured with Paramount Publix Theatres including appearances in New York City, where he also opened Loew's Paradise Theatre, 188th Street in the Bronx. He also appeared in Buffalo, Boston, Indianapolis, Chicago, Baltimore, Minneapolis, San Francisco, Los Angeles, San Antonio, Houston, Atlanta, Washington, D.C., and Dallas. In September 1930 he opened the newly installed Publix No. 1 Wurlitzer at the Palace Theatre in Dallas. Ramsey traveled to England for the summer of 1932 and returned to England the winter of 1932 to 1933 to the Granada Theatre in Tooting (London). During the days that he was a staff organist for the Granada circuit in the London area he was billed as "Mr. X."

Ramsey was one of four organists chosen to open the BBC theatre organ. He published many compositions including "This Lovely Rose," "Her Name Is Mary," "Rodeo March," "Evangeline," "Growing Old Together," "Maureen O'Dare," and "Britain Remember!"

In 1950 Ramsey returned to Canada and became minister of music in a Calgary church. He retired to the small town of Salmon Arm near Vancouver, British Columbia. He died there February 2, 1976.

Ramsey often billed himself professionally as "Harold Ramsbottom." His name appears in two spellings, "Ramsay" and "Ramsey."

RICHMOND, ROBIN (1912-) Richmond was born in Queens Gate, London, on April 21, 1912. Neither of his parents was musical, although his father, a doctor, made sundry attempts at playing the violin. He was educated at Westminster School, in the precincts of Westminster Abbey, London. On leaving Westminster, Richmond went to London University to continue law studies, but after three unsuccessful tries, he gave up hope of ever passing the exams and turned to his organ hobby as a full-time job. One of his first jobs was at a Mission Hall in Lambeth, where it was the organist's job to play for the silent films during the week and to accompany the services on Sunday. Fired after disobeying the minister for using the percussion while accompanying hymns, he saw his chance to strike new ground when the Hammond electronic organ first appeared, and he purchased the first two in England. He made his debut in the West End revue "It's In The Bag," in which two special scenes were produced for him. Then he went to Holland where he played at the Palais de Dance, Scheveningen opposite Benny Carter and his orchestra. Engagements at Laaren, Zaandvoort, Amsterdam, and Hilversum followed before he returned to this country to join the Two Leslies in "Radio Pie." After a tour of the music halls he formed a dance band featuring the Hammond at the Hammersmith Palais de Dance, which he broadcast frequently. He was appointed organist at the Paramount, Tottenham Court Road, and then joined the Variety Department of the BBC and stayed there until March 1946, whcn he left to join Gaumont-British. Not only has he broadcast from theatre organs, but he has appeared in more BBC featured shows than perhaps any other organist. Shows include "Variety Bandbox," "Itma," "Palace of Varieties," "Navy Mixture," "Shipmates Ashore," "Picture Parade," and others as well as his own particular show, "Organ-grinders' Swing," and more recently, "The Organist Entertains."

REEVE, DOUGLAS Reeve is the name that has been and always will be associated with the Dome, Brighton, but they did not officially meet until 1941 when, the Dome having been converted into a dance hall, he was appointed dance organist as relief to the dance band. He was appointed borough organist when the Dome was reconverted into a concert hall in 1946.

Reeve was born in Brighton. He learned the piano at an early age.

At the age of fourteen he became a pupil of Terance Casey at the Regent Cinema, who was making recording and broadcasting fame for himself and Brighton with a two manual, nine rank Wurlitzer. Under Terance Casey's expert teaching he soon mastered the cinema organ techniques, and was appointed assistant organist at another Brighton cinema, the Savoy, which had a three manual, twelve rank Compton. Reginald Foort was the musical director of the circuit, and on a visit to Brighton he was so impressed with Reeve's playing that he engaged him for a tour of the circuit, billed as "The Wonder Boy Organist." Later he settled in the London area, at the Regal, Golders Green, and had his first broadcast in 1937 at the old BBC theatre organ. With the outbreak of World War II, he, like many other organists, was drafted, but on being invalided out of the Army in 1941, he returned to his home town, Brighton, and became the dance organist at the Dome.

RIO, ROSA Rosa Rio began her musical instruction at the Eastman School of Music in Rochester, New York. Her teacher was theatre organ great, John Hammond, whom she eventually married. Upon graduating from Eastman, she took theatre organist positions in Syracuse, Loew's Burnside Theatre in New York, and Loew's Willard Theatre in Richmond Hill, Long Island. She did short stints at some of the other Loew's houses in the New York City area before moving to New Orleans to the Saenger Theatre with its magnificent Robert Morton organ. Saenger Theatres comprised a chain of houses in the South, and Rosa Rio toured most of them.

Eventually, as the Depression and sound films made theatre organists' positions scarce, Rosa Rio traveled north to the Paramount Theatre in Scranton, Pennsylvania, and then in 1933, to the Brooklyn Fox. She was the last regular organist to play this organ and also the organs of the RKO Albee and the Brooklyn Paramount. Rio also played at the RKO Patio Theatre in Brooklyn. Later she closed the Crown Theatre in New London, Connecticut.

Since so many theatres were closing out the use of their pipe organs, Rosa Rio accepted a position as staff organist with the NBC Radio Network. It was by means of radio that she became best known. She played a great many soap operas and dramatic radio shows such as "Cavalcade of America," "Front Page Farrell," "The Shadow," "Town Hall Tonight," and "When a Girl Marries." Her longest running radio show was "My True Story." She played as many as thirteen shows per week, five days per week. In addition to these shows, Rosa had her own network broadcasts at various times, one of which was known as "Rosa Rio Rhythms." She is believed to be the first network organist to play the electronic organ and piano simultaneously.

With the death of the "golden era" of radio came the development of television soap operas and dramas. Rosa played for a number of those shows before moving to Shelton, Connecticut, in 1960 where, as the wife of Bill Yeoman, professional radio announcer, she now teaches and does occasional radio and television work, and is frequently found on the concert circuit.

RODWELL, BRYAN (1929-) Born June 1929 at Keighley, Yorkshire, England, Rodwell began his musical training on piano at the age of eight years. At age fourteen he went on tour with the Youth Symphony Orchestra conducted by Henry Croudson. After studying organ at his local parish church and from two theatre organists, Norman Briggs (New Victoria, Bradford) and Charles Saxby (Odeon, Leeds), Rodwell joined the ABC circuit in 1946 and was appointed to the Forum, Southampton.

Rodwell served with the RAF for two years, but he found time for some radio broadcasting, including a broadcast from the BBC theatre organ. After his RAF years, Rodwell returned to the ABC circuit in 1949 and was appointed to the Ritz, Hereford, where he remained until 1951. He then joined the Granada circuit with whom he remained until 1956. He continues to tour, playing concerts on electronic and pipe organs, doing radio broadcasting and recording, and also playing the piano professionally.

SAVAGE, DUDLEY (1920-) Born Penzance in 1920, Savage began a theatre organ course at the age of sixteen and toured England in 1936–37 as the "Cornish Wonder Boy Organist." He was appointed resident organist at the Royal, Plymouth, in 1938. He has been a frequent broadcaster in England and has broadcast organ from South Africa as well as several piano recitals on all-India radio. He joined the army in 1940 and went to India in 1942; he was captain in the Devonshire Regiment (attached to Indian Army). Has also broadcast in the regional programs on a Hammond organ installed in his father-in-law's home in Plymouth. For some years he was organist of the Regal, Plymouth.

For over twenty-two years Dudley Savage has been playing requests for sick people in the hospital and at home on the organ of the ABC Theatre, Plymouth, in his weekly "As Prescribed" program for listeners in the former South and West Region of the BBC. In September 1968 it was decided to discontinue the series, but such was the outcry that the program was restored to the schedules three months later and today is heard all over England on Sunday mornings.

SELLERS, EDNA J. (1899-) Edna Jane Smith Sellers was born August 23, 1899, in a small Iowa town of Manilla, near Council Bluffs, just across the river from Omaha, Nebraska. She took her first music lessons from the organist of the Manilla Presbyterian Church. By the time she was eighteen, the big city beckoned. Sellers moved to Chicago and got a job selling phonograph records in the Wurlitzer store. Within six months she landed her first theatre job in Chicago at the Boston Theatre on Clark Street where she accompanied the "silents" on a small pipe organ. She met and married Preston H. Sellers, Jr., a theatre organist.

Edna had joined the Senate organ staff, Chicago, prior to the birth of their son Preston H. Sellers, III, in 1927. Thereafter the Sellers were assigned to the Marbro where a second console was added to the Wurlitzer. After their daughter Barbara's birth in 1930 the Sellers performed there in tandem.

They also appeared at other Chicago theatres, the Paradise, the State-Lake, the Granada, the Tivoli, the Uptown, and most of the large B & K houses.

In the mid–1930s Edna and Preston Sellers launched careers in radio. Edna went to WGN in 1936 when the studios were still in the Tribune Tower.

Edna found time to play at WBBM and WENR on their Wurlitzers. She also played at station WKY in Oklahoma City for a period of time and then returned to Chicago where she soloed at the Oriental for three years.

By 1946 Edna had semi-retired from radio work, but she continued restaurant and club appearances.

SELLERS, PRESTON H., JR. (1898–1962) Preston Sellers was born in St. Louis, Missouri, February 24, 1898, to Sallie and Preston H. Sellers, Sr. He received his education in East St. Louis. He married Edna Jane Smith, a professional organist, and he began playing the theatre organ in 1915, spending four years with the Lubliner and Trinz chain and four years with Balaban and Katz, doing organ presentations, novelties, and community singing. He opened Chicago's Belmont Theatre Wurlitzer (three manuals, fifteen ranks) in 1926.

He did a considerable amount of radio broadcasting in the Chicago area and was staff organist for radio station WGN, Chicago (three manual, eleven rank Kimball-Wurlitzer).

Preston Sellers died of a heart attack in 1962.

(See also SELLERS, EDNA J.)

SENG, JOHN (1939-) Born July 6, 1939, in Evanston, Illinois, Seng received his bachelor of arts degree from Loyola University and studied music at the American Conservatory in Chicago. He spent three years (1955–58) as staff organist for NBC, Chicago, followed by an eleven-year stint playing concerts and consulting for two major organ manufacturers, Wurlitzer and Hammond. Beginning in the late 1960s Seng became involved in the writing and production of radio and television commercials. His credits include themes for McDonald's, United Artists, Greyhound, and others.

Seng's Columbia record album, "Dream Awhile," was used for seven years as theme music on the "Today Show" and probably received more "air play" than any other organ record.

Seng has appeared as guest performer on the "Today Show," the "Tonight Show," and the "Breakfast Club" and as guest soloist at Chicago's Orchestra Hall and Radio City Music Hall, New York. More recently he has been involved as a consultant to the Yamaha Company in the development of GX–1, the world's first polyphonic synthesizer.

Seng's television and film keyboard credits include; "Kojak," *Buck Rogers in the 25th Century*, "Magnum PI," "Nero Wolf," *Alien, Superman, The Empire Strikes Back*, and *The Chosen*, among others. In the midst of his extensive work as a film musician in Hollywood he still finds time for a limited number of theatre pipe organ concerts every year.

SHAW, GERALD (1911–1974) Born April 15, 1911, at seventeen Shaw became "music and all trades" master at a preparatory school in St. Leonards-on-Sea. In 1930 he had three lessons from Dr. Tootell at Marble Arch Pavilion. In 1932 when the Regal Cinema was built in St. Leonards-on-Sea, he was appointed for the opening. Besides ordinary duties, the job included a daily recital of an hour.

Other theatres where Shaw appeared include the Regal, Glasgow; the Astoria, Brixton; the Paramount, Glasgow; the Manchester, Odeon, and the Odeon, Swiss Cottage, London, from which he broadcast regularly. During this period, the Rank Organization was expanding its theatre empire overseas and through this, Shaw was called upon to open and play the only theatre organ in the Middle East at the Rivoli, Cairo. The organ was a four manual, ten rank Compton and was broadcast by Shaw on Egyptian radio. He followed this engagement by playing a three manual Compton Theatrone at the São Jorge Cinema in Lisbon.

Returning to Great Britain, he played at the Metropole, Victoria, London, and the Odeon, Marble Arch. He remained there as the last resident organist. He then moved to the Odeon, Leicester Square, where he remained for a number of years. From here he made numerous broadcasts and played daily for intermissions on the magnificent five manual, sixteen rank Compton. He played for many film premieres, royal film shows, charity performances, and club meetings for the various theatre organ enthusiasts' clubs. Compositions include "Red Cross Salute," official march of the County of London Red Cross.

He died suddenly on April 26, 1974, England's last full-time theatre organist.

SMART, CHARLES (1897-) Smart was born at Calne, Wiltshire, on December 4, 1897. He passed his Royal College of Organists exam for solo organ in 1921 and was winner at London Musical Competition Festival for organ solo in 1920. He recorded for Decca in 1933–38 and spent some time with the Variety Department BBC shows in addition to solo appearances: "Moon River," "Band Waggon," "Kentucky Minstrels," "Bandstand," "Navy Mixture," and "Armchair Mel." He led a small band known as the "Moonrakers," built round the "Novachord." He appeared in *Band Waggon* film, and made the film recording in *Lisbon Story*, and in the film *Black Narcissus*. During World War I, he served with Royal Garrison Artillery.

TIMS, F. ROWLAND (1887–1955) Tims was born in Truro, England, in 1887. His early training was at Truro Cathedral, Cornwall, where he was a choirboy and later pupil/assistant organist. From 1907 to 1918 he held church organ appointments at Horsham and Croydon. After World War I, Tims toured the halls with a portable concert pipe organ (similar to Pattman). Around 1925 he became resident organist at the Capitol, Haymarket, London (five manual Hill, Norman and Beard orchestral pipe organ—not a unit organ) where he began broadcasting and recording. During his residence the Hill, Norman and Beard was replaced by a Compton three manual, nine rank unit organ. He played Union Cinemas in 1934 (Adelphi, Slough), then moved to the Paramount, Liverpool in 1934 where he began broadcasting again the following year. In 1937 he opened the Compton at the Ritz, Birkenhead, and later broadcast from there. In 1938 he succeeded Harold Coombs at the (three manual, eight rank) Compton of the Capitol, Aberdeen, where he stayed until he retired in 1950. He continued to play a church organ in Aberdeen for several years until just before his death in 1955.

TORCH, SIDNEY One of the theatre organists to appear on the scene and gain great popularity in Great Britain during the sound film era was Sidney Torch. A splendid musician, Torch specialized in a snappy style of organ playing which was completely unique. Rather than imitating the orchestra as some of the older generation of theatre organists had done, Torch imitated the "swing" dance bands which were attaining great popularity. He gained a following beginning in the early 1930s at the Dominion Theatre, Walthamstow, where he taught himself to play the organ. He had previously been a pianist in Emanuel Starkey's orchestra at the Regal Theatre, Marble Arch.

Torch set the style for British theatre organ playing in the 1930s. It was a rapid fire, staccato method which emphasized rhythm. Soon Torch had many imitators. Torch's recordings of tunes like "Twelfth Street Rag" and "The Orient Express" sold widely. He moved back to the Regal Theatre, Marble Arch, this time as organist in the early 1930s. A few years later he left to open the four manual, fifteen rank Christie at the Regal Theatre, Edmonton. Many regarded this instrument as Christie's finest and as one of the great monuments to the British theatre organ builder's art.

In 1937 Torch moved to the State Theatre, Kilburn, and after World War II he formed an orchestra which he conducted until his recent retirement. He never returned to the console after the war.

TUDOR, STANLEY Tudor began his career as assistant and then organist of a North Staffordshire church in England. While at school he won many prizes for his musical ability on piano and other instruments. Leaving school at fourteen he became solo pianist at the Capitol Cinema, Hanley, broadcasting every day on the Stoke-on-Trent radio station. Tudor moved to the Hippodrome as organist, and at the end of 1931 he gave up his church position and toured Gaumont-British theatres in London, his base theatre being Gaumont, Hammersmith. He opened the Gaumont, Manchester, and was there when called to the Royal Air Force in World War II. While serving with the military, he did occasional radio broadcasts and straight organ recitals. He returned after the war to the Gaumont, Manchester the organ with which he was identified for many years.

VELAZCO, EMIL Emil Velazco graduated from the Chicago Musical College, and after he received his degree began teaching piano and music theory there. He served a term in World War I in France with the 332nd Field Artillery. When he returned to this country, he played the piano with a number of dance orchestras, eventually finding his way to the theatre organ and working for the Stanley, Paramount, and Publix Theatre circuits. He is remembered for his appearance at the Palace Theatre in Dallas, Texas in the early 1920s.

Velazco was hired, along with Deszo Von D'Antalffy, and Dr. C.A.J. Parmentier to open the three console Kimball organ in the Roxy Theatre, New York, in March 1927. Although he rehearsed for the opening, his illness a few days beforehand prevented his appearing. He never played the Roxy Theatre publicly.

Sometime after the Roxy Theatre opened, Arthur Hammerstein built the Hammerstein Theatre at Broadway and 54th Street. A three manual, horseshoe console Welte theatre organ (fourteen to eighteen ranks, approximately) was installed on a center lift, not for accompanying silent pictures but for legitimate theatre productions. Emil Velazco was appointed organist there.

For a period of time Velazco broadcast over station WOR in New York with a program entitled "The Witching Hour." In the early part of 1928 he opened the Velazco Organ Studios at 7th Avenue and 50th Street in New York for the training of theatre organists. Here he had projection equipment and all facilities set up like a miniature theatre, which permitted his students to work under simulated conditions. The studio boasted both a two manual Welte-Mignon practice organ and a three manual Kimball pipe organ, which was also used by Velazco in many of his broadcasts.

During World War II Velazco was stationed at the Naval Photo Lab in Washington, D.C. He was in charge of composing and conducting background music for films. After the war he moved to Argentina in the employ of an electronics firm.

WALLACE, OLIVER (1893–1968) Oliver Wallace was born in London, England, in 1893, moving to Seattle, Washington, while still a boy. He got his start playing piano in the Dream Theatre in Seattle, but when he had a chance to try the small Estey pipe organ in the Sherman-Clay Music Store, he convinced the theatre owner to install it in the Dream.

Around 1913 Wallace was playing at the Clemmer Theatre in Seattle. His unique style of organ playing had made him so popular in the city that one musician said of him that he could have been elected mayor.

Jesse Crawford recalled going to the Seattle Clemmer Theatre just to hear Wallace play the show. He said it was as good as taking an organ lesson. Wallace was an excellent organist and showman and numbers of other organists drew inspiration from his work.

When the Liberty Theatre opened in Seattle with its now famous Wurlitzer, Henry B. Murtagh was at the console. Wallace eventually got the position and remained at this post into the mid-twenties.

Wallace became organist of Grauman's Rialto Theatre in Los Angeles, where he was billed on the marquee as "Wallace at the Wurlitzer." His entire career seems to have centered in the western United States.

Wallace's last and perhaps most important position was as musical director for Walt Disney Enterprises—a post that he held at the time of his death at age seventy-five in the 1960s. His most enduring claim to fame was as the composer of the long-time favorite, "Hindustan."

WEAVER, EDDIE (1907-) Edward J. Weaver has the good fortune of holding down an organist's job at a theatre that has practically always featured its outstanding pipe organ. Weaver is organist of the beautiful Byrd Theatre in Richmond, Virginia. The four manual, seventeen rank Wurlitzer installed over the proscenium arch, is one of the most beautiful sounding original installations in the world.

Born in Catasauqua, Pennsylvania, November 1, 1907, Eddie Weaver's first piano lessons were from his mother. He later studied violin and studied classical organ at Rochester's Eastman School of Music for a year. An opportunity to play theatre organ accompaniment to silent films in the Lafayette Theatre, Batavia, New York, and the promise of one hundred dollars if he'd learn how, were sufficient to change the professional direction of his life. Among his organ teachers was Henry Murtagh, then in Buffalo. Weaver took the train to Buffalo once a week for lessons. When Murtagh transferred to New York City in 1926, he was able to get a job for Weaver with the Paramount circuit. Paramount sent Weaver to Florida to open the new Coral Gables Theatre. One month later Paramount sent Weaver back to Florida to open the Tampa Theatre. After six months in Tampa he moved to the Olympia Theatre, New Haven, Connecticut, where he remained for ten years.

Weaver fronted his own fifteen-piece band for a while, directing from the console of a Hammond organ. In 1937 he joined the staff of the largest department store in Virginia—Miller and Rhoads, Richmond, as organist and pianist of their Tea Room, where daily style shows are held. He played three to four daily shows at the Loew's Theatre Wurlitzer starting in 1937, for an unbelievable term of twenty-four years. The Byrd Theatre has been featuring him at least twice daily at their famous Wurlitzer since 1961. He also plays for special events, conventions and programs at the Mosque Auditorium and finds time for radio broadcasting and personal appearances.

WHITE, LEW (1903–1955) Lew White, one of America's best-known organists, was on the organ staff at New York's fabulous Roxy Theatre when it opened in 1927. Born in 1903 of a musical family, he was trained for a career as a concert pianist before taking up the study of the organ. His father, Herman White, had been his early teacher of piano. When Lew White began his organ studies, he turned to Dr. Alexander H. Matthews of the University of Pennsylvania as instructor.

Lew White began his career as a theatre organist in 1918 and spent eight years as premier organist for the Stanley Theatre chain before being engaged by Sam Rothafel ("Roxy") to open New York's Roxy Theatre. Emil Velazco, Deszo Von D'Antalffy, and Dr. C.A.J. Parmentier were the organists scheduled to open the three console Kimball at the Roxy Theatre, but Velazco became quite ill three or four days before the opening and Lew White was brought in as a replacement. Opening night saw Lew White, Deszo Von D'Antalffy, and Dr. C.A.J. Parmentier at the consoles. A few months previous to the opening of the Roxy, Lew White opened his own theatre organ school in the Brunswick Building at the corner of Broadway and 53rd Street, New York City. There were a two manual Kimball and a three manual Kimball pipe organ in this studio. White began broadcasting over NBC and began making pipe organ rolls for the Aeolian Duo-Art Company. He left the Roxy Theatre a year after it opened to devote time to his organ school and his broadcasting and composing.

On Saturday, March 9, 1929, White returned to the Roxy as chief organist. His broadcasts on the Red Network of WEAF on Saturday evenings and on the Blue Network of WJZ on Monday evenings brought him mail from thousands of listeners as far away as British Guiana.

When Radio City Music Hall opened in 1932, included in the complex of facilities was a smaller theatre, the RKO Center Theatre. Lew White broadcast from this theatre in addition to his regular Sunday morning broadcasts, which originated in his studio.

In later years White played organ themes for soap operas and other dramatic radio series such as "Portia Faces Life," "Grand Central Station," and "Inner Sanctum," and he operated a Hammond Organ School at Three East 43rd Street in New York City. He recorded some long-playing records on the Hammond organ for the MGM label prior to his death on March 3, 1955.

WRIGHT, GEORGE (1920-) Wright was born in Orland, California, north of San Francisco, August 28, 1920. His mother had been a theatre organist, and at an early age he was hearing the organ accompaniment of silent pictures in theatres. Eventually the family moved to Stockton, California, and he began organ lessons from Mrs. Inez McNeil, organist at the Fox California Theatre in Stockton. His first engagement was at the Shanghai Terrace Bowl, a Chinese nightclub in Oakland, California, which boasted a two manual, six rank Wurlitzer. The organ was used as a part of the evening's entertainment and was broadcast nightly over an Oakland radio station.

In 1941 Wright joined radio station KFRC in San Francisco. During these same years Wright was called to the San Francisco Fox Theatre as organist for its Saturday night community sings.

In November 1944 Wright was invited to go to New York to play for the Jack Berch Show on NBC, and he stayed for several years. He did guest appearances with Paul Whiteman, Percy Faith, Bing Crosby, Perry Como, conducted his own orchestra on the Robert Q. Lewis Show, and began a seven-year stint playing in a trio with Charles Magnante, accordionist, and guitarist Tony Mottola for a Prudential Insurance Company-sponsored radio show on NBC. A lifelong dream was realized when Wright became chief organist of the New York Paramount Theatre—a post he was to hold from 1949 until 1951.

In 1951 Wright returned to California as ABC's musical director for the West Coast. He served as organist and choirmaster of the Redemptorist Church, Whittier, California. He continues to give theatre organ concerts across the country and is known to multitudes of people through a considerable number of spectacular theatre organ recordings.

APPENDIX 2
THEATRE ORGAN LISTINGS

The lists of theatre organs that follow are partial listings only. They are arranged in alphabetical order according to country or state. Organs are described as to size as follows: a listing reading "2/6—1927" means the organ had two manuals (keyboards) and six ranks (sets) of pipes and was installed in 1927.

ALASKA

MANUFACTURER	LOCATION	NOTATIONS	ORGANISTS
Kimball	Capitol Theatre, Juneau	Installed in early 1900s	Carl Beery Davis
Kimball	Goss Theatre, Juneau (Colesium)		
Kimball	Goss Theatre, Ketchikan		
Kimball	Goss Theatre, Juneau (20th Century)	Theatre built 1939. Organ moved from Colesium Theatre. (This instrument was installed in the State Office Building, Juneau, in 1976.)	Franklin Butte

ALASKA (Continued)

MANUFACTURER	LOCATION	NOTATIONS	ORGANISTS
Kimball	Empress Theatre, Anchorage		Marian Grace Ollerenschaw
Kimball	Empress Theatre, Fairbanks		Marian Grace Ollerenschaw

NOTE: There were no original Wurlitzer or Robert Morton installations in Alaska. Today there is at least one Wurlitzer in a private residence and a Robert Morton organ in a pizza parlor in Anchorage.

ARGENTINA

MANUFACTURER	LOCATION	NOTATIONS	ORGANISTS
Wurlitzer	Señor Cario's Theatre, Buenos Aires	2/7—1926	Julio Perceval

AUSTRALIA

Theatre organs reached Australia early, only a few years after they began to be installed in large numbers in the United States. The two most widely known builders were Christie and Wurlitzer. Compton, England's most prolific builder, exported no instruments to Australia. Christie, based in England, established a factory in Melbourne but only one complete instrument was built there. The rest were imports.

MANUFACTURER	LOCATION	NOTATIONS	ORGANISTS
Wurlitzer	Melba Theatre, Melbourne	2/4—shipped from factory in 1917	Charles Tuckwell
Wurlitzer	Majestic, Melbourne	2/4—1919 (piano/console)	Will Westbrook
Wurlitzer	Deluxe, Melbourne	2/7—1922	Horace Weber
Wurlitzer	Capitol, Melbourne	3/15	Newell Alton Stanfield Holliday
Wurlitzer	Prince Edward, Sydney	2/10	Noreen Hennessey Knight Barnett
Wurlitzer	Arcadia, Chatswood, NSW	2/10—1926	Nicholas Robins Eddie Horton
Wurlitzer	Capitol, Sydney (a 3,200-seat house)	3/15—1928	Jean Penhall Fred Scholl

MANUFACTURER	LOCATION	NOTATIONS	ORGANISTS
Wurlitzer	Regent, Melbourne	4/21—1929	Lionel Carrick Stanfield Holliday Tony Fenelon
Wurlitzer	Regent, Adelaide	3/15—1928	Knight Barnett Penn Hughes
Wurlitzer	State, Melbourne (twin consoles)	4/21	Aubrey Whelan
Wurlitzer	State, Sydney	4/21	Manny Aarons
Wurlitzer	Regent, Brisbane	3/15—1929	Reubert Hayes
Christie	Victory, Kogarah, NSW	2/7—1929	Eddie Horton
Christie	Kings, Gordon, NSW	2/8—1929	Muriel Jeavons
Christie	Duke of York, Eastwood, Sydney	2/7—1932	Stanley Cummins
Christie	Palatial, Burwood, Sydney	3/10—1930	Knight Barnett
Christie	Lyceum, Sydney	2/9—1930	Manny Aarons
Christie	Roxy, Parramatta, NSW	3/10—1930	Knight Barnett
Christie	Ritz, Concord, NSW	2/5—1930	Penn Hughes
Christie	Astra, Parramatta, NSW	2/5—1937	Nicholas Robins
Robert Morton	Seaview Theatre, Glenelg, Adelaide	(Photoplayer)	Penn Hughes

AUSTRIA

MANUFACTURER	LOCATION	NOTATIONS	ORGANISTS
Christie	Apollo Cinema, Vienna	2/7	William G. Barnes
Kilgen	La Scalla, Vienna	3/10	
Oskalyd	Palast Kino, Vienna		

BELGIUM

MANUFACTURER	LOCATION	NOTATIONS	ORGANISTS
Standaart	Roxy/Empire, Antwerp	3/11	
Wurlitzer	Marivaux, Liege	2/8	
Wurlitzer	Palace, Liege	2/8	
Wurlitzer	Plaza (Churchill), Brussels	2/4	

CANADA

The only Canadian company that can rightfully be considered a manufacturer of theatre pipe organs was the Warren Pipe Organ Company, which traces its origins back to 1895 in the vicinity of Toronto, Ontario. The famous Canadian organ building firm, Casavant Frères of St. Hyacinthe, Quebec, did install an organ or two in theatres, and the Franklin-Legge Organ Company of Toronto installed several instruments in theatres as well. Almost all other instruments in Canadian theatres were imports.

MANUFACTURER	LOCATION	NOTATIONS	ORGANISTS
Warren	Capitol Theatre, Montreal	4/28	H. Norton Payne Leo LeSieur
Warren	Palace, Montreal	3/14	
Warren	Belle, Belleville	2/7	
Warren	Trent, Trenton	2/7	
Warren	Loew's Uptown, Toronto	3/14	Horace Lapp
Warren	Loew's Winter Garden, Toronto	3/12	Horace Lapp
Warren	Pantages (Imperial), Toronto	28 ranks	Kathleen Stokes
Warren	Capitol, Ottawa	4/17	
Casavant	Capitol, Quebec City	3/14	
Franklin-Legge	Radio station CKCO, Ottawa (formerly in Imperial Theatre, Ottawa)		
Hillgreen-Lane	Odeon-Carlton, Toronto	3/19—1948	Al Bollington Bobby Jones Colin Corbett

MANUFACTURER	LOCATION	NOTATIONS	ORGANISTS
Wurlitzer	Davis, Montreal	2/5—1916	
Wurlitzer	Loew's, Toronto	3/13	Kathleen Stokes
Wurlitzer	Orpheum, Vancouver	3/13	Sydney Kelland Harold Ramsey
Wurlitzer	Capitol, Vancouver	3/15	
Wurlitzer	Midway, Montreal	2/5	Leo LeSieur
Wurlitzer	Berliner Residence, Montreal (H. S. Berliner was inventor of the lateral disc phonograph record)	3/13	
Wurlitzer	Shea's Hippodrome, Toronto (now in Casa Loma, Toronto)	3/15	Quentin Maclean Ernest Hunt Horace Lapp Harry O'Grady Colin Corbett Kathleen Stokes

CZECHOSLOVAKIA

MANUFACTURER	LOCATION	NOTATIONS	ORGANISTS
Joseph Metzler	Unitania Theatre, Prague	2/9	
Rieger	D-49 Theatre, Prague	3/12	
Rieger	Berenek Cinema, Prague	3 manual	
(Built in Czech. Builder unknown)	Alhambra Ballroom, Prague		
Christie	Metropol Theatre, Prague	1929	

NOTE: The best-known Czechoslovakian theatre organist was H. J. Habig. Others included Jaroslav Vojtek and Jiri Traxler.

DENMARK

MANUFACTURER	LOCATION	NOTATIONS	ORGANISTS
Marcussen and Son of Apenrade, Denmark	Danish Broadcasting Corp., Copenhagen	Installed in 1939	
Wurlitzer	Paladium Theatre, Copenhagen	3/7 (this was the only Wurlitzer installed in Denmark)	Mogens Kilde
Oskalyd	Palasttheatre	2 manual	

EGYPT

MANUFACTURER	LOCATION	NOTATIONS	ORGANISTS
Compton	Rivoli Theatre, Cairo	4/10	Gerald Shaw

NOTE: The only theatre pipe organ known to have been installed in the Middle East.

FRANCE

MANUFACTURER	LOCATION	NOTATIONS	ORGANISTS
Christie	Gaumont Palace Theatre, Paris	4/14	Tommy Desserre Georges Guestem
Wurlitzer	Madeline Theatre, Paris	2/5—1926	
Wurlitzer	Paramount, Paris	2/10—1927	
Cavaille-Coll	Cine-Olympia, Paris	2/11—1930	Gilbert Leroy Leo Stin

GERMANY

The majority of German theatre organs were built by Welte. The bulk of Welte's business was the building of residence pipe organs with and without player attachments. The company also built many church and concert instruments. The Welte factories were destroyed by bombing near the end of World War II. Other companies building and installing organs in theatres include Hupfield of Leipzig (now in East Germany), Rieger of Jagerndorf, Steinmeyer of Oettingen, Weise of Plattling, and Walcker of Ludwigsburg who built Oskalyd organs. A number of Wurlitzer theatre organs were imported from the United States.

MANUFACTURER	LOCATION	NOTATIONS	ORGANISTS
Welte	North German Broadcasting House, Hamburg	3/27—1928 (eventually a 4th manual [Hammond] was added)	Gerhard Gregor
Welte	Metropol Theatre, Bonn	2 manual—1929	
Welte	Schauburg, Buer	3/16	
Welte	Capitol, Düsseldorf	2 manual	
Welte	Neue Philharmonie, Berlin	2 manual	
Welte	Stella-Palast, Berlin	2 manual	
Welte	Roxy-Palast, Frankfurt		
Wurlitzer	Phoebus Palast, Nuremberg	2/6—1927	Dr. George Tootell
Wurlitzer	Kristall Palast, Berlin	2/6—1928	
Wurlitzer	Alhambra, Berlin	2/6—1928	
Wurlitzer	Europa, Düsseldorf	2/6—1928	
Wurlitzer	Union, Munich	2/6—1928	Paul Mania
Wurlitzer	Litchberg Spielhaus, Essen	2/9—1928	
Wurlitzer	Residence of Werner Von Siemens, Berlin	4/15—1929	Horst Schimmelpfenning
Christie	Bavaria Theatre, Berlin	2 manual—1929	George Tootell
Christie	Capitol Kino/UFA Palast, Cologne	2 manual—1929	George Tootell
Christie	New Kino, Dortmund	2 manual	George Tootell

NOTE: Many of these organs and theatres were destroyed in World War II.

GREAT BRITAIN

The theatre (cinema) organ in Great Britain has had a long and fascinating history. From London comes the earliest known occasion on which organ music was used to accompany motion pictures. On February 12, 1896, French inventors Louis and Auguste Lumiere, whose Cinematographe had been introduced in Paris a few months before, staged a public showing in which a small reed organ or harmonium was used to mask the noise of the projector and provide some background music. The organ was equipped with a cylinder of compressed air, which was used with startling effect to accompany a film sequence of a train puffing into the station. The audience was electrified by such realism and thus began the motion picture era in Britain.

The golden era of the theatre organ in Britain occurred a decade after that of the United States. In America motion picture palaces reached their zenith in the late 1920s, but it was the decade of the 1930s that brought the organ-equipped super cinema to England and the development of a radically different theatre organ design toward relatively small but forceful instruments.

The theatre organ in England can be said with some truth to have come about because of a musician's strike. An early theatre, the Picture House, Tamworth, Staffordshire, featured an orchestra for motion picture accompaniment. The orchestra members went out on strike in 1908, and the owner contacted James Taylor of the John Compton Organ Company. The result was the installation of a Harper player piano coupled to six ranks of pipes plus some drum effects. Taylor himself played the instrument, which was a great success. Photoplayers of this type never became as popular in England as they were in America.

John Compton was to become the largest builder of theatre pipe organs in Britain. By 1926 the prestigious London firm of organ builders, Hill, Norman and Beard, had begun manufacturing theatre pipe organs under the name "Christie." Other builders also began to produce theatre organs. Rutt built the "Organestra" and Jardine the "Symphonique." Ingram, Conacher, Hilsdon, Fitton and Hayley, and Blackett and Howden also installed unit organs in theatres.

MANUFACTURER	LOCATION	NOTATIONS	ORGANISTS
Compton "Kinestra"[1]	County Kinema, Sutton, Surrey	3/14—1921	Hubert Selby
Compton	The Pavilion, Shepherd's Bush, London	4/17—1923 (enlarged to 4/19 in 1927)	Quentin Maclean
Wurlitzer	Picture House, Walsall	2/6—1924	Jack Courtnay
Wurlitzer	New Gallery Cinema, London	2/8—1925	Reginald Foort

MANUFACTURER	LOCATION	NOTATIONS	ORGANISTS
Wurlitzer[2]	Plaza, London (Paramount circuit)	3/15—1926	Charles Smart Maurice Meier
Christie[3]	Regal, Marble Arch, London	4/37—1928	Quentin Maclean Sidney Torch
Christie	Davis Theatre, Croydon, London	4/23—1928	Alex Taylor
Wurlitzer	Empire Theatre, Leicester Square, London[4]	4/20—1928	Sandy MacPherson
Wurlitzer	Paramount, Manchester	4/20—1930	Henry Croudson
Wurlitzer	Paramount, Leeds	3/19—1932	Cecil Chadwick Eric Lord
Wurlitzer	Paramount, Newcastle	3/19—1931	Eric Lord
Wurlitzer	Trocadero, Elephant and Castle, London	4/21—1930	Quentin Maclean
Wurlitzer[5]	Granada, Tooting	4/14—1931	Alex Taylor Robinson Cleaver Harold Ramsay Stuart Barrie
Wurlitzer	Granadas: North Cheam, Harrow, Clapham Junction, Greenford, Welling and Slough (6 identical instruments)	3/8—1937–38	Granada team of organists
Wurlitzer	Tower Ballroom, Blackpool	3/14—1935	Reginald Dixon Ernest Broadbent
Christie	Granada, Walthamstow (two consoles)	3/12	Granada team of organists

GREAT BRITAIN (Continued)

MANUFACTURER	LOCATION	NOTATIONS	ORGANISTS
Compton	Astoria, Brixton	3/13—1929	G. T. Pattman
Compton	Astoria, Old Kent Road	3/12—1930	Elton Roberts
Compton	Astoria, Finsbury Park	3/13—1930 (later enlarged to 3/15 with Melotone added)	Charles Saxby
Compton[6]	Astoria, Streatham	3/12—1930	Al Bollington Charles Saxby
Compton	Odeon, Leicester Square, London	5/17—1937	James Bell John Howlett Gerald Shaw
Christie[7]	The Dome, Brighton	4/41 dual purpose concert and theatre instrument—1936	Douglas Reeve
Jardine	Stoll, Kingsway, London	3/17—1929	Herbert Griffiths
Christie	Regal, Edmonton	4/15—1934	Sidney Torch Vic Hammett
Wurlitzer	State, Kilburn	4/16—1937	Sidney Torch Louis Mordish
Wurlitzer	Opera House, Blackpool	3/13—1939	Horace Finch
Wurlitzer	Granada, Kingston	3/10—1939	Granada team of organists
Marshall Sykes	Cecil Theatre, Hull	1955	Norman Coverdale

Beginning in 1932, organ consoles equipped with glass sides through which shown multicolored lights became very popular in England. New theatre organs and existing instruments had these lighting systems added. The public referred to the glass-enclosed lighting as "fruit-jelly surrounds." The organist could control the colors he wanted by a series of push buttons or colored stop tablets, or he could turn the device on and let it cycle from one blend of colors to the next. Asbestos padding was thoughtfully provided on the underside of organ benches equipped with colored light units.

Close to the time of the invention of the Hammond organ in the United States, Leslie Bourne of the John Compton Company developed an electronic device which generated tones from electrostatic discs. He called his device an "Electrone" when it was introduced in 1935. It came to be known very shortly as the "Melotone." It produced certain imitative organ sounds, and stop tablets were labeled "Vibraphone, Marimba, Krummhorn, Cor Anglais," and so on.

In 1957 the Granada chain removed all organists from the payroll leaving a few with the ABC chain and three with the Rank chain. By 1970 all were dismissed except for Gerald Shaw at the Odeon, Leicester Square, London. Shaw remained as Britain's only full-time theatre organist until his death in 1975. Reginald Dixon, perhaps one of the best-known citizens of England, remained at the Wurlitzer in the Tower Ballroom, Blackpool, England's major resort, until he retired in 1969. His replacement, Ernest Broadbent, has also retired, but the Tower organ remains fully staffed by a younger generation of theatre organists.

NOTES: 1. The Kinestra was a name derived from the words "kinema" and "orchestra." The name was phased out around 1928.

2. This organ was installed on the first console lift in Britain. To inaugurate the instrument, Paramount brought in the American organist Albert Hay Malotte. It was Malotte who later composed the familiar musical setting for "The Lord's Prayer."

3. This was the largest unified theatre organ in Europe.

4. This was MGM's flagship theatre in Britain.

5. The top manual of this instrument controlled percussions only. This was the flagship theatre for the Granada chain.

6. The Astoria theatres were part of the Paramount chain. Each of the above were twin-console pipe organs.

7. This was one of the last major Christie organs built. No new Christie pipe organs were installed in theatres after 1937.

HAWAII

MANUFACTURER	LOCATION	NOTATIONS	ORGANISTS
	Lahaina, Maui	Seeburg-type photoplayer	
	Liberty Theatre, Honolulu	2m photoplayer w/ roll player	
	Empire Theatre, Honolulu	1m photoplayer; replaced by Liberty Theatre organ, 1921	Mabel Fernandez John DeMello

HAWAII (Continued)

MANUFACTURER	LOCATION	NOTATIONS	ORGANISTS
Robert Morton	Empire Theatre, Hilo	2/4 photo-player, moved to church in Hilo, then private residence	Rose Kumoo
Robert Morton	Palace Theatre, Hilo	3/7, installed 1929, $37,500; moved 1940 to Hilo Theatre	Edwin Sawtelle Harold Rouse Alice Blue John DeMello
Robert Morton	Princess Theatre, Honolulu	4/16—1922–69 $35,000. Theatre razed 1969, organ moved to Hawaii Theatre.	Edwin Sawtelle Mildred Van Iwegen Josephine Sosnowsky Don George Virginia Smith Earl Bond George Lake John DeMello Phillip Dooley
Robert Morton	Hawaii Theatre, Honolulu (had twin consoles for a while)	4/16—1922–39. Moved to Waikiki Theatre, 1939. Replaced by organ from Princess Theatre, 1971. Still in use.	Edwin Sawtelle Mildred Van Iwegen Fred Scholl Don George Alice Blue Baron Hartsough
Buhl and Blashfield	Kaimuki Playhouse, Honolulu	3/14—1925–54. Moved to a church, then private residence. Theatre razed 1982.	John DeMello Josephine Sosnowsky

MANUFACTURER	LOCATION	NOTATIONS	ORGANISTS
Wicks	Star Theatre, Honolulu	2/4—1928–32 $15,000. Sold to funeral parlor in Oakland.	John DeMello
Robert Morton	Waikiki Theatre, Honolulu (now called Waikiki III)	Organ moved from Hawaii Theatre, 1939; still in use	Edwin Sawtelle Robert Hornung John DeMello Frank Loney Robert Alder
Robert Morton	Hilo Theatre, Hilo	Organ moved from Palace Theatre 1940. Moved to private residence 1964. Theatre later razed.	John DeMello Bernice AhNin

HUNGARY

MANUFACTURER	LOCATION	NOTATIONS	ORGANISTS
Oskalyd	UFA Palast, Budapest	2 manual	

INDIA

MANUFACTURER	LOCATION	NOTATIONS	ORGANISTS
Wurlitzer	Mr. Madan's Theatre, Calcutta	2/8—1928	

IRELAND

MANUFACTURER	LOCATION	NOTATIONS	ORGANISTS
Wurlitzer	Classic Cinema, Belfast	2/8—1926	
Compton	Savoy Cinema, Cork (a 2,300-seat house)	3/12—1932	Fred Bridgman

IRELAND (Continued)

MANUFACTURER	LOCATION	NOTATIONS	ORGANISTS
Compton	Savoy Cinema, Dublin	3/14—1929	Gordon Spicer Philip Dore
Compton	Savoy Cinema, Limerick	3/7—1935	Jack Courtnay
Compton	Theatre Royal, Dublin	4/16—1935	Alban Chambers Gordon Spicer
Compton	Ritz Cinema, Belfast	4/10	Joseph Seal

JAPAN

MANUFACTURER	LOCATION	NOTATIONS	ORGANISTS
Wurlitzer	Mitsukoshi Department Store, Tokyo	3/12—1930	Hiroshi Matsugawa

MEXICO

Four Wurlitzer pipe organs were shipped to Mexico, all of them to Mexico City churches and religious institutions. The largest and most famous was a four manual instrument in the Our Lady of Guadalupe Roman Catholic Church in 1931.

NETHERLANDS

The most famous Dutch builder of theatre organs was Messers. Standaart and Company. Located in Schiedam near Rotterdam, it began producing theatre organs as early as 1919. By the time the company went out of business in 1952, it had built thirty-three organs ranging in size from two manual, four rank to four manual, twenty-two rank instruments. Theo Strunk from the Standaart firm started his own organ business and built a few instruments. Messers. Dekker of Goes, basically a builder of church organs, constructed a few theatre organs which were called "The Golden Oriole." Other theatre organs in Holland were imports, several of which were from the United States. It is believed that 70 percent of Dutch theatre organs were destroyed by enemy bombing during World War II.

MANUFACTURER	LOCATION	NOTATIONS	ORGANISTS
Standaart	Passage Theatre, Schiedam	3/10—1933	Cor Standaart Joop Walvis
Standaart	VARA Broadcasting Studios, Hilversum	3/13—1929	Johan Jong Cor Steyn
Standaart	Houbeyns Dancing, Leeuwarden (moved to ABC residence, Leeuwarden, 1969)	3/7—1949	Taco Tiemersma
Strunk	Asta Theatre, Hague	4/22—1936	Piet Leechburgh Jos Carpay Louis Zaewyn
Strunk	City Theatre, Amsterdam	4/17—1936	Cor Steyn Bernard Drukker
Wurlitzer	Tuschinski Theatre, Amsterdam	2/5—1923 (enlarged by Standaart to 4/10)	Fred Wolffers Jan Mekkes Pierre Palla René de Rooy
Wurlitzer	Grand Theatre, Rotterdam	2/4—1929	Les Ott
Wurlitzer	Carré Cinema, Amsterdam	2/8—1929	Jan Mekkes Jos Carpay
Dekker	NCRV Radio Studio, Hilversum (moved to the Lutheran Church, Alkmaar)	3/19—1927	
Compton	AVRO Radio Studio, Hilversum	4/22—1936	Pierre Palla

NEW ZEALAND

Theatre organs have been known in New Zealand since before World War I. No theatre organs were manufactured in New Zealand itself. Instruments were imported from England and the United States.

MANUFACTURER	LOCATION	NOTATIONS	ORGANISTS
Wurlitzer	Strand Theatre, Auckland	2/4—1913 (photoplayer)	Johnnie Shaw
Wurlitzer	Deluxe, Wellington	2/10—1926	Reg Maddams Manny Aarons Roland Lavin Henry Rudolph
Wurlitzer	Regent, Auckland	2/8	Maurice Carbines Eddie Horton Knight Barnett Dorothea Ryan Norman Dawe
Wurlitzer	Cozy, Palmerston North	2/5—1927 (piano console)	
Wurlitzer	Cozy, Masterton	2/4—1927 (photoplayer)	
Wurlitzer	Civic, Auckland (largest theatre organ in New Zealand. Installed on highest organ lift in the world—could rise thirty-seven feet from its down position)	3/16	Fred Scholl Ewart Lynne Charles Tuckwell Barrie Brettoner
Christie	Empire, Dunedin	2/10	Leslie Harvey Penn Hughes

Note: Many of the organists listed here also appeared at other New Zealand theatres. Theatre organists from Australia also appeared frequently at New Zealand theatres.

PANAMA

In 1962 a three manual, twenty-seven rank Wurlitzer formerly installed in the Stanley Theatre, Atlantic City, New Jersey, was installed in the El Bombarde Lounge of the Hilton Hotel, Panama City.

POLAND

MANUFACTURER	LOCATION	NOTATIONS	ORGANISTS
Wurlitzer	Colosseum Theatre, Warsaw	2/8—1928	

PORTUGAL

MANUFACTURER	LOCATION	NOTATIONS	ORGANISTS
Compton	São Jorge Cinema, Lisbon	3 manual Theatrone organ using same type of tone generation as Melotone units.	Gerald Shaw

RUSSIA (see USSR)

SOUTH AFRICA

MANUFACTURER	LOCATION	NOTATIONS	ORGANISTS
Estey	Princess Theatre, Durban	Installed 1926	William Bohm
Wurlitzer	Alhambra, Cape Town	2/8—1929	Max Bruce
Wurlitzer	Bijou, Johannesburg	2/8 (organ moved here in 1931 from the Alhambra, Cape Town)	Max Bruce
Wurlitzer	Metro, Johannesburg	3/13—1933	Charles Parkhouse Dean Herrick Tommy McLennan

SOUTH AFRICA (Continued)

MANUFACTURER	LOCATION	NOTATIONS	ORGANISTS
Wurlitzer	Metro, Durban	3/13—1937	
Wurlitzer[1]	20th Century Fox, Johannesburg	4/16	Dean Herrick[2]
Wurlitzer	Plaza, Johannesburg	2/8—1931	
Möller	Leslie Wersman residence	3/13—horseshow console with roll-player attachment	

NOTES: 1. This was the last theatre organ built at the Wurlitzer factory, North Tonawanda, New York. It was constructed in 1939. The theatre opened in March 1940. A second console was added later by a South African company and plaved by organist Frances Friedman.

2. Dean Herrick became the best known of all theatre organists in South Africa after many years of personal appearances and an even longer period of regular broadcasts. Born in Chicago, Illinois, he moved to South Africa in 1937 for a one year's engagement at the Metro Theatre, Johannesburg, and decided to remain in that country. Other theatre organists in South Africa included Frank Lean, Simmie Yutar, and Ken Espen.

SPAIN

MANUFACTURER	LOCATION	NOTATIONS	ORGANISTS
Wurlitzer	Real Cinema, Madrid	3/11—1924	

SWEDEN

MANUFACTURER	LOCATION	NOTATIONS	ORGANISTS
Wurlitzer	Cosmorama Theatre, Gothenburg	2/7—1925 (organ shipped to theatre but installed in private residence)	Miss Benna Moe

MANUFACTURER	LOCATION	NOTATIONS	ORGANISTS
Wurlitzer	Scandia Theatre, Stockholm	2/7—1926 (organ later moved to Stockholm Town Hall)	Willard Ringstrand

SWITZERLAND

MANUFACTURER	LOCATION	NOTATIONS	ORGANISTS
Welte	Capitol Theatre, Zurich		
Welte	Splendid-Palace, Berne		
Welte	Capitol Theatre, Berne		
Welte	Palace Cinema, Basel		
Welte	Apollo Theatre, Zurich		Herman Kuppers
Oskalyd	La Scala, Zurich	2 manual	

NOTE: In 1982 a three manual, eight rank Wurlitzer formerly installed in the Granada Cinema, Clapham Junction, England, was installed at Claperede, Geneva.

USSR (Russia)

MANUFACTURER	LOCATION	NOTATIONS	ORGANISTS
Oskalyd	State Theatre, Odessa	3 manual	

NOTES ON SOURCES

The source materials upon which this book is based fall into three major categories: (1) books, (2) articles, and (3) interviews.

BOOKS

THE THEATRE PIPE ORGAN

The theatre pipe organ flourished for such a brief period in the early decades of this century that few books were ever written about it. Several books about pipe organs in general contain limited references to the theatre pipe organ. William H. Barnes, noted organ consultant, in collaboration with Edward B. Gammons, director of music at the Groton School, Groton, Massachusetts, has written, *Two Centuries of American Organ Building*, a valuable resource book containing a subsection of thirteen pages devoted to the theatre pipe organ.[1]

Most fascinating and authoritative of the newer books concerning the pipe organ is Orpha Ochse, *The History of the Organ in the United States*. This work is particularly useful in tracing the historical threads of the builders and companies that eventually produced instruments for theatres in addition to producing classical instruments. Good coverage is given to the ideas of Robert Hope-Jones and views of him by certain of his contemporaries, including George Ashdown Audsley.

George L. Miller, *The Recent Revolution in Organ Building* (originally published in 1913 but reprinted by the Vestal Press, Vestal, New York, in 1969), is a splendid little volume beginning with the history of the pipe organ and dealing especially with the prominent organ builders of the turn of the century. Miller is particularly impressed with the work of Robert Hope-Jones and provides a view of the man and his work as seen through the eyes of a contemporary.

Geoffrey Wyatt of England has authored a brief treatise on the theatre organ (or "cinema" organ as it is called in England), *At the Mighty Organ*, which contains many photographs of British organs and organists. The text traces the development of the theatre organ in Great Britain to the present.

There are a number of other books which, although not devoted entirely to the theatre organ, make some significant contribution to knowledge about it. Worthy of mention are two books by Q. David Bowers, *Put Another Nickel In* and *Encyclopedia of Automatic Musical Instruments*. Both books are devoted to the history of coin-operated pianos, orchestrions, and similar instruments. Thus they deal with one of the evolutionary steps in the development of the theatre pipe organ.

Cynthia A. Hoover, associate curator, Division of Musical Instruments of the National Museum of History and Technology has written *Music Machines—American Style*. This brief book tells how the machinery of music making has developed and includes some coverage of musical accompaniment of silent pictures. It is profusely illustrated.

For those who are interested chiefly in the mechanism of the theatre pipe organ, Richard Whitworth, *The Cinema and Theatre Organ*, is highly recommended. Recently reprinted by the Organ Literature Foundation, Braintree, Massachusetts, it provides the most clear and lucid explanation of the technical intricacies of the theatre organ ever to find its way into print.

Another source of information on the mechanism of the theatre pipe organ is an unpublished manuscript by Lou Marder, *The Encyclopedia of the Cinema and Theatre Organ*. It represented the creative energies of more than ten years of Marder's life. When Marder died suddenly in the early 1970s, the two-volume manuscript was given to well-known Hawaiian theatre organist John DeMello. DeMello, in turn, loaned it to this author in January 1976.

A number of catalogs of theatre organ manufacturers have been reprinted by the Vestal Press, Vestal, New York. Included are several catalogs of the Wurlitzer Company and catalogs of Kilgen, Link, Marr and Colton, and other companies. These are valuable research tools.

Van Allen Bradley's book, *Music for the Millions*, is a history of the Kimball Company. Included is a brief history of its pipe organ business, including reference to its Roxy Theatre (New York City) installations and other outstanding instruments.

Judd Walton of Vallejo, California, who probably knows more about the specifications of Wurlitzer theatre pipe organs than anyone else, produced his book, *The Wurlitzer Theatre Organ Revised Installation List*, in 1973. This resource book was essential to the writing of the history of the theatre pipe organ.

Jack Courtney, British theatre organist, edited *Theatre Organ World*, a book published in England in 1946, which was a compilation of articles on the theatre organ and biographical sketches of organists mainly from England and the British Empire. Very little information is included relating to the United States.

THEATRE ORGANISTS

There have been only three full-length biographies of theatre organists published the world over, to this author's knowledge. *The Cinema Organ*, Reginald Foort's autobiography, originally published in England in 1932 and reprinted by Vestal Press in 1970, includes a simple description of the theatre pipe organ and how it works. Foort describes how he became a theatre organist and gives a full description of making pipe organ records and broadcasting the organ over radio. A complete bibliography of Reginald Foort's theatre organ records is included.

Jesse Crawford, Poet of the Organ, Wizard of the Mighty Wurlitzer by John W. Landon (this author) was the first full-length biography of an American theatre organist ever published. It was also the most thorough in its research. Released by Vestal Press in 1974, it was based upon Dr. Landon's Ph.D. dissertation. Part of the research done for the dissertation and the Crawford book were transferable to this project—the writing of a general history of the theatre pipe organ.

The remaining biography, *Reginald Dixon* by Peter Ashman, was published in England in 1972. Although brief, it covers the career of this world-famous theatre organist long associated with the Tower Ballroom, Blackpool, England.

RESOURCE BOOKS ON MUSIC

Many books on various facets of music were consulted. Especially useful were those relating to popular music of the 1920s and 1930s. Jack Burton's various "blue books" were used: *The Blue Book of Broadway Musicals*, *The Blue Book of Hollywood Musicals*, and *The Blue Book of Tin Pan Alley*. Orin Keepnews and Bill Grover, *A Pictorial History of Jazz*, helps to provide the flavor of that era. Miles Kreuger (ed.), *The Movie Musical from Vitaphone to 42nd Street*, gives the reader a glimpse of that important art form. Julius Matfield, *Variety Music Cavalcade: 1920–1961*, and Nat Shapiro, *Popular Music: An Annotated Index of American Popular Songs* (4 volumes), are most useful in studying popular music written in this country.

Most useful and most complete in this category was Roger D. Kinkle, *The Complete Encyclopedia of Popular Music and Jazz, 1900–1950*. Its four volumes include a chronological list of popular songs, biographies of composers and performing artists including some theatre organists, and various listings by serial number of the popular music output of several American phonograph record manufacturers. Also useful were Edward B. Marks, *They All Sang*; an autobiographical account of the famed popular music publisher, David Ewen, *The Life and Death of Tin Pan Alley* (Ewen believes that the death of Tin Pan Alley coincided with the birth of talking pictures), and a host of biographies of popular and jazz musicians such as W.C. Handy, Fats Waller and others.

MOTION PICTURE ACCOMPANIMENT

When theatres began to install organs in sufficient numbers, various publishing houses sensed that a market was opening for books on how to accompany motion pictures and music especially prepared for this purpose.

George W. Beynon, *Musical Presentation of Motion Pictures*, and Edith Lang and George West, *Musical Accompaniment of Moving Pictures*, both date from about 1920 and are an excellent means of discovering what this art was all about. George Tootell, one of Britain's outstanding pioneer theatre organists, wrote a book on a similar theme, *How to Play the Cinema Organ—A Practical Book by a Practical Player*. Tootell, an accomplished musician who appeared throughout Europe as well as his native England, was also gifted with a sense of humor. His book is helpful in completing a self-administered "short course" on silent film accompaniment.

The last in this group qualifies as a genuine "period piece," C. Roy Carter, *Theatre Organist's Secrets: A Collection of Successful Imitations, Tricks and Effects for Motion Picture Accompaniment on the Pipe Organ*, published in Los Angeles about 1920. This booklet is discussed fully in Chapter One of this book.

HOLLYWOOD AND THE HISTORY OF MOTION PICTURES

The current wave of nostalgia has generated a wealth of books about Hollywood and the history of motion pictures. It would be impossible to survey them all. There were several which were especially useful in this research effort.

Benjamin B. Hampton, *History of the American Film Industry*, Mrs. D. W. Griffith, *When the Movies Were Young*, Daniel Blum, *A New Pictorial History of the Talkies*, Richard Griffith, *The Talkies*, Roy Stuart, *Immortals of the Screen*, and John M. Smith and Tim Cawkwell, *The World Encyclopedia of the Film* all provide information about motion pictures necessary to the writing of this book. During a significant portion of its life the theatre organ was a part of the package of motion picture entertainment.

One book stands by itself offering a different perspective on Hollywood and mass entertainment. Hortense Powdermaker, an anthropologist, viewed Hollywood as a "dream factory."[2]

HISTORY OF THE 1920s AND 1930s

To understand the historical context in which the theatre organ came to its zenith and then declined, the author selectively read books which describe these two decades from the standpoint of popular culture.

The most popular account of the 1920s is probably Frederick Lewis Allen's *Only Yesterday*. Written in an entertaining journalistic style, just as the decade drew to a close, it has been so widely read that some writers, including Roderick Nash, believe it has completely colored our view of that era. It does paint a vivid picture of the 1920s as an era of wonderful nonsense and makes some references to popular music. The book is especially useful in its chapters on the revolution in manners and morals and on "the ballyhoo years." Allen also wrote about the decade of the thirties using a similar approach in his book, *Since Yesterday*.

Mark Sullivan in volume six (*The Twenties*) of his *Our Times* series gives the most adequate coverage of popular music of any serious historian whose works were examined.

Other historians who wrote from somewhat different points of view include Paul Carter, *The Twenties in America*, George E. Mowry, *The Twenties: Fords, Flappers and Fanatics*, and Roderick Nash, *The Nervous Generation*.

The stock market crash and the Depression, which played a part in the demise of the theatre organ, are covered in Frederick Lewis Allen, *Since Yesterday*, Paul Conkin, *The New Deal*, and William E. Leuchtenburg, *Franklin D. Roosevelt and the New Deal*. Leuchtenburg provides the most masterful study of this period of history.

Of direct usefulness were books concerned with popular culture. Russel Nye, *The Unembarrassed Muse: The Popular Arts in America*, is a history of literature and entertainment in the first two centuries of the United States. It is comprehensive in scope and scholarly in approach.

Ralph K. Andrist et al. have edited *The American Heritage History of the 20's and 30's*. It deals at length with life as experienced by the ordinary American and is profusely illustrated. The motion picture is a subject treated at length.

Two books with a similar focus are volumes 3 and 4 of the *Time-Life* series, *This Fabulous Century*, each covering a decade, *1920–30*, and *1930–40*, respectively. Of special value are the photographs which bring an added touch of realism to the sparse narrative.

Other books that were useful include Lloyd Morris, *Not So Long Ago*, Allen Churchill, *Remember When*, Paul Sann, *The Lawless Decade*, James D. Horan, *The Desperate Years*, and the *Time Capsules* for various years following the introduction of *Time Magazine* in 1923. Each *Capsule* has sections on "Cinema," "Music," and "Theatre," which contain condensations of particular items of interest in each of these areas for a given year. To read them is somewhat like consulting the pages of newspapers of past years.

Isabel Leighton has edited a marvelous book, *The Aspirin Age*, which a reader can scarcely put down until finished. Covering the events between the two world wars, it includes selections by a number of outstanding writers.

Except for a one-page introduction, there is no narrative at all in Edgar Jones, *Those Were the Good Old Days*. A fifty-year period from 1880 to 1930 was selected, and a vast representative collection of magazine advertisements is chronologically presented from that time. A great many conclusions about the advertising and consuming public may be deduced from careful examination of this book.

RADIO AND PHONOGRAPH RECORDS

Both radio and phonograph records were entertainment media through which the theatre pipe organ became known to millions. Irving Settel, *A Pictorial History of Radio*, includes a wealth of photographs from radio's golden era. Noted radio and television editor of the New York *Daily News*, Ben Gross, has written his recollections, *I Looked and I Listened*. The result is an interesting informal history of radio and television, the large portion being devoted to radio.

Frank Buxton and Bill Owen, *The Big Broadcast, 1920–1950,* is perhaps the best source book of information about radio broadcasts, who starred in them, and even the names of the organists supplying theme music for the soap operas and other programs.

Mary Jane Higby wrote her autobiography, *Tune In Tomorrow*, and tells of her career on radio. She appeared in everything from the "soaps," as soap operas were called, to the more serious, dramatic shows. She also remembers and comments about some of the organists on radio. This author enjoyed a brief correspondence with Mary Jane Higby about radio's golden days.

Jane Woodfin, *Of Mikes and Men*, provides a humorous autobiographical account of her career in radio. Joseph Julian, *This Was Radio*, provides a more serious account of what happened to radio personalities during the anti-Communist crusades in post-World War II America. Jim Harmon, *The Great Radio Comedians*, recalls this facet of radio entertainment.

A general history of the phonograph is provided in Oliver Read and Walter L. Welch, *From Tin Foil to Stereo*, 2nd edition. The most authoritative book on the history of recorded sound, it suffers from too much repetition and offers more detail than the general reader is likely to appreciate.

One very specialized tool of research was *The Victor Master Book*, volume 2, compiled by Brian Rust. This indefatigable phonograph record researcher has compiled the complete list of master discs cut and issued from the beginning of electrical recording by Victor in 1925 until 1936. Most of the theatre organ discs recorded by Victor in the 78 rpm days were issued during these years including almost the entire output of Jesse Crawford's Victor records. Rust broadens his approach to other record companies and to a host of show business personalities in his book, *The Complete Entertainment Discography*.

Melvin H. Doner and R. G. Mander completed a most ambitious research project when they published *Theatre Organ Discs of the World* in 1958. It listed every known theatre organ record made since the beginning of recorded sound.

A veritable encyclopedia of show business history is *Show Biz* by the editors of *Variety* magazine, Abel Green and Joe Laurie, Jr., who take their material from the pages of *Variety*'s past issues. This book deserves special mention for, as a history of show business, it is without peer. The subtitle, "From Vaude to Video," gives some idea of the scope of the book.

Related to theatre entertainment is an unusual book by Guy Morgan, *Red Roses Every Night*, published in England following World War II. It is an account of the role British cinemas played in maintaining morale even during the bombing raids in the darkest days of the war. Theatre organists had a part in this through playing for community singing in the theatres and through radio broadcasts of pipe organ music.

MOTION PICTURE THEATRE ARCHITECTURE

Although a number of books on motion picture theatre architecture have been released in recent years, there is one which is so important and useful in compiling a history of the theatre pipe organ that it deserves special mention. Ben M. Hall, *The Best Remaining Seats*, was first published in 1961 and has since been reprinted. It is devoted to the history of the movie palace from storefront theatres to motion picture cathedrals. The book was carefully researched and is an encyclopedia of the motion picture theatre. Profusely illustrated, the book shows not only the interiors and exteriors of many famous movie palaces, but also includes a wealth of photographs of theatre organs, organists, and popular musicians of that bygone era. The student of architectural history will find the book exciting. So does the theatre organ enthusiast, the nostalgia lover, and the writer of popular history.

ARTICLES

Due to the relative absence of material in books regarding theatre pipe organs, hundreds of articles were located in various periodicals. Those used in the preparation of this manuscript are carefully entered in the Bibliography. The vast majority of these articles appeared in *Theatre Organ* (including the *Tibia* and *Bombarde*) and *Console* magazines. *Music* magazine and *Diapason* also provided some articles.

The author, when researching the life of Jesse Crawford, spent many weeks at the Library of Congress in Washington, D.C., during 1970 pouring over the back issues of periodicals. Weekly reviews of various organ solos and soloists appeared in the *Exhibitor's Herald-World*, *Moving Picture World*, and *Motion Picture Herald*—the same publication which went through many name changes. Back issues were read of *Better Music, The American Organ Monthly, Pacific Coast Musician, The Motion Picture Projectionist, The Pacific Coast Musical Review, The Music World* (official journal of the National Association of Organists), *Melody for the Photoplay Musician, Jacob's Orchestra Monthly*, and others.

In some cases biographical information was gathered from printed notes on long-playing record jackets. In each such instance, these articles are carefully footnoted.

INTERVIEWS AND CORRESPONDENCE

The history of the theatre pipe organ could never have been written without the use of interviews with persons who had knowledge of various facets of the story. The Acknowledgments at the front of this book constitute a partial list of those consulted. The author spent a total of ten years researching the theatre organ. In 1966, having just finished his master's degree, the author began collecting material on the theatre organ with an eye to the future and possibly writing a book on the subject. Three years later, having embarked upon study toward a Ph.D. degree, the author decided to write a biography of Jesse Crawford, a lifelong idol, as his doctoral dissertation. Extensive research of Crawford's life involved gathering materials on the theatre pipe organ in general. An idea began to take shape. First the biography of Crawford's life would be written. Then the author would build upon that research to write the first complete history of the theatre pipe organ, its builders, and the artists who played it. The doctoral dissertation was completed in 1972 and after extensive rewriting and revision, the Jesse Crawford biography rolled off the presses September 29, 1974. The last words of this manuscript are being written on an April day in 1982.

The amount of time and energy that have been expended in this decade of research is difficult to comprehend. A total of ten secretaries have worked at the research, sometimes four simultaneously. Literally thousands of letters have been written and sent all around the world. Today the correspondence fills several file cabinets.

The author has personally heard almost every theatre organist of importance in the United States and Britain. He has traveled virtually around the world seeking out theatre organs and organists. Nearly every one of the fifty states in the union has been visited, and several trips have been made to England and Scotland beginning in 1966.

One of the world's most complete collections of 78 rpm records of theatre pipe organ music has been assembled and the collection includes sizeable numbers of long-playing and stereo discs and tapes. Written materials of all sorts relating to theatre pipe organs have been gathered.

Every chapter of the American Theatre Organ Society has been contacted by letter at least twice. Extensive correspondence has been engaged in to gather as much biographical information about as many theatre organists as possible, all over the world.

Continuing correspondence has been carried on with various experts in the theatre organ field over several years. Letters of special importance are cited as footnotes in the body of this book. Unfortunately it is impossible to note the names of all who have given help by letter or by spoken word toward the completion of this vast research project.

Of the many hundreds of interviews conducted, one remains forever clear in the author's memory. Farny Wurlitzer, President Emeritus of the Wurlitzer Company, was interviewed June 5, 1971, in his home in Kenmore, New York, a suburb of Buffalo. Although up in years and suffering from ill health, his mental powers were unimpaired. A delightful afternoon was spent listening to his reminiscences. He told of the development of the Wurlitzer Company, his recollections of Robert Hope-Jones, the evolution of the theatre organ, his unwavering belief in its marketability and how circumstances bore him out, and eventually the conversation wandered off to include his account of a business trip he took for the Wurlitzer Company to San Francisco in 1906 when the city was still in ruins from the earthquake. When the afternoon was over, it was difficult to tell whether the interviewer or interviewee had enjoyed it more.

CONCLUSION

Material regarding the theatre pipe organ continues to come to light. More research can and should be undertaken to focus in greater depth upon certain aspects of the story. However, drawn from every conceivable source, sufficient material has been assembled to permit the writing of a general history of this unique musical instrument—the theatre pipe organ.

NOTES

1. All books referred to in this chapter are listed in the Bibliography, which follows.
2. Hortense Powdermaker, *Hollywood, The Dream Factory* (see full entry in the Bibliography, which follows).

SELECTED BIBLIOGRAPHY

Allen, Frederick Lewis. *Only Yesterday*. New York: Harper Brothers, 1931.

Anderson, John. *The American Theatre*. New York: Dial Press, 1938.

Andrist, Ralph K. et a1. eds. *The American Heritage History of the 20's and 30's*. New York: American Heritage Publishing Company, Inc., 1970.

Armour, Richard, ed. *Give Me Liberty*. New York: The World Publishing Company, 1969.

ASCAP Biograghical Dictionary of Composers, Authors and Publishers. New York: American Society of Composers, Authors and Publishers, 1966.

Ashman, Peter. *Reginald Dixon*. Welwyn, Garden City, Hertfordshire, England: Privately printed by author, 1972.

Audsley, George Ashdown. *The Organ of the Twentieth Century*. New York: Dodd, Mead and Company, 1919; reprint ed., New York: Dover Publications, Inc., 1970.

Barnes, William H, and Gammons, Edward B. *Two Centuries of American Organ Building*. Glen Rock, N.J.: J. Fischer and Bro., 1970.

Berg, Charles Merrell. *An Investigation of the Motives for and Realization of Music to Accompany the American Silent Film, 1896–1927*. New York: Arno Press, 1976.

Beynon, George W. *Musical Presentation of Motion Pictures*. New York: Schirmer, n.d.

Blum, Daniel. *A New Pictorial History of the Talkies*. 2d ed, revised. New York: G. P. Putnam's Sons, 1968.

Bowers, Q. David. *Encyclopedia of Automatic Musical Instruments*. Vestal, N.Y.: Vestal Press, 1972.

———. *Put Another Nickel In*. Vestal, N.Y.: Vestal Press, 1966.

Bradley, Van Allen. *Music for the Millions*. Chicago: Henry Regnery Company, 1957.

Burton, Jack. *The Blue Book of Broadway Musicals*. Watkins Glen, N.Y.: Century House, 1952.

———. *The Blue Book of Hollywood Muscials*. Watkins Glen, N.Y.: Century House, 1953.

———. *The Blue Book of Tin Pan Alley*. Watkins Glen, N.Y. Century House, 1950.

Buxton, Fran, and Owen, Bill. *The Big Broadcast, 1920–1950*. New York: Viking Press, 1972.

Carter, C. Roy. *Theatre Organists' Secrets: A Collection of Successful Imitations, Tricks and Effects for Motion Picture Accompaniment on the Pipe Organ*. Los Angeles, n.d.

Carter, Paul. *The Twenties in America*. New York: Thomas Y. Crowell Company, 1968.

Churchill, Allen. *Remember When*. New York: Golden Press, Inc., 1967.

Conkin, Paul. *The New Deal*. New York: Thomas Y. Crowell Company, 1967.

Corbett, Ruth. *Daddy Danced the Charleston*. New York: A. S. Barnes and Company, 1970.

Courtney, Jack. *Theatre Organ World*. London: Tucker and Oxley, Ltd., 1946.

Doner, Melvin H., and Mander, R. G. *Theatre Organ Discs of the World*. Winona, Minn.; Privately printed, 1958.

Edey, Maitland et al., eds. *This Fabulous Century;* vol. 3, *1920–1930*. New York: Time-Life Books, 1969.

———. *This Fabulous Century*; vol. 4, *1930–1940*. New York: Time-Life Books, 1969.

Elvin, Laurence. *Organ Blowing: Its History and Development*. Lincoln, England: Laurence Elvin, 1971.

Ewen, David. *American Popular Songs*. New York: Random House, 1966.

———. *The Life and Death of Tin Pan Alley*. New York: Funk and Wagnalls Company, Inc., 1964.

———. *Panorama of American Popular Music*. Englewood Cliffs, N.J.: Prentice-Hall, Inc., 1957.

Farnsworth, Marjorie. *The Ziegfeld Follies*. New York: Crown Publishers, 1956.

Foort, Reginald. *The Cinema Organ*. 2d ed., revised. Vestal, N.Y.: Vestal Press, 1970.

Goldberg, Isaac. *Tin Pan Alley*, New York: John Day Company, 1930.

Green, Abel, and Laurie, Joe, Jr. *Show Biz*. New York: Henry Holt & Company, 1951.

Green, Stanley. *Ring Bells! Sing Songs*! New Rochelle, N.Y.: Arlington House, 1971.

Griffith, Mrs. D. W. *When the Movies Were Young*. 2d ed. New York: Dover Publications, Inc., 1969.

Griffith, Richard. *The Talkies*. New York: Dover Publications, Inc., 1971.

Gross, Ben. *I Looked and I Listened*. New Rochelle, N.Y.: Arlington House, 1970.

Hadden, Briton, et al., eds. *Time Capsule/1923*. New York: Time-Life Books, 1967.

———. *Time Capsule/1927*. New York: Time-Life Books, 1968.

———. *Time Capsule/1929*. New York: Time-Life Books, 1967.

Hadlock, Richard. *Jazz Masters of the Twenties*. New York: The Macmillan Company, 1965.

Hall, Ben M. *The Best Remaining Seats*. New York: Clarkson N. Potter, Inc., 1961.

Hampton, Benjamin B. *History of the American Film Industry*. 2d ed. New York: Dover Publications, Inc., 1970.

Handy, William Christopher. *Father of the Blues*. New York: The Macmillan Company, 1941.

Harmon, Jim. *The Great Radio Comedians*. Garden City, N.Y.: Doubleday and Company, Inc., 1970.

Higby, Mary Jane. *Tune in Tomorrow*. New York: Cowles Educational Corporation, 1968.

Hoover, Cynthia A. *Music Machines—American Style*. Washington, D.C.: Smithsonian Institution Press, 1971.

Horan, James D. *The Desperate Years*. New York: Bonanza Books, 1962.

Hortsmann, Henry C., and Tousley, Victor H. *Motion Picture Operation*. Chicago: Frederick J. Drake and Company, 1923.

International Motion Picture Almanac. Chicago: Quigley Publishing Company, 1930.

Jobes, Gertrude. *Motion Picture Empire*. Hamden, Conn.: Archon Books, 1966.

Jones, Edgar R. *Those Were the Good Old Days*. New York: Simon and Schuster, 1959.

Julian, Joseph. *This Was Radio*. New York: Viking Press, 1975.

Keepnews, Orrin, and Grauer, Bill, Jr. *A Pictorial History of Jazz*. 2d ed. revised. New York: Crown Publishers, Inc., 1966.

Kilgen Wonder Organ: The Voice of the Silent Drama. Kilgen catalog, 1927; Reprint ed., Vestal, N.Y.: Vestal Press, n.d.

Kinkle, Roger D. *The Complete Encyclopedia of Popular Music and Jazz, 1900–1950*, vol 1, *Music Year by Year, 1900–1950*. vol. 2, *Biographies, A through K*. vol. 3, *Biographies, L through Z*. vol. 4, *Indexes and Appendices*. New Rochelle, N.Y.: Arlington House, 1974.

Kirkeby, Ed, et al. *Ain't Misbehavin'*. New York: Dodd, Mead & Company, 1966.

Kreuger, Miles, ed. *The Movie Musical from Vitaphone to 42nd Street*. New York: Dover Publications, Inc., 1975.

Landon, John W. *Jesse Crawford, The Poet of the Organ; Wizard of the Mighty Wurlitzer*. Vestal, N.Y.: Vestal Press, 1974.

Lang, Edith, and West, George. *Musical Accompaniment of Moving Pictures*. Boston: The Boston Music Company, 1920.

Leighton, Isabel, ed. *The Aspirin Age, 1919–1941*. New York: Simon and Schuster, 1949.

Leuchtenburg, William E. *Franklin D. Roosevelt and the New Deal*. New York: Harper and Row, 1963.

Lewine, Richard, and Simon, Alfred, ed. *Encyclopedia of Theatre Music*. New York: Crown Publishers, Inc., 1961.

Marder, Lou. *The Encyclopedia of the Cinema and Theatre Organ*. Unpublished book manuscript dating from approximately 1970.

Marks, Edward B. *They All Sang*. New York: Viking Press, 1934.

Mattfield, Julius. *Variety Music Cavalcade: 1920–1961*. Englewood Cliffs, N.J.: Prentice-Hall, Inc., 1962.

Miller, George Laing. *The Recent Revolution in Organ Building*. 2d ed. New York; The Charles Francis Press, 1913; reprint ed., Vestal, N.Y.: Vestal Press, 1969.

Morgan, Guy. *Red Roses Every Night*. London: Quality Press, 1948.

Morris, Lloyd. *Not So Long Ago*. New York: Random House, 1949.

Mowry, George E. *The Twenties: Fords, Flappers and Fanatics*. Englewood Cliffs, N.J.: Prentice-Hall, Inc., 1963.

Nash, Roderick. *The Nervous Generation*. Chicago: Rand McNally, 1970.

Nye, Russel. *The Unembarressed Muse: The Popular Arts in America*. New York: Dial Press, 1970.

Ochse, Orpha. *The History of the Organ in the United States*. Bloomington: Indiana University Press, 1975.

Osgood, Henry D. *So This Is Jazz*. Boston: Little, Brown and Company, 1926.

Powdermaker, Hortense. *Hollywood, The Dream Factory*. Boston: Little, Brown and Company, 1950.

Read, Oliver, and Welch, Walter L. *From Tin Foil to Stereo*. 2d. ed. Indianapolis: Howard W. Sams and Co., Inc., 1976.

Rust, Brian. *The Complete Entertainment Discography*. New Rochelle, N.Y.: Arlington House, 1973.

———. *The Victor Master Book*. vol. 2: *1925–1936*. Stanhope, N.J.: Walter C. Allen, 1970.

Sann, Paul. *The Lawless Decade*. New York: Bonanza Books, 1957.

Sarris, Andrew. *The American Cinema*. New York: E. P. Dutton & Company, Inc., 1968.

Settel, Irving. *A Pictorial History of Radio*. New York: Grosset & Dunlap, 1967.

Shapiro, Nat. *Popular Music: An Annotated Index of American Popular Songs*. vol. 1, *1950–1959*. vol. 2, *1940–1949*. vol. 3, *1930–1939*. vol. 4, *1920–1929*. New York: Adrian Press, 1964.

Skolle, John. *The Lady of the Casa*. Santa Fe, N.M.: Rydal Press, 1959.

Smith, John M., and Cawkwell, Tim, eds. *The World Encyclopedia of the Film*. New York: World Publishing, 1972.

Sobel, Bernard. *A Pictorial History of Vaudeville*. New York: Crown Publishers, 1961.

Spaeth, Sigmund. *A History of Popular Music in America*. New York: Random House, 1948.

Stuart, Roy. *Immortals of the Screen*. New York: Bonanza Books, 1965.

Student's Dictionary of Musical Terms. New York: Hansen Publications, 1954.

Sullivan, Mark. *The Twenties*, vol. 4 of *Our Times*. New York: Charles Scribner's Sons, 1935.

Sumner, William Leslie. *The Organ: Its Evolution, Principles of Construction and Use*. New York: St. Martin's Press, Inc., 1962.

Tootell, George. *How to Play the Cinema Organ—A Practical Book by a Practical Player*. London: W. Paxton and Co., Ltd., n.d.

Walton, Judd. *The Wurlitzer Theatre Organ Revised Installations List*. Privately printed, 1973.

Whitworth, Reginald. *The Cinema and Theatre Organ*. London: Musical Opinion, 1932; reprint ed., Nashua, N.H.: The Organ Literature Foundation, n.d..

Woodfin, Jane. *Of Mikes and Men*. New York: McGraw-Hill Book Company, Inc., 1951.

Wurlitzer Unit Organ. N.p, Reprint ed. Vestal. N.Y.: Vestal Press, n.d.

Wyatt, Goeffrey. *At the Mighty Organ*. Oxford, England: Oxford Illustrated Press, 1974.

INDEX

ABOUT THE AUTHOR

JOHN W. LANDON is Associate Professor and Coordinator of the Undergraduate Program in Social Work at the University of Kentucky College of Social Work. For twenty-eight years he has been organist of the Paramount Theatre in Anderson, Indiana. He has written *From These Men* and *Jesse Crawford, Poet of the Organ,* and articles for the *Journal of Popular Film* and *Human Services in the Rural Environment.*